# MASTERING

Kate Chapman

# FRENCH

D0234132

# MACMILLAN MASTER SERIES

Banking
Basic Management
Biology
British Politics
Business Communication
Chemistry
COBOL Programming
Commerce
Computer Programming
Computers
Data Processing
Economics
Electronics
English Grammar
English Language
English Literature
French
German
Hairdressing
Italian
Keyboarding
Marketing
Mathematics
Modern British History
Modern World History
Nutrition
Office Practice
Pascal Programming
Physics
Principles of Accounts
Spanish
Statistics
Study Skills
Typewriting Skills
Word Processing

# MASTERING

# FRENCH

## E. NEATHER

EDITORIAL CONSULTANT
BETTY PARR

**MACMILLAN**

First published 1982
Reprinted 1983 (twice), 1985

Published by
MACMILLAN EDUCATION LTD
Houndmills, Basingstoke, Hampshire RG21 2XS
and London
Companies and representatives
throughout the world

ISBN 0 333 32346 7 (hardcover)
ISBN 0 333 32347 5 (paperback)
Cassette ISBN 0 333 34058 2

Printed in Great Britain by
Camelot Press Ltd
Southampton

# CONTENTS

# CONTENTS

# CONTENTS

# SERIES EDITOR'S PREFACE

The first language books in the Master Series, which are intended primarily for adult beginners without a teacher, should fill a notable gap in an otherwise well cultivated field. The publishers make no promises of instant mastery, and recognise that no one slim volume can contain more than the basic essentials of any living language. It is believed, however, that these initial books provide a carefully planned introduction to the language and a secure foundation for further study, for which it is hoped that the Master Series will ultimately give additional help.

Existing publications seem either to concentrate on teaching 'how to survive' or else to adopt a mainly academic approach. In these new books, the publishers aim to assist not only those studying a language for practical – generally touristic or commercial – purposes, but also those wishing to acquire a more formal knowledge of the grammar and structures of the language, with the intention of extending their skills of reading and writing by subsequent study. The dual aims of these books are made clear from the start, so that students may determine their own learning procedures and work through the material in ways best suited to their needs and capacity. The main emphasis is placed on understanding and speaking the language, but due attention has been paid to the importance of reading, especially for interpreting instructions and seeking information, and of writing, for such practical tasks as filling in forms, making reservations and writing simple letters.

The author's introduction clearly explains the content and presentation of the course. The table of contents is specific and informative and the student may see at a glance the ground to be covered. It is advisable to study the introduction very closely, so as to make best use of the carefully structured teaching and reference material throughout the book.

Mastery of the spoken language presents one of the greatest problems to the student working alone; without considerable linguistic experience, it is impossible to develop an ear for the sounds and intonation of a language by reading the printed page. Each book contains a detailed and helpful guide to pronunciation but there is also a most useful adjunct in the form of a cassette, containing an introductory section on pronunciation, and all the dialogues in the book. All material is spoken by native speakers. This cassette is invaluable for all languages in the Series, but for French it may be regarded as virtually indispensable. If the admirable pronunciation guide in *Mastering French* is intelligently used in conjunction with the cassette, the traditional difficulties of acquiring a good French pronunciation should be overcome.

The authors of the language books in the Master Series, who are all gifted and successful teachers of individuality and experience, have tried to ensure that those who use these books thoughtfully may experience the pleasure of successful language study without the direct intervention of a teacher. All concerned with the project hope that the books will establish for the learner a continuing involvement with the infinite variety and endless fascination of languages.

BETTY PARR

*Editorial Consultant*

# INTRODUCTION: HOW TO USE THIS BOOK

This introduction to French is intended for complete beginners in the language but it also offers a valuable refresher course for those who have previously learned a little French but now find that it has grown 'rusty'.

As explained in the Series Editor's preface, the book has a dual aim. Firstly, it seeks to provide a grounding in the basic skills of communicating in French for students intending to spend holidays in France, for those who are involved in business activities with French companies, and for those individuals and families who participate in the expanding number of 'twinnings' between French and English communities.

Secondly, this course offers the first stages in French for students whose aims may not be solely concerned with the spoken language and 'survival' situations, but who wish to acquire the basis of a more formal knowledge of the grammar and structures of the language with a view to developing a reading knowledge, or to extend writing skills at a later date. Existing beginners' courses seem to divide between those that teach how to 'survive abroad' and those which are wholeheartedly academic. The twofold aim of this course will be clear right from the contents page through all the chapters.

On the contents page you will see that each chapter is presented under three headings:

1 *Theme*: this expresses the main communicative aim of the chapter.
2 *Topic*: this sets out the situation or area of information in which the communicative theme is developed through dialogues.
3 *Grammar*: here the main elements of formal grammar are listed.

Those students whose main concern is with speaking and understanding will probably not wish to pursue the details of the grammatical points raised. Therefore each chapter presents the exercises in two sections. Firstly, there is, for all students, a section which is concerned with the main communicative aims of the chapter. Secondly, there is a section which is optional, and which provides practice of a more formal kind, such as translation, for those wishing to gain greater insight into the grammatical forms.

Similarly the section in each chapter entitled 'Explanations' sets out the essential information required to cope with the grammatical material of the chapter. In addition, however, each chapter refers the student to the grammatical summary at the back of the book for further details.

Students can obviously choose their own learning strategy; either to work methodically through all the material from chapter to chapter, or to cover the communicative material first and return to the details at a later date.

Selecting the content of a first language book is always difficult, since learners' needs vary considerably, but the proposals of the Threshold Level of language learning published under the auspices of the Council of Europe, have provided a useful point of reference for this book as also has the basic vocabulary of 'Le Français Fondamental' (Level 1).

## ORGANISATION OF CHAPTERS

Each chapter begins with a series of dialogues, or, in some cases, other material such as letters, which introduce the new topics and grammatical structures.

The vocabulary follows, with English equivalents, organised so that there is a section of vocabulary for each dialogue, to make reference easier. Each of these sections is divided into sub-sections grouping together (i) useful expressions, (ii) nouns, grouped according to their gender, and (iii) other words. All the vocabulary lists present the words in the order in which they occur in the dialogues. Next follows a series of explanations which clarify new grammatical material, and finally come the exercises, presented in two sections as has already been explained.

As described in the series editor's preface there is also a cassette to help students who are using this book. The cassette contains an introductory section on pronunciation and all the dialogues in the book. Sections of the book included on the cassette are indicated by the symbol ▭.

## REFERENCE MATERIAL

In the reference section the student will find the dialogues of the first five chapters fully translated, to assist with initial learning problems. A key provides answers to all exercises and a grammar reference section presents a summary of all the grammatical forms introduced in the book. A guide to pronunciation is provided as a supplement to the cassette. Finally a short bibliography is provided to guide the student in the choice of further reference material and opportunities for hearing French.

## TYPOGRAPHY

It is an aid to studying a foreign language from a textbook if the language can be distinguished easily from the English text. In this book the French is therefore set in a different typeface:

Votre passeport, s'il vous plaît.

This will help the reader, particularly in explanatory sections where the two languages occur side by side.

## ACKNOWLEDGEMENTS

In the preparation of this book I have relied heavily upon the help and advice of a number of French friends, but in particular my thanks are due to Madame Isabelle Rodrigues, who read the text with meticulous care and a native speaker's eye for correct French. I would also like to thank Miss Caroline James for typing the manuscript, with great care and considerable speed, and my secretary, Mrs Lila Backhouse, for her willingness to shoulder whatever burdens I push in her direction. Above all my thanks and appreciation are due to my wife Elisabeth for her never-failing support and concern at every stage of preparation and writing.

E. N.

# I TEACHING UNITS

# CHAPTER 1

# GREETINGS, INTRODUCTIONS, GOODBYES

## 1.1 DIALOGUES 📼

### (a) Dialogue 1

John and Mary Smith and their two children are off to spend their summer holidays in France. They drive off the ferry and a policeman of the immigration service checks their documents.

*Agent*: Bonjour, monsieur. Votre passeport, s'il vous plaît.

*John Smith*: Bonjour, monsieur. Voilà mon passeport.

*Agent*: Merci, monsieur. Alors, vous êtes bien John Smith?

*John*: Oui, monsieur. C'est bien ça. Et voilà ma femme et mes deux enfants.

*Agent*: Bonjour, madame.

*Mary*: Bonjour, monsieur.

*Agent*: Vous restez combien de temps en France?

*John*: Trois semaines.

*Agent*: Très bien, monsieur. Alors, voilà votre passeport. Au revoir et bon séjour.

*John*: Merci, monsieur. Au revoir.

### (b) Dialogue 2   À l'Hôtel   At the Hotel

The family drive to Caen, where they are booked into a hotel.

*John*: Bonjour, monsieur. Je suis Monsieur Smith. Vous avez une chambre pour ma famille.

*Hôtelier*: Ah, oui! Bonjour, Monsieur Smith; bonjour, Madame Smith.

*Mary*: Bonjour, monsieur. Et voilà nos deux enfants, Catherine et Robert.

*Hôtelier*: Bonjour, les enfants. Alors, monsieur, vous restez trois semaines, c'est bien ça?

*John*: Oui, c'est ça.

*Hôtelier*: Très bien, monsieur. Alors, c'est la chambre numéro cinq. Voilà votre clef.

*John*: Merci, monsieur.

*Hôtelier*: À bientôt, monsieur. Au revoir, madame.

## (c) Dialogue 3

After settling in, the Smiths leave the hotel to call on Monsieur Michel Lebrun, to whom they have been given a letter of introduction by a friend. They call at his office and are first dealt with by a secretary.

*John*: Pardon, madame. Est-ce que Monsieur Lebrun est là, s'il vous plaît? Je m'appelle John Smith.

*Secrétaire*: Ah, oui, vous êtes Monsieur Smith. Monsieur Lebrun est là. Un moment, s'il vous plaît.

(She buzzes and Monsieur Lebrun comes into the office.)

*Lebrun*: Bonjour, Monsieur Smith. Très heureux de faire votre connaissance.

*John*: Bonjour, Monsieur Lebrun. Je vous présente ma femme, Mary, et nos deux enfants, Catherine et Robert.

*Lebrun*: Enchanté, madame. Bonjour, les enfants. Eh bien, est-ce que vous êtes libres ce soir? Vous pouvez dîner chez nous?

*John*: Avec plaisir.

*Mary*: Vous êtes très gentil.

*Lebrun*: Alors, à sept heures ce soir.

*John*: Merci bien, et au revoir, monsieur.

*Lebrun*: Au revoir, monsieur. Au revoir, madame. Au revoir, les enfants. À bientôt.

## (d) Dialogue 4

The Smiths turn up for supper at 7.00 pm, as invited. Monsieur Lebrun opens the door.

*Lebrun*: Bonsoir, Monsieur Smith. Bonsoir, madame. Comment allez-vous?

*John*: Très bien, merci, monsieur. Et vous?

*Lebrun*: Bien, merci. Entrez, s'il vous plaît. (He calls his wife) Nicole, Monsieur et Madame Smith et les enfants sont là.

*Madame Lebrun*: Bonsoir, Monsieur Smith. Bonsoir, Madame Smith.

*John*: Enchanté, madame. Et voilà nos enfants, Catherine et Robert.

*Madame Lebrun*: Bonsoir, les enfants.

*Caen — vue generale sur la ville*

Photograph: J. Allan Cash

## 1.2 VOCABULARY

### (a) Dialogue 1
#### (i) Useful expressions

| | |
|---|---|
| bonjour | good morning; good afternoon |
| s'il vous plaît | please |
| voilà | here is; this is |
| c'est ça | |
| c'est bien ça | } that's right; that is so |
| combien de temps? | how long |
| au revoir | goodbye |
| bon séjour | have a nice stay |

#### (iii) Nouns – Masculine

| | |
|---|---|
| le jour | day |
| l'agent | policeman |
| le passeport | passport |
| l'enfant | child (boy) |

#### Nouns – Feminine

| | |
|---|---|
| la femme | wife; woman |
| la semaine | week |
| l'enfant | child (girl) |

(iii) **Other words**

| | | | |
|---|---|---|---|
| bon | good | France | France |
| votre | your | trois | three |
| mon | | très | very |
| ma | my | merci | thank you |
| mes | | alors | so; well |
| bien | fine; well | oui | yes |
| vous restez | you remain; | et | and |
| | you stay | deux | two |
| en | in | | |

**(b) Dialogue 2**

(i) **Useful expressions**

à bientôt        goodbye for now; see you later

(ii) **Nouns – Masc.**      **Nouns – Fem.**

| | | | |
|---|---|---|---|
| l'hôtel | hotel | la chambre | bedroom |
| l'hôtelier | hotel | la famille | family |
| | proprietor | la clef | key |
| le numéro | number | | |

(iii) **Other words**

| | |
|---|---|
| je suis | I am |
| vous avez | you have; you've got |
| pour | for |
| nos | our |
| c'est | it is |
| cinq | five |

**(c) Dialogue 3**

(i) **Useful expressions**

| | |
|---|---|
| je m'appelle ... | my name is ... |
| très heureux de faire votre connaissance | pleased to meet you; how do you do? |
| je vous présente ... | may I introduce ... |
| enchanté | delighted; it's a pleasure; how do you do? |
| eh bien ... | well now ... |
| chez nous | at home with us |
| à sept heures | at seven o'clock |
| merci bien | many thanks; thank you very much |

(ii) **Nouns – Masc.**      **Nouns – Fem.**

| | | | |
|---|---|---|---|
| le moment | moment | la secrétaire | secretary |

| le soir | evening | la connaissance | acquaintance |
| le plaisir | pleasure | | |

(iii) **Other words**

| pardon | excuse me | vous pouvez | you can |
| est | is | dîner | to have |
| là | there | | supper/ |
| | (sometimes used for | | dinner |
| | 'here' − see (d)) | | |
| vous êtes | you are | avec | with |
| heureux | happy; | gentil | kind; nice |
| | pleased | | |
| libres | free | ce | this |

**(d) Dialogue 4**

  **(i) Useful expressions**

| bonsoir | good evening |
| comment allez-vous? | how are you? |

  **(ii) Other words**

| entrez | come in |
| sont | are |
| là | here (occasional use) |

## 1.3 EXPLANATIONS

**(a) Forms of address**

Monsieur is the equivalent of 'Mr', as in Monsieur Lebrun.
Madame is the equivalent of 'Mrs', as in Madame Lebrun.
In addition to these uses as titles, however, French makes much more use of monsieur and madame. They might be translated 'sir' and 'madam' in some circumstances, but more often English would not use any form of title, as when French says Bonjour, monsieur, or Au revoir, madame. In these cases English says only 'good morning', or 'goodbye'. Note that bonjour is used as a greeting throughout the day, that is, it means both 'good morning' and 'good afternoon'.

**(b) Conversational** *extras*

Ordinary conversation in any language is 'oiled' by certain little expressions which occur and recur, sometimes without adding a great deal to the meaning of what is expressed, but forming an important part of everyday communication, for example; 'Now, what shall we do?'; 'Well, I just don't know'. French makes use of alors in rather the same way as English uses 'well' and 'now' in these examples. Bien or eh bien have rather similar uses. It is hard to translate these words or to give them a precise meaning. Watch out for the ways they occur in conversation. Bien is also used to emphasise or underline a statement, for example; C′est bien ça − That's *quite* right'; Vous êtes bien Monsieur Smith? − 'You *are* Mr Smith, aren't you?'

**(c) Gender − masculine or feminine** − *grammar ref 2.1*
All French nouns are classed as either masculine or feminine. Although it is usually true to say that male persons, occupations and so on are of the masculine gender and female persons, occupations and so on are of the feminine gender, there is no overall rule to help you guess the gender of a word. In the vocabulary of each chapter in this book, masculine and feminine nouns are listed separately, and you should learn each word together with the word for 'the', which is le for masculine and la for feminine words. For example, in the vocabulary you will find le passeport and la chambre.

You will also note from the vocabulary that when a noun begins with a vowel, both le and la become l′, and the word is pronounced as though it began with 'l', for example: l′agent.

**(d) Plurals** − *grammar ref 2.2*
The great majority of nouns in French form the plural, like English nouns, by adding s. When words are used in the plural the word for 'the' changes to les, for all words, whether masculine or feminine, for example: les passeports; les chambres. Note that this plural s does not usually affect the pronunciation of a word.

**(e) Expressing possession** − *grammar ref 3.5*
There are several cases in the dialogues where characters refer to possession, for example: 'your passport'; 'my children'; 'my wife'; 'our children'. You will have noticed that the French word expressing possession may change its form, for example: John Smith refers to ma femme − 'my wife'; nos enfants − 'our children'. The word expressing possession changes according to whether the noun following is masculine or feminine, singular or plural.

Because it is le passeport, 'my passport' is translated mon passeport. Because it is la chambre, 'my bedroom' is translated ma chambre. Because it is les enfants, 'my children' is translated mes enfants.

The dialogues also introduce ways of saying 'our' and 'your'.

Votre means 'your' for both masculine and feminine nouns, for example: votre enfant; votre clef.

Vos is used for 'your' with all words in the plural, for example: vos enfants; vos clefs.

Notre means 'our' for both masculine and feminine words, for example; notre séjour; notre chambre.

Nos means 'our' for all words in the plural, for example: nos enfants; nos chambres.

**(f) Putting the question** – *grammar ref 5.11*

From the dialogues you will notice that there are two ways of asking a question presented in this chapter.

(i) A question may be asked by giving a rising intonation to any statement (that is, the last word is pronounced on a higher note than the rest of the sentence). For example, vous êtes John Smith, with the voice dropping at the end of the sentence is a statement meaning 'You are John Smith'. Vous êtes John Smith?, with the voice rising at the end of the sentence makes this into a question, 'Are you John Smith?' Similarly, when John Smith books into his hotel he says, Vous avez une chambre pour ma famille, which is a statement. He could equally well have made it a question by raising his voice at the end of the sentence. Vous avez une chambre pour ma famille?

(ii) A question can be asked by putting the little phrase est-ce que ... in front of any statement. For example, Monsieur Lebrun asks, Est-ce que vous êtes libres ce soir?; Est-ce que vous pouvez dîner chez nous?

## 1.4 EXERCISES

**Section A**

**(a) Exercise 1**

Play the part of John Smith in the following short exchanges based on the dialogues.

(i) **Entry formalities**

*Agent*:   Bonjour, monsieur. Votre passeport, s'il vous plaît.
*John Smith*:   . . . . . .
*Agent*:   Vous êtes Monsieur John Smith?
*John Smith*:   . . . . . .
*Agent*:   Vous restez combien de temps en France?
*John Smith*:   . . . . . .
*Agent*:   Merci bien. Au revoir, monsieur.
*John Smith*:   . . . . . .

(ii) **At the hotel**

*Hôtelier*: Bonjour, monsieur. Vous restez bien trois semaines?

*John Smith*: ......

*Hôtelier*: Alors, la chambre numéro cinq. Voilà votre clef, monsieur.

*John Smith*: ......

(iii) **At Lebrun's office. John Smith first introduces his wife**

*John Smith*: ......

*Lebrun*: Enchanté de faire votre connaissance, Madame Smith. Alors, Monsieur Smith, est-ce que vous pouvez dîner chez nous ce soir?

*John Smith*: ......

*Lebrun*: Alors, à sept heures ce soir. Au revoir, monsieur. Au revoir madame.

*John Smith*: ......

(iv) **At Lebrun's home**

*Lebrun*: Bonsoir, monsieur. Bonsoir, madame. Entrez. Je vous présente ma femme, Nicole.

*John Smith*: ......

**(b) Exercise 2**

Here are some answers. What do you think the questions were? For example, Oui, je suis Monsieur Smith, would be the answer to the question Vous êtes Monsieur Smith?; or Est-ce que vous êtes Monsieur Smith?

  (i) Oui, je suis Mary Smith.

 (ii) Oui, avec plaisir.

(iii) Très bien, merci. Et vous?

(iv) Oui, Monsieur Lebrun est là.

 (v) Oui, vous avez la chambre numéro cinq.

**Section B**

**(c) Exercise 3**

Translate into French

   (i) My name is John Smith.

  (ii) Here is my passport.

 (iii) Have you got a room for my family?

— (iv) How long are you staying in France?

  (v) May I introduce my wife? I'm very pleased to meet you.

 (vi) Can you have supper with us this evening?

(vii) It's room number five. Here is your key.

(viii) You are very kind. See you soon.

**(d). Exercise 4**

Practise replying to the following questions using the appropriate form of the possessive adjective ('my', 'your', and so on).

Example: C'est votre passeport? Oui, c'est mon passeport.

  (i) C'est votre femme?
 (ii) C'est votre clef?
(iii) C'est votre chambre?
 (iv) C'est votre enfant?

Follow the same pattern, but this time answer for yourself and your wife.

Example: C'est votre clef? Oui, c'est notre clef.

  (v) C'est votre chambre?
 (vi) C'est votre passeport?
(vii) C'est votre enfant?
(viii) C'est votre hôtel?

Further practice exercises will be found in Chapter 20.

rencontrer

notre (l'hôtel
notrotel

# CHAPTER 2

# CAN I...?

# WHAT WOULD YOU LIKE?

# I'M VERY SORRY

## 2.1 Dialogues 📼

### (a) Dialogue 1   À la Banque   At the Bank

Already short of money, John Smith goes along to the bank to cash a cheque.

*Employé de banque*:  . Bonjour, monsieur. Vous désirez?

*John*:   Bonjour, monsieur. Est-ce que je peux changer cinquante livres en francs, s'il vous plaît.

*Employé*:   Certainement, monsieur. Vous pouvez changer un chèque, ou alors de l'argent liquide. Qu'est-ce que vous préférez?

*John*:   Je peux changer un chèque anglais?

*Employé*:   Mais oui, monsieur. Avec le système eurochèque vous pouvez changer un chèque anglais si vous présentez votre carte bancaire.

*John*:   Bien. Alors voilà ma carte et voilà un chèque de cinquante livres.

*Employé*:   Merci, monsieur. Est-ce que je peux voir votre passeport, s'il vous plaît?

*John*:   Voilà mon passeport.

*Employé*:   Merci, monsieur. Bon alors, passez à la caisse, s'il vous plaît.

### (b) Dialogue 2   Au café   At the café

John meets up with his wife and children and they go for mid-morning refreshment. They take a table on the terrasse of a café and the waitress comes to take their order.

*Serveuse*:   Bonjour, monsieur. Qu'est-ce que vous prenez?

*John*:   Je voudrais un café crème.

*Mary*:   Moi, je voudrais un café noir. Et deux oranginas pour les enfants.

*À la banque*

Photograph: Roger-Viollet

*Serveuse*: Alors, un café crème, un café noir et deux oranginas. C'est tout?

*John*: Apportez aussi deux glaces pour les petits, s'il vous plaît.

*Serveuse*: Oui, monsieur. Quel parfum? Il y a vanille, fraise ou chocolat.

*Mary*: Alors, chocolat, s'il vous plaît.

*Serveuse*: Bien, madame.

(When they have finished, John asks the waitress for the bill.)

*John*: Mademoiselle, l'addition, s'il vous plaît.

*Serveuse*: Oui, monsieur. Alors, deux cafés, ça fait trois francs soixante, deux oranginas, ça fait huit francs et deux glaces quatre francs. Alors, quinze francs soixante en tout, monsieur.

*John*: Le service est compris?

*La terrasse*

Photograph: Ken Lambert

*Serveuse*:   Oui, monsieur. Le service est compris.
*John*:   Eh bien, voilà. Merci, mademoiselle.
*Serveuse*:   Merci bien, monsieur. Au revoir, monsieur. Au revoir, madame.

### (c) Dialogue 3   Retour à l'hôtel   Back to the hotel

The family return to their hotel at midday to discover a slight hitch. John asks the hotel manager for his key.

*John*:   Pardon, monsieur. Je peux avoir la clef de la chambre numéro cinq, s'il vous plaît.
*Hôtelier*:   Voilà, monsieur. Je suis désolé, monsieur, mais il y a un petit problème.
*John*:   Pourquoi?
*Hôtelier*:   Parce que votre chambre n'est pas tout à fait prête. La femme de chambre fait les lits.
*John*:   Ça ne fait rien. Est-ce qu'on peut déjeuner?
*Hôtelier*:   Je regrette beaucoup, monsieur. Le déjeuner n'est pas tout à fait prêt.

ça n' fait rien

*John*: Mais pourquoi? Il est déjà midi et demi.

*Hôtelier*: Parce qu'il y a un problème avec le personnel, monsieur. Ce n'est pas grave. C'est une grève.

*John*: Une grève! Pourquoi?

*Hôtelier*: Ce n'est vraiment pas important, monsieur. Tout est réglé maintenant. Vous pouvez déjeuner dans dix minutes.

*John*: Bien.

## 2.2 VOCABULARY

### (a) Dialogue 1

#### (i) Nouns – Masc.

| | | Nouns – Fem. | |
|---|---|---|---|
| un employé | employee | la banque | bank |
| le franc | franc | la livre | pound |
| le chèque | cheque | la carte | card |
| l'argent | money | la carte bancaire | banker's card |
| de l'argent liquide | cash | la caisse | cash-desk |
| le système | system | | |

#### (ii) Other words

| | | | |
|---|---|---|---|
| désirer | to want; to wish | préférer | to prefer |
| je peux (pouvoir) | I can | anglais | English |
| | | mais | but |
| changer | to change | si | if |
| cinquante | fifty | présenter | to present |
| certainement | certainly | bancaire | bank (*adjective*) |
| ou (alors) | or (else) | voir | to see |
| vous pouvez (pouvoir) | you can | passer | to pass, move on to |
| liquide | liquid | | |

### (b) Dialogue 2

#### (i) Useful expressions

| | |
|---|---|
| qu'est-ce que vous prenez? | what would you like? |
| je voudrais . . . | I'd like . . . |
| ça fait . . . | that comes to . . . |
| le service est compris? | is a service charge included? |

#### (ii) Nouns – Masc.

| | | Nouns – Fem. | |
|---|---|---|---|
| le café | coffee | la terrasse | tables on pavement |

| le café crème | white coffee | la serveuse | waitress |
|---|---|---|---|
| un orangina | fizzy orange | la glace | ice (cream) |
| les petits | the little ones; children | la vanille | vanilla |
| | | la fraise | strawberry |
| le parfum | flavour; perfume | une addition | bill |
| le chocolat | chocolate | | |
| le service | service | | |

(iii) **Other words**

| | | | |
|---|---|---|---|
| vous prenez (prendre) | you take | quel? | which?; what? |
| tout | all | soixante | sixty |
| apporter | to bring | huit | eight |
| aussi | also | quatre | four |
| petit | small; little | quinze | fifteen |

## (c) Dialogue 3

### (i) Useful expressions

| | |
|---|---|
| je suis désolé | |
| je regrette beaucoup | I'm very sorry |
| ça ne fait rien | it doesn't matter |
| il est midi et demi | it's half past midday |
| tout est réglé | everything is settled |

### (ii) Nouns – Masc. / Nouns – Fem.

| **Nouns – Masc.** | | **Nouns – Fem.** | |
|---|---|---|---|
| le problème | problem | la femme de chambre | chambermaid |
| le lit | bed | la grève | strike |
| le personnel | staff | la minute | minute |

### (iii) Other words

| | | | |
|---|---|---|---|
| avoir | to have | on | one |
| il y a | there is; there are | déjeuner | to have lunch |
| | | beaucoup | much; a lot |
| pourquoi? | why? | déjà | already |
| parce que... | because... | grave | serious |
| tout à fait | completely, quite | vraiment | really |
| | | important | important |
| prêt(e) | ready | maintenant | now |
| fait (faire) | makes; is making | dans | in |
| | | dix | ten |

## 2.3 EXPLANATIONS

### (a) Verbs

When you look up a verb in a dictionary or other list of words, the form you find is called the infinitive. From the infinitive you can usually work out what the present tense of the verb will be. For example, from the English infinitive 'to see', you can expect to say 'I see'; 'he sees', and so on. Sometimes verbs are irregular, which means that the form of the present tense cannot be worked out automatically in this way. If you find the verb 'to be' in a word list, there is no way you can guess that the present tense is 'I am'; 'he is', and so on. Some of the most common verbs in English and French are irregular in this way, but the great majority of verbs follow a regular pattern. In future the vocabulary of each chapter will give the infinitive forms of all regular verbs introduced, and you will find the pattern of the present tense, and all other parts of the verb, in section 5 of the grammar reference section. In the case of irregular verbs, the form of the verb found in the chapter will be given in the vocabulary, followed by the infinitive in brackets, for example: je peux (pouvoir). A complete list of the irregular verbs introduced in this book is in *grammar ref. 5.1 (c) and (d)*.

The majority of regular verbs in French have an infinitive ending in -er, for example: changer; désirer. *See grammar ref. 5.1 (a)*. In the present tense the French verb may render two possible forms of the English verb, for example: je change can mean 'I change' or 'I am changing'; elle fait — 'she makes' or 'she is making'.

### (b) Can I ...? May I ...?

'I can' or 'I may' are expressed in French by je peux. To make this into a question, that is 'can I?', you should follow the procedure explained in Chapter 1, sec. 1.3 (f). *Either* keep the same order of words and express the question with a rising intonation (je peux?); *or* start the question with Est-ce que ... (Est-ce que je peux?). You may want to add a further idea, as when English says, 'Can I see ...?' or 'May I pay?' In French, this further idea is always expressed by the infinitive of the verb. The English examples just given are expressed in French like this: Est-ce que je peux voir?; Est-ce que je peux payer? You will find other examples in the dialogues of the chapter, for example: Est-ce que je peux changer un chèque?; Est-ce que je peux voir votre passeport?

In Chapter 1 you have already met an example of how to say, 'Can you ...?' (*or,* 'you can') — Vous pouvez dîner ce soir? Further examples occur in this chapter, for example: Vous pouvez changer un chèque.

### (c) Giving commands and instructions

Giving a command, or telling someone to do something is expressed by using the form of the verb that is found after vous, but in this case, vous is dropped. For example, vous payez means 'you pay', and vous apportez means 'you bring'. If you drop vous, you are giving commands, for example: Payez à la caisse; Apportez deux glaces. Of course, such commands can sound very impolite, in French, as in English, but the effect can always be softened by adding 'please', for example: Passez à la caisse, s'il vous plaît.

### (d) Expressing the negative *grammar ref. 5.10*

There are some examples in the dialogues of the present tense used in its negative form, for example: La chambre n'est pas tout à fait prête. In this example, ne has become n' because it precedes a vowel, but apart from this small variation, the pattern of forming the negative remains constant for all verbs. If you wish to render the English 'not', you do it in French with two little words, one on each side of the verb, ne . . . pas. You have learned that je peux means 'I can', so je ne peux pas means 'I cannot'. Similarly, 'we are not able to pay' is translated nous ne pouvons pas payer. (It should be mentioned that modern spoken French often drops ne, so that you will hear je peux pas; c'est pas grave. These forms are technically incorrect but commonly heard.)

### (e) The indefinite article *grammar ref 1.2*

In Chapter 1 it was explained that there are two genders in French and that the definite article ('the') may be either le, la, l' or les. The same distinction is made with the indefinite article ('a', 'an'). Masculine words have the indefinite article un (for example; un chèque – 'a cheque'), whereas feminine words have une (for example: une serveuse – 'a waitress'). In the plural, English may have no article at all, for example; 'cheques'; 'waitresses'. In French it is not normally possible for a noun to stand alone, with no article, so the word des is used in the plural, and may be seen as equivalent to English 'some', for example: des chèques, 'cheques', or 'some cheques'; des serveuses – 'waitresses' or 'some waitresses'. (In subsequent vocabularies nouns beginning with a vowel will be shown with the indefinite article, since l' does not make the gender clear.

### (f) More about putting questions *grammar ref 5.11*

Besides what has already been said about asking questions, there are also many cases where a question is put by using a word such as 'what?' 'why?' and so on. In this chapter two such forms are introduced:

(i) 'what' — qu'est-ce que?, for example: qu'est-ce que vous prenez — 'what are you taking?' (that is, 'what would you like?')

(ii) 'Why' — pourquoi? This can either stand by itself (see dialogue (c)) or be combined with est-ce que, for example: Pourquoi est-ce que la chambre n'est pas prête? — 'Why isn't the bedroom ready?' The answer to a pourquoi question usually begins parce que ... ('because ...').

## (g) Background information

### (i) Banks

It is not usual in French banks for every person at the counter to act as a cashier. The counter staff deal with any necessary documentation and administration, but the money is issued by a cashier at a cash-desk which is usually protectively enclosed in some way.

### (ii) Cafés

La terrasse is the French name for the tables that are set out on the pavement so that you can sit and watch the world go by as you take your refreshment. It is usually the case that you sit and wait at the table until served and do not pay until you are ready to leave. Even if you buy drinks at the bar instead of waiting at a table, you do not pay until you are ready to go. 'A waitress' is une serveuse, but you address her as mademoiselle (unless she is more mature, in which case, madame). A waiter is un garçon (this word also means 'boy'), and you address him as garçon, or, more usually, monsieur.

### (iii) Prices

There are 100 centimes to one franc. Prices are written and expressed as follows:

| | |
|---|---|
| 0F40 | quarante centimes |
| 3F | trois francs |
| 4F60 | quatre francs soixante (*or*, quatre soixante) |
| 50F30 | cinquante francs trente (*or*, cinquante trente) |

(A complete list of numerals is given on pages 238−9, and this should be referred to in future when numerals appear in the dialogues.)

## 2.4 EXERCISES

### Section A

### (a) Exercise 1

In each of the sentences given below you are asked if you want to do something and you answer yes, can I ...? adding something to your answer as indicated.

Example: Vous voulez changer un chèque?

(Do you want to change a cheque?)

Oui, est-ce que je peux changer un chèque de cinquante livres?
(Yes, can I change a cheque for £50?)

(i)     Vous voulez changer un chèque?
— (Yes, ask if you can change it into francs.)

(ii)    Vous voulez voir mon passeport?
(Yes, ask if you can see the passport.)

(iii)   Vous voulez aller à votre chambre?
(Yes, ask if you can have the key.)

(iv)   Vous voulez manger, monsieur?
— (Yes, ask if you can have lunch.)

## (b) Exercise 2

Below are listed some items on a café menu. Using these items and the phrase je voudrais ('I'd like') complete the following dialogue with a waitress, taking the part of John Smith.

café crème; café noir; orangina; glaces (fraise, chocolat)

*Serveuse*:   Bonjour, monsieur. Qu'est-ce que vous prenez?

*John S*:   ......

*Serveuse*:   Bien, monsieur. Un café crème, un café noir et deux oranginas. C'est tout?

*John S*:   ......

*Serveuse*:   Alors, deux glaces pour les enfants. Quel parfum? Il y a fraise et chocolat.

*John S*:   ......

*Serveuse*:   Alors, deux glaces, parfum chocolat. Merci, monsieur.

Try to make up other short dialogues using the few items given above.

## (c) Exercise 3

Below are given three questions asking what? and three asking why? Following the example given, reply to each of these questions expressing a personal preference if you are given a choice. (Un thé is 'tea'.)

Example:   Qu'est-ce que vous preférez, un café crème, un café noir ou un thé?

Answer:   Je préfère un café noir. (Or whichever your personal preference happens to be.)

(i)     Qu'est-ce que vous préférez changer, monsieur, un chèque ou de l'argent liquide?

(ii)    Qu'est-ce que vous préférez, madame, un café ou un thé?

(iii)   Qu'est-ce que vous préférez, monsieur, fraise ou chocolat?

Example:   Pourquoi est-ce que vous allez à la banque?

Answer: Parce que je voudrais changer un chèque.
(iv)    Pourquoi est-ce que vous allez au café?
        (Because you'd like a coffee.)
(v)     Pourquoi est-ce que vous allez à l'hôtel?
        (Because you'd like to have lunch.)
(vi)    Pourquoi est-ce que la chambre n'est pas prête?
        (Because there is a small problem.)

When you have written out the answers to the above questions, cover up the questions and try to work them out correctly from your answers.

**Section B**

**(d) Exercise 4**
Translate into French
  (i) Can I change £10 into francs please?
 (ii) Certainly, sir. Would you rather (est-ce que vous préférez) change a cheque or cash?
(iii) Can I see your passport please?
 (iv) I'd like one coffee with milk and one black coffee, please.
  (v) Can I have the key to room five, please?
 (vi) I'm sorry, sir, your room is not quite ready.
(vii) Why isn't the room ready?
(viii) Because there is a small problem.
 (ix) You can lunch in ten minutes.

**(e) Exercise 5**
(i) Here is a list of verb infinitives and a list of nouns. As they are written at the moment, the verbs and the nouns do not match up. See how many sentences you can make by linking up est-ce que je peux? with a combination of verb and noun.

|  |  |  |
|---|---|---|
|  | changer | le café |
|  | présenter | une semaine |
|  | payer | chez vous |
| est-ce que | apporter | ce soir |
| je peux | rester | un chèque |
|  | dîner | l'addition |
|  | voir | ma carte |
|  | déjeuner | ma femme |
|  |  | le menu |

(ii) When you have written out all the correct sentences you can find, answer 'yes' to all the questions posed.
    Example: Oui, vous pouvez déjeuner chez nous.

# CHAPTER 3

# WHERE IS IT?

# HOW DO I GET THERE?

## 3.1 DIALOGUES 📼

**(a) Dialogue 1    Au Syndicat d'Initiative    At the Information Bureau**

*John Smith*:    Bonjour, madame. C'est la première fois que nous sommes à Caen. Est-ce que vous avez des renseignements sur la ville, s'il vous plaît?

*Dame*:    Avec plaisir, monsieur. Voilà un plan de la ville et voilà le guide officiel. Vous voulez des renseignements sur les monuments principaux?

*John*:    Oui, s'il vous plaît.

*Dame*:    Eh bien, sur le plan vous voyez ici le château. Devant l'entrée principale du château, vous voyez l'église Saint-Pierre.

*Mary*:    C'est l'église avec une grande flèche?

*Dame*:    Oui, c'est bien ça, madame. Alors, suivez la rue Saint-Pierre et la rue Écuyère, traversez la Place Fontette et l'église Saint-Étienne est sur la gauche.

*John*:    Ah oui, elle est très connue. Et près de l'église, qu'est-ce que c'est?

*Dame*:    C'est l'Hôtel de Ville. Vous pouvez visiter aussi le Port de Caen.

*Mary*:    Il y a un port ici, à Caen?

*Dame*:    Oui, madame, il y a un port très important. Le Jardin des Plantes est aussi très intéressant.

*John*:    Très bien. Alors merci beaucoup, madame.

*Dame*:    Je vous en prie, monsieur. Bon séjour à Caen.

**(b) Dialogue 2**

They decide to go first to Saint-Étienne but manage to get lost despite the plan. John Smith stops a passer-by.

*Church of Saint-Étienne*

*John*: Pardon, monsieur, pour aller à l'église Saint-Étienne, s'il vous plaît.

*Passant*: L'église Saint-Étienne, eh bien, vous allez tout droit, vous traversez la Place Fontette, vous prenez la première rue à droite et l'église est sur votre gauche.

*John*: C'est loin d'ici?

*Passant*: Ah non, monsieur. Dix minutes à pied, seulement.

*John*: Merci beaucoup, monsieur.

*Passant*: De rien.

**(c) Dialogue 3**

Having looked round the church they decide to go to the castle.

*John*: Pardon, monsieur, pour aller au château, s'il vous plaît?

*Passant*: Au château. C'est assez loin, monsieur.

*John*: Ah bon?

*Passant*: Oui, à pied il faut une demi-heure, au moins, surtout avec les enfants. Prenez l'autobus.

*John*: C'est une bonne idée. Où est l'arrêt d'autobus?

*Passant*: Là, devant l'Hôtel de Ville.

*John*: Merci, monsieur, vous êtes bien aimable.

*Passant*: Je vous en prie, monsieur.

*... ici le château*

Photograph: J. Allan Cash

**(d) Dialogue 4**

They get on the bus. Most passengers getting on seem to have tickets already. John speaks to the driver.

*John*:   Deux adultes et deux enfants, s'il vous plaît.

*Chauffeur*:   Vous allez où, monsieur?

*John*:   Au château.

*Chauffeur*:   Alors huit francs quarante (8F40). Merci. N'oubliez pas d'oblitérer vos billets. Voilà votre monnaie.

*John*:   Merci, monsieur.

**(e) Dialogue 5**

After the château they decide to take the children to see the ships in the port of Caen.

*John*:   Pardon, monsieur. Vous savez, où est le Port de Caen?

*Passant*:   Je regrette, monsieur, je ne sais pas. Je suis étranger ici.

*John*:   Pardon, madame, pour aller au port, s'il vous plaît?

*Dame*:   Vous allez tout droit, vous traversez la Place Courtonne et le Bassin Saint Pierre est sur votre droite.

*John*:   Merci, madame. C'est loin d'ici?

*Dame*:   Non, pas du tout. À deux cents (200) mètres, environ.

*John*:   Merci, madame.

*Dame*:   De rien, monsieur.

## 3.2 VOCABULARY

**(a) Dialogue 1**

  (i) **Useful expressions**

| | |
|---|---|
| sur la gauche | on the left |
| qu'est-ce que c'est? | what's this? |
| merci beaucoup | thanks very much |
| je vous en prie | don't mention it; you're welcome |

  (ii) **Nouns – Masc.**

| | | | |
|---|---|---|---|
| les ren- | information | la fois | time |
| seignements | | la ville | town |
| – le plan | plan | une éntrée | entrance |
| le guide | guide | une église | church |
| le monument | monument; | la flèche | spire |
| | public | la rue | street |
| | building | la place | square |
| le château | castle | la plante | plant |

**Nouns – Fem.**

| | |
|---|---|
| le port | port |
| le jardin | garden |

(iii) **Other words**

| | | | |
|---|---|---|---|
| première | first | vous voyez | you see |
| nous | we are | (voir) | |
| sommes | | ici | here |
| (être) | | devant | in front of |
| à | to | grand(-e) | big |
| sur | on | suivez | follow |
| de | of; from | (suivre) | |
| officiel(-le) | official | traverser | to cross |
| vous voulez | you want | connu(-e) | well-known |
| (vouloir) | | près de | near |
| principal(-e) | main, | visiter | to visit |
| | principal | intéressant | interesting |
| | | (-e) | |

**(b) Dialogue 2**

(i) **Useful expressions**

| | |
|---|---|
| pour aller à | how do I get to ...? |
| tout droit | straight ahead |
| à droite | to the right |
| à pied | on foot |
| de rien | don't mention it; you're welcome |

(ii) **Nouns – Masc.**

| | |
|---|---|
| le pied | foot |

(iii) **Other words**

| | |
|---|---|
| vous allez (aller) | you go |
| loin (de) | far (from) |
| seulement | only |

**(c) Dialogue 3**

(i) **Useful expressions**

| | |
|---|---|
| ah bon? | oh really? |
| il faut une demi-heure | you need half an hour |
| au moins | at least |

(ii)

| **Nouns – Masc.** | | **Nouns – Fem.** | |
|---|---|---|---|
| un autobus | bus | une demi- | half an hour |
| un arrêt | stop | heure | |

| un Hôtel de Ville | town-hall | une idée | idea |
|---|---|---|---|

**(iii) Other words**

| assez | quite |
|---|---|
| surtout | above all; especially |
| bon (bonne) | good |
| où? | where? |
| aimable | nice; kind |

**(d) Dialogue 4**

**(i) Nouns – Masc.**    **Nouns – Fem.**

| un adulte | adult | la monnaie | small change |
|---|---|---|---|
| le billet | ticket | | |

**(ii) Other words**

| oublier | to forget |
|---|---|
| oblitérer | to stamp; to cancel a ticket |

**(e) Dialogue 5**

**(i) Useful expressions**

| sur votre droite | on your right |
|---|---|
| pas du tout | not at all |
| à deux cents mètres | two hundred metres away |

**(ii) Nouns – Masc.**

| un étranger | stranger; foreigner |
|---|---|
| le bassin | dock |

**(iii) Other words**

| vous savez (savoir) | you know |
|---|---|
| je sais (savoir) | I know |
| environ | approximately; about |

## 3.3 Explanations

**(a) Asking the way**

There are various possibilities:

(i) Just state the name of the place you want to find, for example:
Pardon monsieur, le château, s'il vous plaît.

(ii) Use the phrase *où est?* – 'where is?' for example: Pardon,
monsieur, où est le château, s'il vous plaît?

(iii) Use the expression pour aller à, meaning roughly, 'how do I get
to?' In the answers you receive you will need to distinguish between

the sound of tout droit – 'straight on', and à droite – 'to the right'. The only difference in pronunciation between droit and droite is that you can hear the 't' pronounced in the latter. Droit = *drwa*; droite = *drwat*.

**(b) Prepositions** *grammar ref 7*
Prepositions are the words that indicate position, such as devant – 'in front of', and près de – 'near'. In many cases, such as these two examples, prepositions in English and French have exactly the same meaning, and can be translated directly into the other language. But it is also true the prepositions can be some of the trickiest parts of a foreign language because they can be used with a variety of meanings which are not exactly equivalent to the mother tongue of the learner. (Think of the variety of meanings for the English preposition 'on' in such examples as 'on the table'; 'on parole'; 'on account'; 'have one on me', and so on. Amongst the most common French prepositions which can be used in a variety of ways are à and de.
(i) à can change its form depending on the definite article which follows, for example:

à + le = au     – vous allez au château
à + la = à la     – vous allez à la gare (railway station)
à + l' = à l'     – vous allez à l'église
à + les = aux     – vous allez aux églises

We have already met à in a number of different uses, for example:
meaning 'to' in vous allez à l'église;
meaning 'at' or 'in' when used with the name of a town, such as à Caen;
in the phrases à droite; à gauche, when giving directions;
in the expression à pied – 'on foot';
when expressing distance, for example: le port est à deux cents mètres – 'the port is 200 metres away'.
(ii) de is used particularly to express possession, as in le port de Caen, meaning 'the port belonging to Caen'; l'Hôtel de Ville – 'the Town Hall'. When combined with the definite article, de also undergoes some changes; de la and de l' show no change of form, but de le becomes du (for example: l'entrée du château), and de les becomes des (for example: le Jardin des Plantes). Often de can be translated 'of' (for example: 'the port of Caen'). At other times, English might not use a preposition at all, for example: l'entrée du château would be 'the castle entrance', and le Jardin des Plantes is what we would call 'the Botanical Gardens'. Similarly un arrêt d'autobus is 'a bus stop'.

**(c) Adjectives** *grammar ref 3*

Adjectives are words used for describing appearances or characteristics.

(i) The usual position of the adjective in French is after the noun it is describing, for example: une personne aimable − 'a nice person'; l'entrée principale − 'the main entrance'; le guide officiel − 'the official guide'. A small number of quite common adjectives do precede the noun. In the dialogues we met une bonne idée; une grande flèche. (*See grammar ref. 3.3 for a full list*).

(ii) French adjectives change their form according to whether they are used with a masculine or a feminine noun. The rule for the great majority of adjectives is that they add -e to become feminine. Sometimes this only makes a change in the written language and no difference can be heard in the spoken language, for example: le château principal; l'entrée principale. In other cases there is a difference in pronunciation, particularly if the adjective ends with a consonant such as 'd' or 't', for example: prêt/prête (Le déjeuner est prêt; La chambre est prête.)

In some cases there may be other changes in spelling besides adding -e, for example: bon/bonne; officiel/officielle. All these agreements obviously have a more important part to play in the written than in the spoken language, since many of the variations are simply a result of spelling conventions. The grammar summary sets out the complete picture (*3.1*) and future vocabularies will give, in brackets, the feminine form of the adjective, for example: principal(-e).

Both masculine and feminine forms of adjectives add -s in the plural. Here again, there may often by no difference in pronunciation, for example: une église principale; des églises principales.

There are a small number of irregular forms in the plural, for example: adjectives ending in -al form a masculine plural ending in -aux, − principal − principaux. (The feminine form is regular, for example: principale − principales.) (*See grammar ref. 3.2.*)

**(d) More about the imperative**

In this chapter there are several further examples of the imperative, (introduced in Chapter 2.3 (c)), for example: suivez!; traversez!; prenez! There is also an example of a negative imperative, for example: n'oubliez pas! − 'do not forget'. Forming the negative of commands therefore follows the same pattern as that already explained for the present tense (2.3 (d)), that is, ne precedes the verb and pas follows it. Look at these further examples:

Ne traversez pas la rue!; N'allez pas au port!

**(e) Some notes on items of vocabulary**

(i) It has already been explained that to say 'where is . . . ?' you use où est . . . ?, for example: Où est le château? Où can also be combined with est-ce que if the question contains a verb, for example: Où est-ce que vous allez? – 'where are you going?'

Another way of putting the same question is given by the bus-driver in Dialogue 4; Vous allez où?

(ii) Note the question Qu'est-ce que c'est? meaning 'what's that?' or 'what's this?' It is usually followed by an answer beginning c'est . . . , for example: Qu'est-ce que c'est? – C'est un château. (It's the castle.)

(iii) Il y a is a very common phrase in everyday French, already met in Chapter 2 in the example il y a un problème. It means 'there is', and also 'there are'. The word voilà, introduced in Chapter 1, means 'here is' or 'here are' when the object(s) is/are right in front of you. For example, Voilà mon passeport, because you've actually got it in your hand. Il y a is not so specific, for instance, Il y a un port à Caen – 'There is a port in Caen'. But if you were standing right in front of the port and pointing it out to someone you would say Voilà le port. When asking questions with il y a, you can either use the rising intonation, for example: Il y a un port ici à Caen? or you can use est-ce que to put the question, for example: Est-ce qu'il y a un château à Caen? (Note that que becomes qu' before a vowel.)

**(f) Background information**

(i) *Le Syndicat d'Initiative* is the name usually given to the information bureau in French towns. Every town has its Syndicat, which will vary from a very large tourist information centre in a big town to a local shopkeeper who acts as a source for information in small places.

(ii) *Public transport.* When the Smiths get on their bus they note that most other passengers seem to have tickets already. This is because, not only will many passengers have season tickets, but it is much cheaper to buy a strip of tickets (known as un carnet). On the bus there is then a machine where passengers stamp their tickets as they get on. The ticket may then be checked by inspectors making random surveys. The verb used for this process of stamping or cancelling the ticket is oblitérer. When travelling by rail in France it is now also the case that tickets have to be cancelled in machines before boarding the train. The verb used by the SNCF (French Railways) is composter. So as you enter a French station you will see signs saying N'oubliez pas de composter.

## 3.4 EXERCISES

### Section A

**(a) Exercise 1**

Here are some of the places marked on the plan of Caen.
(i) le château;  (ii) le Jardin des Plantes;  (iii) le Port de Caen;
(iv) l'église Saint-Étienne;  (v) l'église Saint-Pierre;
(vi) l'Hôtel de Ville.
Make up sentences asking how to get to these places, using any of the ways suggested in 3.3 (a).

**(b) Exercise 2**

You are standing at the Place de la Résistance facing the château.
You are given instructions on how to get to various places. Following the instructions and making use of the plan can you fill in the name of the place you are going to?

(i) Vous allez tout droit. Vous traversez la rue de Bernières. Vous prenez la première à droite et . . . . . . est sur votre gauche.

(ii) Vous allez tout droit. Vous prenez la première à droite. Vous traversez la Place Courtonne et . . . . . . est sur votre droite.

(iii) Vous allez tout droit. Vous traversez la Rue Saint-Pierre et . . . . . . est devant vous.

(iv) Vous prenez la première à gauche. Vous allez tout droit à la Place Gambetta. Vous prenez le Boulevard Bertrand et au bout du boulevard . . . . . . est devant vous.

**(c) Exercise 3**

Complete the following dialogue with a passer-by expressing your intentions as indicated.

*You*: (Ask how you get to the castle.)
*Passant*: Au château, alors, vous allez à pied?
*You*: (Yes, you are on foot.)
*Passant*: Alors, vous allez tout droit, vous prenez la deuxième rue à droite et le château est devant vous.
*You*: (Ask if it is far from here.)
*Passant*: Oui, monsieur, assez loin.
*You*: (Ask if there is a bus.)
*Passant*: Oui, monsieur, il faut cinq minutes seulement en autobus.
*You*: (Ask where the bus-stop is.)
*Passant*: Là, devant l'Hôtel de Ville.
*You*: Thank him and say he is very kind.
*Passant*: De rien, monsieur.

32

*Street plan of Caen*

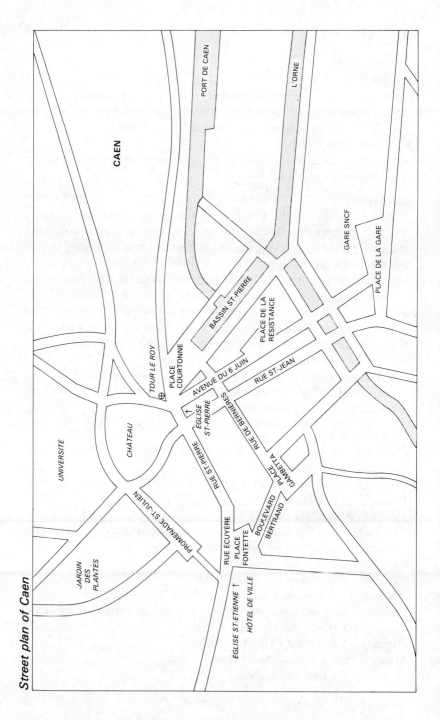

**Section B**

**(d) Exercise 4**
Form sentences using the adjective given in brackets and copying the example given.
Example: Vous allez au château? (intéressant) — Oui, c'est un château intéressant.
  (i) Vous allez au port? (important)
 (ii) Vous allez à l'église? (intéressante)
(iii) Vous allez au château? (connu)
 (iv) Vous avez le guide? (officiel)
  (v) Vous voyez l'entrée? (principale)

**(e) Exercise 5**
Translate into French
   (i) Excuse me, please. How do I get to the castle?
  (ii) I am going (je vais) to the port and to the Saint-Étienne church.
 (iii) I am going to the Information Bureau. Is it far from here?
  (iv) No, it's quite close. About 200 metres away.
   (v) In front of the main entrance to the castle is a church.
  (vi) On your right is a well-known church.
 (vii) Where is the port? I don't know, I'm a stranger here.
(viii) I'm here for the first time.

# CHAPTER 4

# WHAT TIME DOES IT START? WHEN DOES IT OPEN?

## 4.1 DIALOGUES 📼

John Smith makes a number of telephone calls while planning visits in the area.

**(a) Dialogue 1**

*Monsieur au téléphone*: Allô, ici la piscine municipale de Caen.

*John*: Bonjour, monsieur. Quand est-ce que la piscine est ouverte?

*Monsieur*: Ce matin, monsieur, la piscine est ouverte de neuf heures à midi.

*John*: Et l'après-midi, c'est ouvert aussi?

*Monsieur*: Oui, monsieur. L'après-midi la piscine est ouverte de deux heures à six heures.

*John*: Les heures d'ouverture sont les mêmes tous les jours?

*Monsieur*: De lundi à vendredi les heures sont les mêmes. Le samedi la piscine est ouverte jusqu'à neuf heures du soir, et le dimanche de dix heures moins le quart jusqu'à cinq heures et demie.

*John*: Merci beaucoup, monsieur.

**(b) Dialogue 2**

*John*: Allô, c'est le Musée du Débarquement?

*Monsieur*: Allô, oui, monsieur, ici c'est le Musée du Débarquement à Arromanches.

*John*: Alors, je voudrais savoir, monsieur, quand est-ce que le musée est ouvert?

*Monsieur*: Le musée est ouvert tous les jours de neuf heures à midi et de quatorze heures à dix-neuf heures.

*John*: Merci, bien, monsieur.

*Public telephone*

Photograph: Roger-Viollet

**(c) Dialogue 3**
*Dame au téléphone*:  Allô, Syndicat d'Initiative à Lisieux.
*John*:  Bonjour, madame. Je viens à Lisieux avec ma famille et je voudrais savoir s'il y a une visite accompagnée de la Basilique Sainte-Thérèse.
*Dame*:  Oui, monsieur, il y a des visites accompagnées tous les jours de neuf heures à midi et de quatorze heures à seize heures trente.

*John*: Bien. Et quand est-ce qu'il y a le spectacle Son et Lumière à la Basilique?

*Dame*: Le spectacle Son et Lumière est donné tous les soirs, sauf le vendredi, à vingt et une heures trente.

*John*: Merci, madame.

*Dame*: De rien, monsieur.

## (d) Dialogue 4

While John is telephoning, Mary tries to book seats for the theatre.

*Mary*: Bonjour, madame. Est-ce que vous avez deux places pour la représentation de mardi soir?

*Dame à la caisse*: Je suis desolée, madame. Mardi, c'est complet.

*Mary*: Quel dommage! Et mercredi?

*Dame*: Mercredi aussi. Je regrette, mais c'est complet. Il y a des places libres jeudi soir. Voilà deux places à vingt francs.

*Mary*: Bien. Et quand est-ce que la représentation commence?

*Dame*: À sept heures et quart, madame. Il y a un entr'acte à neuf heures moins le quart.

*Mary*: Alors, voilà quarante francs. Merci, madame.


## 4.2 VOCABULARY

### (a) Dialogue 1

#### (i) Useful expressions

| | |
|---|---|
| les heures d'ouverture | the opening times |
| tous les jours | every day |

#### (ii) Nouns – Masc. / Nouns – Fem.

| Nouns – Masc. | | Nouns – Fem. | |
|---|---|---|---|
| le téléphone | telephone | la piscine | swimming pool |
| le matin | morning | | |
| l'après-midi | afternoon | une heure | hour |
| le quart | quarter | l'ouverture | opening |

#### (iii) Other words

| | |
|---|---|
| le monsieur | man; gentleman |
| allô | hello (only on telephone) |
| municipale (-e) | municipal |
| quand? | when? |
| ouvert(-e) | open |
| même | same |
| jusque | until |
| moins | less |

**(b) Dialogue 2**
  (b) **Nouns – Masc.**
    le musée             museum
    le débarquement    landing

  (ii) **Other word**
    savoir             to know

**(c) Dialogue 3**
  (i) **Useful expressions**
    tous les soirs       every evening

  (ii) **Nouns – Masc.**    **Nouns – Fem.**
    le spectacle  show;    la visite    visit
        performance  la Basilique  Basilica
    le son  sound    la lumière  light

  (iii) **Other words**
    je viens (venir)      I come; I am coming
    accompagné(-e)      accompanied; guided
    donné(-e)         given; presented
    sauf             except

**(d) Dialogue 4**
  (i) **Useful expression**
    quel dommage!      what a pity!

  (ii) **Nouns – Masc.**    **Nouns – Fem.**
    un entr'acte  interval  la place  seat (at
    le théâtre  theatre        theatre or
                     cinema)
                la repré-  performance
                sentation

  (iii) **Other words**
    complet(ète)      full up
    commencer      to begin

Note that all numerals and days of the week are to be found in *grammar ref. 9.1 and 9.2.*

## 4.3 EXPLANATIONS

**(a) Telling the time and asking when?** *grammar ref 9.2 (e)*
  (i) The word for 'when?' is quand? It can stand by itself, as, for

example, a response to a statement: Je vais au théâtre. Quand? ('I am going to the theatre. When?'). If you want to form a question such as, 'When are you coming to the theatre?', the most straightforward way is to combine quand with est-ce que, for example:

Quand est-ce que vous venez au théâtre?

(ii) To reply to such a question you need to be able to express time of the clock. The French equivalent for 'o'clock' is heure(s), so that 'one o'clock' is une heure; 'seven o'clock' is sept heures, and so on. The preposition equivalent to 'at' is à, so if the question is Quand est-ce que le spectacle commence?, the answer might be, à sept heures. If the time is not so precise you can say vers sept heures, meaning 'at about 7 o'clock'.

In the dialogues there are other examples of telling the time. Here is a summary of the way they are formed:

**Half past**, for example: 7.30 − sept heures et demie. (The word demie ends with -e, because you are saying literally 'seven hours and a half', and heure is feminine.

**Quarter past**, for example: 7.15 − sept heures et quart.

**Quarter to**, for example: 7.45 − huit heures moins le quart. (Here, French views the clock rather differently from English and says 'eight hours minus the quarter'.)

**Minutes past**, for example: 7.10 − sept heures dix. There is no need to use the word minutes, although it is sometimes included (for instance, when a time check is given on the radio) − sept heures dix minutes.

**Minutes to**, for example: 7.50 − huit heures moins dix.

(iii) **24 hour clock**. This is normally used when giving times of train departures and arrivals, and sometimes with opening times, to avoid any confusion. For example, the man in Dialogue 2 gives the afternoon opening times of the museum as de quatorze heures à dix-neuf heures. When using the 24 hour clock, times between the hours are usually expressed as the number of minutes, for example: 21.30 − vingt et une heures trente: 14.25 − quartorze heures vingt-cinq.

If the 24 hour clock is not used, 'am' and 'pm' can be expressed by adding du matin, du soir, for example: huit heures du matin; six heures du soir.

(iv) **Midday and midnight**. To express these times French does not usually use douze heures. '12 noon' is expressed by midi, and 'midnight' by minuit. Thus '12.30 pm' would be midi et demi. (Note that midi is masculine, and therefore demi does not end in -e as with heure.) 11.45 is minuit moins le quart.

(v) **Opening hours**. There are several examples in the dialogues of the

way in which opening hours are expressed, that is 'from ... to ...'.
For example:

La piscine est ouverte de neuf heures à midi.

(vi) **Written form of the time.** When writing the time, French often
uses the letter h to stand for heures. For example:

Le musée est ouvert tous les jours de 9h à 12h et de 14h à 19h.

Le spectacle est donné à 21h30.

## (b) Days of the week

You will need to learn the days of the week given on p.239. A few
comments about their use might be helpful. The name of the day
usually occurs without the definite article, and with no preposition
equivalent to the English 'on'. 'On Monday I'm going to the
swimming pool' would be expressed, Lundi je vais à la piscine.

When talking about habitual and regular activities, however, the
article is used, for example: 'On Mondays I go to the theatre (that is,
regularly every Monday) — Le lundi je vais au théâtre.

## (c) More about verbs *grammar ref 5.8 (e) (g)*

There are a number of common verbs which are found in combination
with an infinitive. We have already met the verb pouvoir in
combinations such as Vous pouvez changer un chèque, and Je peux
payer. Another verb used in the same way is vouloir — 'to want', for
example:

Je veux savoir — 'I want to know'.

Because je veux, like 'I want' in English, can sometimes sound rather
abrupt, French can use a more polite form, equivalent to 'I would
like' — je voudrais, for example:

Je voudrais savoir quand le musée est ouvert.

## 4.4 EXERCISES

### Section A

### (a) Exercise 1

Here are the opening times of some of the places around Caen. How
would you express these times in French, if you were asked Quand est-
ce que ...... est ouvert(e)?

|  |  |  |  |
|---|---|---|---|
|  | le château |  | 9h – 12: 14h – 18h30 |
|  | la piscine |  | 9h15 – 12h30: 1.45 – 6.15 |
| Quand est-ce que | le musée | est ouvert(e)? | 9h30 – 1h: 2h30 – 5h15 |
|  | la Basilique |  | 9h45 – 12h15: 14h45 – 17h30 |
|  | l'église |  | 8h30 – 11h15: 2h15 – 18h45 |

40

**(b) Exercise 2**
Put the following times into French.

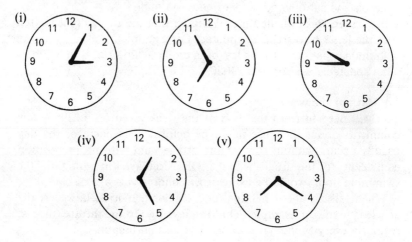

(i) (ii) (iii) (iv) (v)

## Section B

**(c) Exercise 3**

Translate into French
   (i) When is the swimming pool open?
  (ii) This morning the pool is open from 9 o'clock to midday.
 (iii) The museum is open every day from 9.30 until 5 pm.
 (iv) I would like to know if there is a museum at Caen.
  (v) Have you got two seats for Thursday evening's performance?
 (vi) I am very sorry. Thursday's performance is sold out.
(vii) What a pity! When does the performance start on Friday?
(viii) At 7.15. There is an interval at 8.45.

**(d) Exercise 4**
Write out the following sentences giving the correct present-tense form of the verb in brackets.
   (i) Je (venir) à Caen.
  (ii) Je (être) John Smith.
 (iii) La réprésentation (commencer) à sept heures.
 (iv) La femme de chambre (faire) les lits.
  (v) Nous (préférer) le café noir.
 (vi) Quand est-ce que vous (commencer) le déjeuner?
(vii) Vous (pouvoir) visiter le château.
(viii) Les enfants (être) là.

# CHAPTER 5

# CAN YOU COME?

# DO YOU LIKE THIS

# WEATHER?

## 5.1 DIALOGUES 📼

**(a) Dialogue 1  Au petit déjeuner  At breakfast**
While having a leisurely breakfast at the hotel, the Smiths are
visited by their friend Michel Lebrun.

*Lebrun*:  Bonjour, tout le monde. Bon appétit. Comment ça va?

*John*:  Bonjour, Michel. Quel plaisir de vous revoir. Ça va très bien,
merci. Et vous?

*Lebrun*:  Très bien, aussi. Comment se passe votre séjour à Caen?

*Mary*:  Très bien. Nous sommes ravis de notre visite.

*Lebrun*:  Bien. Alors, excusez-moi de déranger votre petit déjeuner,
mais qu'est-ce que vous prévoyez pour aujourd'hui?

*John*:  Ce matin, nous allons faire des courses.

*Mary*:  Oui, ce matin nous voulons acheter des vêtements pour les
enfants. Après cela, nous ne savons pas encore.

*Lebrun*:  Si vous êtes libres à midi, je vous invite à déjeuner au
restaurant avec ma femme et moi.

*John*:  Avec plaisir. Vous êtes très gentil. Les enfants aussi?

*Lebrun*:  Mais bien entendu! Alors, nous allons déjeuner aux
'Cultivateurs' près de l'Avenue du Six Juin. Vous connaissez la rue?

*John*:  Oui, je connais la rue, mais où est le restaurant?

*Lebrun*:  Eh bien, prenez la rue en direction de la rivière, et le
restaurant est sur votre droite au Quai de Juillet. Quand est-ce que
vous voulez manger?

*John*:  Nous sommes à votre disposition.

*Lebrun*:  Alors, venez vers midi et demi. Au revoir et à plus tard.

*John*:  Au revoir et merci.

**(b) Dialogue 2**
John Smith pauses to chat to the hotelier as he hands in his key,
on the way out after breakfast.

*Hôtelier*:   Vous aimez ce temps, monsieur?

*John*:   Ah non! Nous n'avons pas de chance. Il pleut encore. Est-ce qu'il ne fait jamais beau à Caen?

*Hôtelier*:   Mais si, monsieur! Généralement il fait beau en été. Il fait même très chaud quelquefois. Mais la mer n'est pas loin, vous savez; c'est un climat maritime, comme chez vous en Angleterre, et il pleut de temps en temps.

*John*:   Vous croyez qu'il va faire beau plus tard?

*Hôtelier*:   C'est possible. Le temps change vite ici. Regardez! On voit déjà un peu de ciel bleu. Il va y avoir du soleil peut-être. On ne sait jamais.

*John*:   Vous êtes optimiste, monsieur. Mais je crois que nous allons acheter des anoraks pour les enfants quand même. On ne sait jamais, c'est vrai.

*Hôtelier*:   Bonne chance, quand même, monsieur. Amusez-vous bien!

## 5.2 VOCABULARY

### (a) Dialogue 1

#### (i) Useful expressions

| | |
|---|---|
| tout le monde | everybody |
| bon appétit | have a good meal; enjoy your meal |
| comment ça va? | how are you? |
| quel plaisir de vous revoir | how nice to see you again |
| comment se passe votre séjour? | how is your visit going? |
| excusez-moi | excuse me; forgive me |
| faire des courses | to go shopping |
| je vous invite | I invite you |
| bien entendu | of course |
| en direction de | in the direction of |
| à votre disposition | at your disposal |
| à plus tard | see you later |

#### (ii) Nouns – Masc.

| | |
|---|---|
| le petit déjeuner | breakfast |
| un appétit | appetite |
| les vêtements | clothes |
| le restaurant | restaurant |
| le cultivateur | farmer |
| le quai | quay |

#### Nouns – Fem.

| | |
|---|---|
| une avenue | avenue |
| la rivière | river |
| la direction | direction |
| la disposition | disposal; disposition |

(iii) **Other words**

| | | | |
|---|---|---|---|
| nous sommes (être) | we are | après | after |
| | | cela | this; that |
| | | nous savons (savoir) | we know |
| ravi(-e) | delighted | | |
| excuser | to excuse | encore | yet |
| déranger | to disturb | inviter | to invite |
| vous prévoyez (prévoir) | you foresee; have in mind | vous connaissez (connaître) | you know |
| pour | for | je connais (connaître) | I know |
| aujourd'hui | today | | |
| nous allons (aller) | we are going | manger | to eat |
| | | venez (venir) | come |
| nous voulons (vouloir) | we want | plus | more |
| | | tard | late |
| acheter | to buy | | |

(b) **Dialogue 2**

(i) **Useful expressions**

| | |
|---|---|
| il fait beau | it's fine |
| de temps en temps | from time to time |
| on ne sait jamais | you never know |
| il va y avoir du soleil | it's going to be sunny |
| quand même | all the same; nevertheless |
| bonne chance! | good luck! |
| amusez-vous bien! | enjoy yourselves! |

(ii) **Nouns – Masc.**          **Nouns – Fem.**

| | | | |
|---|---|---|---|
| le temps | weather; time | la chance | luck |
| l'été | summer | la mer | sea |
| le climat | climate | | |
| un peu | a little | | |
| le ciel | sky | | |
| le soleil | sun | | |
| un anorak | anorak | | |

(iii) **Other words**

| | | | |
|---|---|---|---|
| aimer | to like | vous croyez (croire) | you think |
| il pleut | it's raining | | |
| encore | again | possible | possible |
| jamais | never | vite | quickly |
| si | yes | regarder | to look (at) |
| généralement | generally | peut-être | perhaps |

| | | | |
|---|---|---|---|
| chaud(-e) | warm; hot | on | one |
| quelquefois | sometimes | bleu(-e) | blue |
| maritime | maritime | optimiste | optimistic |
| comme | like | vrai(-e) | true |

## 5.3 EXPLANATIONS

### (a) More about greetings, good wishes etc.

(i) English has no equivalent for bon appétit! which is what you wish someone in French if they are already eating when you arrive (like Michel Lebrun arriving during the Smiths' breakfast), or if you are about to start a meal together. You respond by saying Merci, or, if the other person is also about to eat, you can wish them Bon appétit! in turn, or say Merci, vous aussi.

(ii) A commonly heard greeting is Ça va? This is a short version of Comment allez-vous?, and means 'How are you?'; 'How are things?' The answer is simply Ça va, or Ça va bien. So you could conceivably hear a hurried conversation like this:

*Michel*:  Ça va?
*John*:  Ça va. Et vous, ça va?
*Michel*:  Ça va. La famille, ça va?
*John*:  Ça va. Les enfants, ça va?
*Michel*:  Ça va. Alors, au revoir.

You will hear the little word ça quite often. It is really a short form of cela, meaning 'this' or 'that'. You have already met the expression c'est ça, meaning 'that's right'. You will also hear comme ça, meaning 'like that', if someone shows you how to do something. If there is anything you want and do not know the French word for, you can always point to it and say Ça, s'il vous plait – it's not very elegant, but it might get you out of a problem!

(iii) In Chapter 1 the policeman wishes the Smiths Bon séjour! – 'have a nice stay!' In Dialogue 2 the hotelier says Bonne chance! – 'good luck!'

### (b) More about verbs

(i) One way in English of expressing future intentions is by using the verb 'to go' followed by an infinitive, for example: 'We are going to visit the castle this morning'. French has an exactly equivalent construction using the verb aller + infinitive, for example:

Nous allons visiter le château ce matin.

Other examples will be found in the dialogues, for example:

Nous allons faire des courses.

(ii) The verb croire means 'to think' or 'to believe', and is used to express opinions. When it starts the sentence it is followed by que, for example:

Je crois que nous allons acheter des anoraks — I think (that) we are going to buy some anoraks'.

(Note that the word 'that' can be left out in English, but must always be included in French.)

It is also possible for the verb croire to come after the statement, for example:

Il va faire beau, je crois — 'It's going to be fine, I think'.

(iii) There are a number of further examples in this chapter of the use of vouloir + infinitive, for example:

Nous voulons acheter des vêtements — 'we want to buy some clothes'.

**(c) Talking about the weather**

The word for 'weather' is le temps. To ask, 'What's the weather like?' you say Quel temps fait-il? (Note that temps not only means 'weather' but also, in some cases, 'time'. In Chapter 1 the policeman asked, Vous restez combien de temps en France?, that is 'how long' or, literally, 'how much time?' Temps can mean 'time' when referring to a period of time. But when you are referring to time by the clock, such as saying 'What time is it?' (Quelle heure est-il?) or, 'the exact time is ...' (l'heure exacte est ...) you use heure.) This is how you talk about the weather in French.

(i) When using an adjective French says il fait ..., for example:

Il fait beau — 'It's fine'; Il fait mauvais — 'It's bad weather'.

(ii) French uses il y a to refer to sun, wind and so on, for example:

Il y a du soleil — 'It's sunny'; Il y a du vent — 'It's windy'.

(Note il va y avoir ... — 'It's going to be ...'

(iii) There are a number of verbs to describe particular weather conditions, for example:

Il pleut — 'It's raining'.

These verbs for describing the weather follow the patterns already learned for asking questions and making negative statements, for example:

Est-ce qu'il pleut? — 'Is it raining?' Il ne fait pas beau — 'It isn't fine weather'.

**(d)** A further form of the negative is introduced in this chapter, namely, jamais — 'never'. This word can stand by itself, for example:

Vous allez au théâtre? – Jamais! ('Do you go to the theatre? – Never!).

When used with a verb, however, ne ... jamais is used, following the same pattern as ne ... pas, for example: Il ne fait jamais beau; on ne sait jamais (literally, 'one never knows'). *See grammar ref. 5.10.*

(e) Although 'yes' is normally rendered in French by oui, a response to a question phrased in the negative is si, for example:
Il ne fait jamais beau? – si!

## 5.4 EXERCISES

### Section A

#### (a) Exercise 1
Say what you are going to do today in answer to the question qu'est-ce que vous prévoyez pour aujourd'hui?

Combine je vais, or, nous allons with a suitable verb and noun from the list below, for example: je vais acheter des vêtements – 'I am going to buy some clothes'.

|  |  |  |  |
|---|---|---|---|
|  | acheter | le château |  |
|  | visiter | le musée |  |
| je vais | voir | au restaurant |  |
| nous allons | manger | un chèque |  |
|  | changer | une glace |  |
|  | déjeuner | des vêtements |  |

#### (b) Exercise 2
Using the same lists of words in sensible combinations (you are unlikely to be buying the château!) respond this time to the question Qu'est-ce que vous voulez faire? – 'What do you want to do?', for example:
Nous voulons acheter une glace; Je veux déjeuner au restaurant.

#### (c) Exercise 3
You really have overloaded your programme! When a French friend tries to fix a time for you to have a meal together there is hardly a moment free. First of all he asks you what you are going to see today, Qu'est-ce que vous allez voir aujourd'hui?. When you tell him all that you have in mind, he retorts, Mon Dieu! Quand est-ce que vous allez faire tout ça? Here is the programme you've made out for yourself. At the castle and town hall you have to be punctual for the guided tour,

but at the other places the times can be more approximate, for example:

Je vais voir le château à neuf heures et demie; Je vais voir le port vers onze heures.

*Programme*

| | |
|---|---|
| Château | 9h30 |
| Église Saint-Pierre | 10h30 |
| Port | 11h |
| Hôtel de Ville | 14h |
| Musée | 15h15 |
| Jardin des Plantes | 16h30 |

Try putting yourself in the place of the person asking the questions about this programme. How would he say, when are you going to visit ...? for each of these items?

## Section B

### (d) Exercise 4

Here is your diary for the coming week of your stay in Caen. Someone asks you Qu'est-ce que vous prévoyez pour la semaine? – 'What plans have you got for the week?' Tell them what you and your family plan to do, for example:

Lundi, nous allons visiter le port; Mercredi matin ... and so on.

| | |
|---|---|
| lundi | le port |
| mardi | le château; le musée |
| mercredi | Lisieux (Basilique); le théâtre (soir) |
| jeudi | Musée du Débarquement (matin); Tapisserie de Bayeux (après-midi) |
| vendredi | faire des courses (matin); déjeuner au restaurant |
| samedi | piscine (matin); la plage (après-midi) |
| dimanche | église Saint-Pierre |

### (e) Exercise 5

Translate into French

(i) I am going to have lunch at half-past twelve.

(ii) I want to visit the port at about a quarter to two.

(iii) If you are free at noon, come to the restaurant.

(iv) Forgive me for disturbing your lunch.

(v) I think that it will be fine later on.

(vi) Isn't it ever fine here?

(vii) The weather changes quickly here. Perhaps it's going to be sunny.

(viii) You never know. I think we are going to buy anoraks nevertheless.

# CHAPTER 6

# DO YOU LIKE IT?

# I'LL HAVE THIS FOR MYSELF

## 6.1 DIALOGUES 📼

**(a) Dialogue 1   On achète des vêtements   Shopping for clothes**

*Vendeuse*:   Bonjour, monsieur. Bonjour, madame. Vous désirez?

*Mary*:   Où sont les vêtements pour enfants, s'il vous plaît, mademoiselle?

*Vendeuse*:   Par ici, madame. Qu'est-ce que vous cherchez?

*Mary*:   Je voudrais des anoraks pour nos deux enfants.

*Vendeuse*:   Oui, madame. Alors, nous avons des anoraks de toutes les tailles et de toutes les couleurs. Est-ce que la fillette préfère un anorak bleu, rouge ou vert?

*Mary*:   Pour elle, un anorak rouge, je crois.

*Vendeuse*:   Et pour le garçon?

*Mary*:   Pour lui, un anorak bleu. Oui, c'est ça.

*Vendeuse*:   Voilà, madame. C'est la taille exacte pour lui et pour elle, je crois. Vous aimez ça?

*Mary*:   Oui, très bien.

*Vendeuse*:   C'est tout, madame?

*Mary*:   C'est tout pour eux. Mon mari cherche un pullover.

*Vendeuse*:   Les pullovers sont au rayon messieurs.

*John*:   Bien, alors. J'y vais. À plus tard.

**(b) Dialogue 2   On achète des vêtements** *(suite)*   **Shopping for clothes** *(continued)*

*Mary*:   Moi, je voudrais un imperméable.

*Vendeuse*:   Oui, madame. Voilà un imperméable rouge. Il est très chic. Ou alors, un imperméable jaune, si vous préférez. Vous voulez essayer le jaune?

*Mary*:   Oui, pour moi c'est préférable, je crois. Je ne porte jamais de rouge.

## On achète des vêtements

Photograph: D. J. Troisfontaines

*Vendeuse*:  Ah oui, madame. Il est très bien.

*Mary*:  Alors je prends les deux anoraks et l'imperméable. Ça fait combien?

*Vendeuse*:  L'anorak de la fillette fait cinquante-neuf francs (59F) et l'anorak du garçon fait cinquante-deux francs (52F). L'imperméable fait trois cent quatre-vingt-dix-neuf francs (399F), alors cinq cent dix francs en tout. Payez à la caisse, s'il vous plaît, madame.

*Mary*:  Oui. Où est la caisse?

*Vendeuse*:  Là-bas, madame, près de l'entrée.

*Mary*:  Merci bien. Ah, voilà mon mari.

*Vendeuse*:  Vous avez votre pullover, monsieur?

*John*:  Non, rien. Il n'y a rien pour moi. Je ne trouve jamais de vêtements à ma taille. Des pullovers énormes et des pullovers minuscules, mais pas un pullover de taille normale, comme moi!

*Vendeuse*:  Je suis desolée, monsieur.

*John*:  Ce n'est pas de votre faute, mademoiselle. Ce n'est rien. Les anoraks des enfants sont jolis et l'imperméable de ma femme est joli aussi.

*Mary*:  Tu aimes mon imperméable?

*John*:  Oui, beaucoup.

**(c) Dialogue 3   Retour à l'hôtel   Return to the hotel**

*Hôtelier*:   Alors vous voyez, monsieur. Il ne pleut plus. C'est fini le
mauvais temps. Vous allez avoir de la chance aujourd'hui, quand
même. Il va faire beau, je crois.

*John*:   Oui, heureusement. Après le déjeuner nous allons faire un
petit tour en voiture, peut-être.

*Hôtelier*:   Ah oui, vers la mer peut-être. Les plages de la région sont
très belles. Vous aimez aller au bord de la mer, madame?

*Mary*:   Oui, beaucoup. Et les enfants adorent ça, quand il y a du
soleil.

*Hôtelier*:   Amusez-vous bien, alors.

## 6.2 VOCABULARY

### (a) Dialogue 1

#### (i) Useful expressions

| | |
|---|---|
| par ici | this way; over here |
| de toutes les tailles | in all sizes |
| j'y vais | I'm going there; I'm on my way. |

#### (ii) Nouns – Masc.

| | | |
|---|---|---|
| le garçon | boy | |
| le pullover | pullover | |
| le rayon | department | |
| le rayon messieurs | the men's department | |

#### Nouns – Fem.

| | |
|---|---|
| la taille | size |
| la couleur | colour |
| la fillette | little girl |

#### (iii) Other words

| | |
|---|---|
| chercher | to look for |
| rouge | red |
| vert(-e) | green |
| exact(-e) | exact |

### (b) Dialogue 2

#### (i) Useful expressions

| | |
|---|---|
| ça fait combien? | what does that come to? |
| à ma taille | in my size |
| ce n'est pas de votre faute | it's not your fault |
| il n'y a rien pour moi | there's nothing for me |
| ce n'est rien | it doesn't matter |

#### (ii) Noun – Masc.

| | |
|---|---|
| un imperméable | raincoat |

#### Noun – Fem.

| | |
|---|---|
| la faute | fault |

(iii) **Other words**

| | | | |
|---|---|---|---|
| chic (no change for the feminine) | | | smart |
| jaune | yellow | rien | nothing |
| essayer | to try | trouver | to find |
| préférable | preferable | trop | too |
| porter | to wear | énorme | enormous |
| je prends (prendre) | I take; I'll take | minuscule | tiny |
| payer | to pay | normal(-e) | normal |
| là-bas | over there | joli(-e) | pretty |

**(c) Dialogue 3**

(i) **Useful expressions**

| | |
|---|---|
| il ne pleut plus | it's not raining any more |
| au bord de la mer | at the sea-side |

(ii) **Noun – Masc.**    **Nouns – Fem.**

| | | | |
|---|---|---|---|
| le tour | tour, trip | la voiture | car |
| | | la plage | beach |

(iii) **Other words**

| | | | |
|---|---|---|---|
| fini(-e) | finished | vers | towards |
| mauvais(-e) | bad | beau (belle) | fine; beautiful |
| heureusement | luckily; happily | adorer | to love; to adore |

## 6.3 EXPLANATIONS

### (a) Expressing likes and dislikes

The verb aimer can mean 'to like', or 'to love'. It can be followed either by a noun, for example:

J'aime le tennis – 'I like tennis',

or by a verb, for example:

J'aime aller à la plage – 'I like going to the beach'

(note that the French verb following aimer is in the infinitive form). The verb can be made stronger by using beaucoup, for example:

J'aime beaucoup faire les courses; J'aime beaucoup la région.

(Note that, unlike English, the adverb beaucoup stays close to the verb.) Asking questions about people's likes is done in the same way, either with a noun, for example:

Vous aimez le tennis? or with the infinitive of a verb, for example:

Est-ce que vous aimez aller à la plage?

### (b) Pronouns grammar ref 4.1 (e)

Pronouns are words which replace nouns to avoid unnecessary repetition. In a series of statements such as, 'My children are still young'; 'My children like swimming'; 'My children go to bed early', it would be unusual to repeat the noun for each statement; the pronoun 'they' would be used instead. Pronouns change according to their position in a sentence. If the pronoun 'they' occurs after a preposition it becomes 'them', for example: 'with them'; 'for them'. In this chapter we meet a number of cases where French pronouns are used after prepositions in this way. For example, we know that the pronoun 'I' is expressed in French as je. After a preposition, English 'I' changes to 'me', for example: 'for me'; 'with me.' In French, je changes to moi, for example: Mary says pour moi, c'est préférable. Look at these other examples from the dialogues: Pour lui un anorak bleu; C'est tout pour eux. Three of the subject pronouns do not change in this position, namely, elle, nous and vous. We say pour elle, un anorak rouge, and in the same way we should say pour vous; avec nous and so on.

## (c) More about verbs

The subject pronouns introduced in this course have so far been limited to je, nous and vous. In this chapter the other pronouns are introduced, so that we now have the complete picture of the verb in the present tense, for instance, we could write out the present tense of the verb être − 'to be':

| je suis | I am | nous sommes | we are |
|---------|------|-------------|--------|
| tu es | you are | vous êtes | you are |
| il est | he is | ils sont | they are |
| elle est | she is | elles sont | they are |

Some of this needs further explanation:

(i) French has two pronouns for 'you'. Mary says to her husband, Tu aimes mon imperméable? The word tu is used to address children or very close friends and relations. Amongst students, schoolchildren and between members of families, tu is common, but for a foreigner it is always safest to stick to the polite form vous when talking to adults. This book does not set out to teach tu, and it is given here for information only.

(ii) You will notice that 'they' is expressed differently according to whether it refers to a group of males (and grammatically masculine objects), or a group of females (and grammatically feminine objects). If a group is mixed, the masculine gender is used.

(iii) There is a further pronoun, very commonly met with in spoken French, namely on. This means 'one', or 'you' or 'people' as in the statements 'One can never tell'; 'People say the weather will improve', and so on. The hotelier says On ne sait jamais − 'You never know'; On voit déjà un peu de ciel bleu − 'You can already see a bit of blue sky'. On is particularly often used as a substitute for nous, for example: one can say;

Qu'est-ce qu'on va faire aujourd'hui? or Qu'est-ce que nous allons faire aujourd'hui?

English would say, for both of these, 'what are we going to do today?'

#### (d) Possession

Chapter 3 has already introduced the idea of possession expressed by de, as in le port de Caen. This chapter contains further examples of such usage. French has no equivalent to the English use of the apostrophe in 'Mary's raincoat'; 'the children's anoraks'. The French way of saying this is l'imperméable de Mary; les anoraks des enfants. You will remember that de changes its form when it links up with le or les. Note the other examples from the text.

l'anorak de la fillette − 'the girl's anorak';
l'imperméable de ma femme − 'my wife's raincoat';
l'anorak du garçon − 'the boy's anorak';
les anoraks des enfants − 'the children's anoraks'.

#### (e) C'est

We have already encountered a number of examples of the little phrase c'est. It can normally be rendered in English by 'it is'; 'this is', or 'that is'. Consider the following examples:

Qu'est-ce que c'est − 'what is it?'
C'est le château − 'it's the castle'
C'est un climat maritime − 'it's a maritime climate'
C'est possible − 'it's possible'
C'est vrai − 'that's true'
C'est tout? − 'is that all?'
C'est de votre faute − 'it's your fault'

You can see that c'est is a useful little phrase with many possible renderings. Note the further examples that occur.

#### (f) More about negatives *grammar ref 5.10*

In this chapter we met two further examples of negative constructions, ne ... rien, and ne ... plus. Ne ... rien means 'nothing', as when John Smith says Il n'y a rien pour moi − 'There is nothing for me'. Like jamais, introduced in the previous chapter, rien can be used with a verb, as in the example given, or stand alone, for example:

Vous avez votre pullover, monsieur? Non, rien.

Ne ... plus means 'no longer', for example:

Il ne pleut plus − 'It's no longer raining'.

**(f) Some notes on items of vocabulary**

(i) Note the various uses of the preposition en, for example: en été − 'in summer'; en Angleterre − 'in England'; en voiture − 'by car'.

(ii) The word tout may be a pronoun meaning 'everything', in which case it doesn't change, for example:

C'est tout? − 'Is that everything?'

But when tout is an adjective meaning 'all', or 'every', in which case it appears before the noun which it qualifies, it has four possible forms depending on whether it is masculine or feminine, singular or plural (tout, toute; tous; toutes). Most of these forms have already been introduced, for example:

tout le monde − 'everybody';

tous les jours − 'every day';

toutes les couleurs − 'every colour'.

(iii) The pronoun y is introduced in one example in this chapter, namely, j'y vais. Y means 'there' and it comes in front of the verb, as in this example, which means 'I am going there'. Further examples and explanations of the use of y will be given in Chapter 14.

(iv) An adjective in French can be used without the noun which it would normally qualify if the meaning is clear, for example:

Vous voulez essayer le jaune? − 'Do you want to try the yellow one?'

French does not need to express the word 'one' which occurs in the English version of this sentence. Note also in Chapter 2.1 (b), Apportez aussi deux glaces pour les petits ('for the little ones' that is, 'the children').

## 6.4 EXERCISES

### Section A

**(a) Exercise 1**

You are asked a series of questions about your personal likes. Some words are new, but you can easily guess them (for instance, le sport). Respond according to your own opinions with one of the possible answers bracketed on the right, for example, you might say:

Non je n'aime pas le sport, or Oui j'aime beaucoup faire les courses.

| | |
|---|---|
| (i) Vous aimez le sport? | Non, je n'aime pas ... |
| (ii) Vous aimez le tennis? | Oui, j'aime ... |
| (iii) Vous aimez le beau temps? | Oui, j'aime beaucoup ... |
| (iv) Vous aimez le rugby | Oui, j'adore ... |
| (v) Vous aimez faire les courses? | Comme ci comme ça (so so) |
| (vi) Vous aimez visiter les musées? | Ça dépend (it all depends) |

(vii) Vous aimez déjeuner au restaurant?     Non, je n'aime pas . . .
(viii) Vous aimez aller au théâtre?                Oui, j'aime . . . etc
 (ix) Vous aimez voir un spectacle de 'son et lumière'?
 (x) Vous aimez aller à la piscine?

When making your replies you can either repeat the whole item as in the examples given or you can use the all-purpose ça, for example:

Vous aimez aller au théâtre? — Oui, j'adore ça.

## (b) Exercise 2

See if you can conduct a conversation about the weather on the following lines. You take part B.

*A*:  Bonjour, monsieur. Il fait encore mauvais aujourd'hui.

*B*:  (Yes the weather is bad again. Is it going to be fine later?)

*A*:  Peut-être, monsieur. On ne sait jamais. Mais il pleut aussi chez vous en Angleterre, non?

*B*:  (Yes, of course. Say it rains a lot in England because there is (parce qu'il y a) a maritime climate. Say that you are out of luck but perhaps there will be (il va y avoir) sunshine later.)

*A*:  Ah oui monsieur. Je suis optimiste. Mais n'oubliez pas votre anorak.

*B*:  (No, you never know. Say you think you will be visiting a museum today.)

*A*:  Ah oui, quand il pleut, un musée, c'est très bien. Amusez-vous bien!

*B*:  (Thank him and say goodbye.)

## (c) Exercise 3

Who is it for?     C'est pour qui?

  (i) L'anorak rouge, c'est pour Catherine? — Oui, c'est pour elle.
 (ii) L'imperméable jaune, c'est pour Mary? — Oui, . . . . . .
(iii) Le pullover bleu, c'est pour John? — Oui, . . . . . .
 (iv) L'anorak bleu, ce n'est pas pour le garçon? — Mais si . . . . . .

(Notice this very French way of putting this sort of question. The English word order is, 'Is the red anorak for Catherine?' French begins by naming the object and then puts the question using c'est with a rising intonation. It can't be done with the following set of questions, because they all refer to people and c'est can usually only refer to objects).

With whom?     Avec qui?

  (v) Les deux enfants sont avec leur père? — Oui, ils sont avec lui.
 (vi) Monsieur Lebrun est avec la famille Smith? — Oui, il est . . . . . .
(vii) L'hôtelier est avec sa femme? — Oui . . . . . .
(viii) Mary est avec les enfants? — Oui . . . . . .

## Section B

**(d) Exercise 4**
Translate into French
  (i) I like the region very much, but it rains a lot.
  (ii) I think that it's going to be fine later.
  (iii) That's possible. One never knows. What are you planning for today?
  (iv) We are going shopping this morning.
  (v) At midday we are going to have lunch in a restaurant.
  (vi) You are lucky! Enjoy yourselves!
  (vii) Catherine's anorak is too small.
  (viii) We have anoraks in all sizes. Do you want a blue or red anorak for her?
  (ix) She prefers the red anorak I think. Yes, that's the exact size for her.
  (x) Good, and I'd like a raincoat for myself.

**(e) Exercise 5**
On the left is a list of objects. On the right is a list of people and places. Indicate possession with the correct form of du, de la, des, de l' or de, for example: l'imperméable de Madame Smith.

| | | | |
|---|---|---|---|
| (i) | le pullover | | la chambre |
| (ii) | le port | | le château |
| (iii) | l'entrée | de | les hommes |
| (iv) | la voiture | de la | la ville |
| (v) | la clef | de l' | Monsieur Lebrun |
| (vi) | le numéro | du | Caen |
| (vii) | la piscine | des | l'enfant |
| (viii) | les vêtements | | la porte (door) |
| (ix) | l'imperméable | | le monsieur |

# CHAPTER 7

# WHAT WOULD YOU LIKE TO EAT? DO YOU WANT TO TRY SOMETHING LOCAL?

## 7.1 DIALOGUES 📼

**(a) Dialogue 1   Au Restaurant   In the Restaurant**

*John Smith*:   Ah, les voilà! Bonjour, Michel, bonjour, Nicole.

*Michel Lebrun*:   Bonjour, mes amis.

*Nicole Lebrun*:   Bonjour, tout le monde. Asseyez-vous, je vous en prie.

*Michel*:   Alors, vous allez prendre un petit apéritif avant de manger?

*Mary*:   Oui, avec plaisir. Pour moi, un martini, s'il vous plaît.

*John*:   Et pour moi, un pernod.

*Michel*:   Bien. Vous voyez, ma femme et moi, nous buvons aussi du martini. Et les enfants?

*Mary*:   Pour eux, des jus de fruit, je crois.

*Michel*:   Garçon! Un martini, un pernod et deux jus de fruit, s'il vous plaît.

*Garçon*:   Oui, monsieur. Des jus d'orange?

*Mary*:   Oui, ça va très bien.

*Michel*:   On peut avoir le menu, s'il vous plaît?

*Garçon*:   Certainement, monsieur. Le voilà.

**(b) Dialogue 2   Au Restaurant *(suite)*   In the Restaurant *(continued)***

*Michel*:   Alors, qu'est-ce que vous aimez comme hors d'oeuvre? Mary, si vous voulez quelque chose de la région il y a un pâté normand, ou alors des moules marinière.

*Mary*:   Je voudrais bien un pâté. J'adore ça!

*John*:   Moi, je vais prendre les moules.

*Michel*:   Et toi, chérie, qu'est-ce que tu prends? Le pâté, les moules ou autre chose?

*Nicole*:   Je vais prendre les escargots.

# MENU

Araignée de Mer Mayonnaise . . . . . . . . . . . . . . . . . . . . . . 48F
Langoustines Mayonnaises . . . . . . . . . . . . . . . . . . . . . . . . 40
6 Huîtres Farcies Florentine . . . . . . . . . . . . . . . . . . . . . . . 30
Soupe de Poisson . . . . . . . . . . . . . . . . . . . . . . . . . . . . . . . 38
Galantine de Saint-Jacques . . . . . . . . . . . . . . . . . . . . . . . 30
Terrine de Foie de Volaille . . . . . . . . . . . . . . . . . . . . . . . . 32
Jambon Cru de Pays . . . . . . . . . . . . . . . . . . . . . . . . . . . . 35
Assiette de Charcuterie . . . . . . . . . . . . . . . . . . . . . . . . . . 25
Artichaut Vinaigrette . . . . . . . . . . . . . . . . . . . . . . . . . . . . 18
Pâté Normand . . . . . . . . . . . . . . . . . . . . . . . . . . . . . . . . . 30
Assiette de Saumon Fumé . . . . . . . . . . . . . . . . . . . . . . . . 38
Pamplemousse Glacé . . . . . . . . . . . . . . . . . . . . . . . . . . . . 15
Melon Glacé . . . . . . . . . . . . . . . . . . . . . . . . . . . . . . . . . . 15
Moules Marinière . . . . . . . . . . . . . . . . . . . . . . . . . . . . . . . 30
6 Escargots . . . . . . . . . . . . . . . . . . . . . . . . . . . . . . . . . . . 30

## POISSONS
Darne de Lieu Meunière . . . . . . . . . . . . . . . . . . . . . . . . . . 38
Friture de Scampi Milanaise . . . . . . . . . . . . . . . . . . . . . . . 35
Maquereau au Vin Blanc Grillé . . . . . . . . . . . . . . . . . . . . . 38
Sole Meunière . . . . . . . . . . . . . . . . . . . . . . . . . . . . . . . . . 65
Suprême de Turbot Sauce Crème . . . . . . . . . . . . . . . . . . . 48

## VIANDES
Escalope de Dinde Pannée Viennoise . . . . . . . . . . . . . . . . 38
Noix d'Entrecôte Béarnaise . . . . . . . . . . . . . . . . . . . . . . . 40
Coq au Vin . . . . . . . . . . . . . . . . . . . . . . . . . . . . . . . . . . . 38
Steak au Poivre . . . . . . . . . . . . . . . . . . . . . . . . . . . . . . . . 45
Canard à l'Orange . . . . . . . . . . . . . . . . . . . . . . . . . . . . . . 42
Escalope Normande . . . . . . . . . . . . . . . . . . . . . . . . . . . . . 40

## DESSERTS
Plateau de Fromages . . . . . . . . . . . . . . . . . . . . . . . . . . . . 18
Corbeille de Fruits . . . . . . . . . . . . . . . . . . . . . . . . . . . . . . 15
Glaces . . . . . . . . . . . . . . . . . . . . . . . . . . . . . . . . . . . . . . . 15
Pêche ou Fraises Melba . . . . . . . . . . . . . . . . . . . . . . . . . . 20
Crème Caramel . . . . . . . . . . . . . . . . . . . . . . . . . . . . . . . . 10
Café Express . . . . . . . . . . . . . . . . . . . . . . . . . . . . . . . . 3.50

*Michel*: Moi aussi, je vais prendre les escargots. Et les enfants?

*Mary*: Pour les enfants? Eh bien, l'assiette de charcuterie, je crois.

*Garçon*: Voilà vos apéritifs, messieurs-dames. Un martini pour madame, un pernod pour monsieur et deux jus d'orange pour les petits. Et qu'est-ce que vous allez prendre comme hors d'oeuvre?

*Michel*: Comme hors d'oeuvre, alors, nous prenons: deux escargots, une fois moules marinière, un pâté et une assiette de charcuterie pour les deux petits.

*Garçon*: Bien, monsieur. Et ensuite?

*Michel*: Nous ne savons pas encore.

*Garçon*: Bien, monsieur. Je reviens dans quelques minutes, alors.

### (c) Dialogue 3  Au Restaurant *(suite)*  In the Restaurant *(continued)*

*Michel*: Comme plat principal, qu'est-ce que vous préférez? Vous voulez encore goûter quelque chose de la région, Mary? Il y a l'escalope normande, ou alors les tripes à la mode de Caen.

*Mary*: Je n'aime pas beaucoup les tripes. Pour moi, c'est un peu trop gras. Mais je voudrais bien essayer l'escalope.

*Michel*: Vous avez raison. L'escalope est délicieuse ici.

*John*: Moi, j'aime beaucoup le steak au poivre.

*Michel*: Vous aimez votre steak saignant ou bien cuit?

*John*: Saignant. C'est meilleur, je crois.

*Michel*: Et toi, chérie, qu'est-ce que tu vas prendre?

*Nicole*: J'hésite entre le coq au vin et le canard à l'orange. Ils sont tous les deux très bons ici, mais le coq est peut-être meilleur, alors, le coq au vin pour moi.

*Michel*: À mon avis, le canard est meilleur. Et les enfants, ils ont faim, je crois. Ils attendent patiemment.

*Mary*: Catherine aime les oeufs, alors, une omelette pour elle. Robert, lui, n'aime pas du tout les oeufs, mais il adore la viande. Alors une escalope pour lui. Mais, il y a des demi-portions pour enfants?

*Michel*: Mais oui, bien entendu. Et comme boisson, alors. Une carafe de vin rouge et une de blanc, je crois, pour plaire à tout le monde.

*Garçon*: Voilà les hors d'oeuvre. Bon appétit, messieurs-dames. Et comme plat principal . . .?

### (d) Dialogue 4  Au Restaurant *(suite et fin)*  In the Restaurant *(continued and concluded)*

*John*: Quel repas délicieux!

*Mary*: Oui, alors. Vraiment excellent!

*Michel*: Et ce n'est pas encore fini! Vous prenez bien un peu de fromage?

*Mary*: Ah oui, c'est vrai. En France, on mange le fromage avant le dessert.

*Nicole*: Oui, les Français trouvent ça plus logique. Et en Normandie nous avons les meilleurs fromages du monde. Le Camembert, le Livarot, le Pont l'Évêque.

*John*: Je ne connais pas le Livarot.

*Michel*: C'est le roi des fromages, mais plus fort que le Camembert. Voilà le plateau des fromages. Vous pouvez choisir. Et après comme dessert?

*Mary*: Moi, je vais prendre une glace, tout simplement. Et des fruits pour les enfants.

*John*: Moi aussi, je vais prendre un fruit.

*Michel*: Garçon! . . .

## 7.2 VOCABULARY.

**(a) Dialogue 1**

(i) **Useful expressions**

| | |
|---|---|
| tout le monde | everybody |
| asseyez-vous | sit down |

(ii) **Nouns – Masc.**  **Nouns – Fem.**

| | | | |
|---|---|---|---|
| un apéritif | aperitif | une orange | orange |
| le jus (de fruit) | (fruit) juice | | |
| le menu | menu | | |

(iii) **Other words**

| | |
|---|---|
| avant | before (time) |
| nous buvons (boire) | we drink: we are drinking |

**(b) Dialogue 2**

(i) **Useful expressions**

| | |
|---|---|
| quelque chose | something |
| autre chose | something else |
| ou alors | or else |

(ii) **Nouns – Masc.**  **Nouns – Fem.**

| | | | |
|---|---|---|---|
| les hors d'oeuvre | hors d'oeuvres | la région | region |
| | | la moule | mussel |

| le pâté | pâté | la chose | thing |
|---|---|---|---|
| un escargot | snail | une assiette | plate |
| | | la charcuterie | cold meats |

### (iii) Other words

| | |
|---|---|
| vous voulez (vouloir) | you want |
| normand(e) | Norman |
| marinier(-ère) | marine (but here, a way of serving mussels) |
| chéri (chérie) | dear; darling |
| autre | other |
| ou | or |
| ensuite | next |
| quelques | some; a few |
| je reviens (revenir) | I return |

## (c) Dialogue 3

### (i) Useful expressions

| | |
|---|---|
| à mon avis | in my opinion |
| pas du tout | not at all |

### (ii) Nouns – Masc.                                   Nouns – Fem.

| le plat | dish | une escalope | cutlet |
|---|---|---|---|
| le steak | steak | les tripes | tripe |
| le poivre | pepper | la mode | fashion |
| le coq | cock | la faim | hunger |
| le vin | wine | une omelette | omelette |
| le canard | duck | la viande | meat |
| un avis | opinion | la portion | portion |
| un oeuf | egg | la boisson | drink |
| | | la carafe | carafe; jug |

### (iii) Other words

| goûter | to taste | hésiter | to hesitate |
|---|---|---|---|
| gras | fat | entre | between |
| essayer | to try | avoir faim | to be hungry |
| avoir raison | to be right | attendre | to wait |
| délicieux-(-euse) | delicious | patiemment | patiently |
| saignant | bloody; rare (meat) | blanc (blanche) | white |
| cuit (-e) | cooked | plaire à | to please |
| meilleur | better | | |

**(d) Dialogue 3**

(i) **Useful expressions**

| | |
|---|---|
| quel repas délicieux! | what a delicious meal! |
| tout simplement | quite simply |

(ii) **Nouns − Masc.**  **Noun − Fem.**

| | | | |
|---|---|---|---|
| le repas | meal | la Française | Frenchwoman |
| le fromage | cheese | | |
| le dessert | dessert | | |
| le Français | Frenchman | | |
| le roi | king | | |
| le plateau | tray | | |
| le plateau des fromages | cheese board | | |
| le fruit | fruit | | |

## 7.3 EXPLANATIONS

### (a) Regular verbs

The regular verbs which have been introduced so far have all had an infinitive ending in -er, as explained in Chapter 2. By far the majority of French regular verbs have this -er ending, but two other types of regular verb are also encountered. One example of each is found in this chapter, namely:

choisir − 'to choose' (infinitive ending in -ir)

attendre − 'to wait' (infinitive ending in -re)

You will find the full present tense of these verbs in *grammar ref. 5.1(a)*

### (b) Comparative of Adjectives *grammar ref 3.4*

We often use adjectives to compare one thing with another. In English we usually do this by adding '-er' to the adjective, as in the statement, 'He is taller than his brother'. Another possibility in English, particularly with adjectives of two or more syllables, is to make the comparative by using the word 'more', for example: 'This garden is more beautiful than any I've seen'. It is this pattern with 'more' that is used in French in almost all cases. The French word for 'more', is plus. One example of this usage has already been seen in an earlier chapter, that is, à plus tard − 'see you later'. In Dialogue 4 of this chapter you will find, c'est plus logique. The comparative form of the adjective often occurs in English with the word 'than', for example:

'taller than' in the example already given, the French equivalent of 'than' is que, as in:

Le Livarot est plus fort que le Camembert — 'Livarot is stronger than Camembert'

Catherine est plus petite que son frère — 'Catherine is smaller than her brother'.

Some commonly occurring adjectives in both English and French are irregular, in that they do not follow the pattern described. For example, English does not say 'gooder', but 'better'. In the same way, the adjective bon has the comparative meilleur — 'better', for example:

Le coq est peut-être meilleur.

If the French comparative appears with the definite article in front, for example: les meilleurs fromages, it means the same as the English superlative, for instance, 'the best cheeses'. If we applied this rule to the examples already given we would find:

le fromage le plus fort — 'the strongest cheese'

Catherine est la plus petite — 'Catherine is the smallest'.

## (c) Adverbs *grammar ref 6*

These are words which can qualify a verb, for example: 'he runs quickly', 'she runs slowly'. Not all English adverbs end in '-ly', but it is quite a common process to make an adverb by adding '-ly' to the adjective. In the same way, French adverbs are often formed by adding -ment to the feminine form of the adjective. Chapter 5 introduced généralement (from générale); heureusement (from heureuse). In this chapter you will find simplement and certainement. Sometimes, adding -ment to the adjective may cause slight changes of spelling and pronunciation. We have met two cases of adjectives ending in ent, namely évident and patient for which the adverbs are évidemment and patiemment. The form of adverbs never varies.

## (d) More about adjectives

English sometimes avoids the repetition of a noun in a sentence like this: 'Here is a red hat and a yellow one'. In French it is sufficient to drop the noun in such a case, and the word 'one' is not translated. For example:

une carafe de vin rouge et une de blanc; des jus de fruit pour les petits (that is, 'the little ones').

## (e) More about disjunctive pronouns *grammar ref 4.1(e)*

These are the pronouns introduced in Chapter 6 as used after prepositions, for example, avec moi; pour lui. They are also used to give emphasis in cases where English uses the voice alone to emphasise, for example:

Moi, je prends une escalope — '*I'll* take a cutlet'.

This seems, to English ears, to be saying the same thing twice over (moi, je ... ) but it is a very characteristic form of expression in French. Other examples are:

Toi, chérie, qu'est-ce que tu prends? — 'What would *you* like, dear?'

Moi, j'aime beaucoup le steak — '*I'm* very fond of steak'.

Robert, lui, n'aime pas du tout les oeufs — '*Robert* doesn't like eggs at all.

These pronouns can also be followed by aussi, for example:

Moi aussi, je vais prendre un fruit — 'I'll have some fruit as well'.

And notice how this sentence is formed with a double subject:

Ma femme et moi, nous buvons aussi du martini — 'My wife and I are drinking martini as well'.

### (f) Use of definite article *grammar ref 1.1 (b)*

There are some differences in usage of the definite article between English and French. For example, English would have no article at all in each of the following examples:

There are some differences in usage of the definite article between English and French. For example, English would have no article at all in each of the following examples:

Catherine aime les oeufs; Moi, j'aime beaucoup le steak.

When words are used in a general sense ('Catherine likes eggs', that is, eggs in general) French uses the definite article, for example:

Le fromage est bon à manger; Je n'aime pas les tripes.

### (g) Verbs and the prepositions that follow them *grammar ref. 5.7*

Numbers of English verbs are followed by prepositions which are essential to their meaning, for example: 'to look for', 'to wait for'. Neither of the French equivalents to these two examples needs a preposition, for example:

Je cherche un pullover; Ils attendent l'autobus.

But there are other examples where French requires a preposition where English has none, for instance:

Pour plaire à tout le monde — 'to please everybody'.

In future vocabularies, such necessary prepositions will be shown with the infinitive, for example: plaire à — 'to please'.

**(h) Notes on items of vocabulary**
(i) Note the use of quel in exclamations, for example:
Quel plaisir de vous revoir! − 'How nice to see you again!';
Quel repas délicieux! − 'What a delicious meal!'
(ii) Avant meaning 'before' can be followed either by a noun, for example: avant le dessert, or by de + infinitive, for example:
avant de manger − 'before eating'.
(iii) Comme means 'as' or 'like', for example,
Comme moi − 'like me'.
But note how often it is used in the restaurant scene, for example:
Qu'est-ce que vous voulez comme boisson?; Comme plat principal, qu'est-ce que vous préférez?
In these cases the most usual English would be, 'What would you like to drink?'; 'What would you like best for your main course?'.
(iv) Oeuf. The pronunciation should be noted. 'One egg' is un oeuf, with f pronounced. In the plural des oeufs, the final fs is not pronounced at all.
(v) Tout means 'all', and occurs in four possible forms (see p. 54). It occurs in numerous idiomatic phrases, for example:
tous les jours − 'every day';
tout le monde − 'everybody';
tout à fait − 'completely'
pas de tout − 'not at all'
(vi) Voilà. Note the use with pronouns:
les voilà − 'there they are';
le voilà − 'here it is'.

## 7.5 EXERCISES

**Section A**

**(a) Exercise 1**
Complete the scene below, taking the part of the person in the restaurant, and making use of the menu on p.58 to place your order.
*Garçon*: Bonjour, monsieur. Vous désirez?
*You*: (Order an aperitif and ask to see the menu.)
*Garçon*: Voilà votre apéritif, monsieur. Et qu'est-ce que vous prenez comme repas?
*You*: Comme hors d'oeuvre je voudrais ... (now order your whole meal, going through main course, cheese board and dessert).

*Garçon*:  Bien, monsieur. Et comme boisson?

*You*:  (Order a carafe of red or white wine.)

*You*:  (At the end of the meal, call over the waiter, ask him for the bill, and ask if the service charge is included.)

**(b) Exercise 2**

You are offered a range of possibilities from the menu. Using the phrases given, accept or refuse each item.

    (i)   Vous voulez l'escalope?

| | | | |
|---|---|---|---|
| (ii) | ... le pâté | | J'aime beaucoup ça |
| (iii) | ... les tripes | Oui, s'il vous plaît | J'adore ça |
| (iv) | ... les escargots | Avec plaisir | Je n'aime pas ça |
| (v) | ... le canard? | Non, merci | Je n'aime pas |
| (vi) | ... le coq au vin? | |    beaucoup ... |
| (vii) | ... une glace? | | Je déteste ... |

**(c) Exercise 3**

From the three columns below, see how many sentences you can form which make sense, for example:

    Le théâtre est plus intéressant que le cinéma.

If you don't agree with the statements, turn them round, for example:

    Le cinéma est plus intéressant que le théâtre.

| | | | |
|---|---|---|---|
| (i) | Le climat français | est plus fort que | en Angleterre |
| (ii) | Le Jardin des Plantes | est plus beau que | le port |
| (iii) | La couleur rouge | est plus chic que | votre anorak |
| (iv) | Dans le Midi il fait | plus chaud que | le cinéma |
| (v) | Le Livarot | est plus belle que | son frère |
| (vi) | Le théâtre | est plus délicieux que | le Camembert |
| (vii) | Mon imperméable | est plus intéressant que | la couleur jaune |
| (viii) | Catherine | est meilleur que | le climat anglais |
| | | est plus petite que | |

**Section B**

**(d) Exercise 4**

Translate into French

    (i) Please sit down. Would you like an aperitif before eating?

    (ii) Yes please, I'll have a martini.

    (iii) I think the children will have fruit juice.

    (iv) Can we have the menu please? Certainly sir.

(v) I'd like the pâté and my wife will have the snails.
(vi) I don't like meat very much. I'll have an omelette.
(vii) In my opinion, the duck is better.
(viii) They are hungry, I think, but they are waiting patiently.
(ix) What would you like to drink? A carafe of red wine.
(x) What a delicious meal! And it isn't finsished yet!

## (e) Exercise 5
Replace the infinitive in brackets with the correct form of the verb.
(i) Les enfants (attendre) patiemment.
(ii) Robert, lui (aimer) la viande.
(iii) Je (revenir) dans quelques minutes.
(iv) Qu'est-ce que vous (vouloir) comme apéritif?
(v) Elle (prendre) le canard, mais lui (préférer) le coq.
(vi) Nous (être) ravis de notre visite.

# CHAPTER 8

# WHAT'S YOUR JOB? WHERE ARE YOU FROM? HOW DO YOU SPEND YOUR TIME?

## 8.1 DIALOGUES 📼

**(a) Dialogue 1   Un sondage   A public opinion poll**
John Smith has paid an early call to the Syndicat d'Initiative to pick up more information about the excursion they are planning for today. As he leaves he is stopped by a young lady conducting some market research on tourism in Normandy.

*Demoiselle*: Excusez-moi, monsieur. Est-ce que vous êtes en vacances ici?

*John*: Oui.

*Demoiselle*: La municipalité de Caen fait un sondage sur le tourisme dans la ville et dans la région. Est-ce que vous avez quelques minutes pour répondre à des questions?

*John*: Mais oui. Je ne suis pas pressé.

*Demoiselle*: Bien, alors, vous venez d'où, monsieur?

*John*: Je viens d'Angleterre.

*Demoiselle*: Vraiment? Vous parlez bien français. Et comment vous appelez-vous, monsieur, votre prénom et votre nom de famille?

*John*: John Smith.

*Demoiselle*: Vous êtes seul ici ou avec votre famille?

*John*: Je suis avec ma famille.

*Demoiselle*: Vous êtes combien de personnes en tout?

*John*: Nous sommes quatre. Il y a ma femme, mon fils, ma fille et moi.

*Demoiselle*: Et où est-ce que vous logez pendant votre séjour, au camping ou à l'hôtel?

*John*: Pendant notre séjour à Caen nous sommes dans un hôtel. Mais on a l'intention de se promener quelques jours dans la région, et pour cette excursion, on va faire du camping.

*Demoiselle*: Vous restez combien de temps à Caen?

*John*: Nous sommes ici depuis quatre jours, et nous allons rester encore quinze jours avant de rentrer.

*Demoiselle*: Et quelle est votre profession?

*John*: Je suis professeur de français dans une école secondaire.

*Demoiselle*: Ah, c'est pour ça que vous parlez si bien français. Donc, ce n'est pas votre première visite en France?

*John*: Non, sûrement pas. Je viens en France chaque année, si possible.

*Demoiselle*: Et vous connaissez bien la Normandie?

*John*: Pas du tout. En général, on passe les vacances dans le Midi ou à Paris. C'est notre première visite à Caen.

*Demoiselle*: Et quelles sont vos impressions?

*John*: Nous sommes tout à fait ravis de notre visite. Nous aimons beaucoup la ville, et les gens sont très aimables.

*Demoiselle*: Comment est-ce que vous passez votre temps ici?

*John*: Eh bien, d'habitude, on se lève assez tard − ce sont les vacances après tout. Après le petit déjeuner, ça dépend. Quelquefois on se promène en ville, on visite les monuments, ou alors on fait des excursions à la mer. Il y a beaucoup d'endroits à visiter et tellement de choses à voir.

*Demoiselle*: Vous êtes satisfait, alors?

*John*: Oui, à part le temps. Aujourd'hui, il y a du vent encore et un ciel gris.

*Demoiselle*: Qu'est-ce que vous prévoyez pour aujourd'hui?

*John*: C'est aujourd'hui le jour de marché à Dives sur Mer, et je crois que le vieux marché de Dives est très intéressant.

*Demoiselle*: Bien, alors, monsieur. C'est tout. Je vous remercie beaucoup.

*John*: Mais de rien. Au revoir, mademoiselle.

**(b) Dialogue 2   Retour à l'hôtel   Return to the hotel**

John Smith returns to the hotel and to a problem. As he enters, the manager tells him that his son is lost and Mrs Smith has called the police.

*Hôtelier*: Ah, Monsieur Smith! Vous voilà enfin! Votre petit garçon est perdu et votre femme est très inquiète.

*John*: Ah, mon Dieu! Où est-elle?

*Hôtelier*: Elle est dans le salon avec un agent de police.
...... 

*Agent*: Calmez-vous, madame. Votre fils ne peut pas être loin. Faites une description de lui, s'il vous plaît. Il a quel âge?

*Mary*: Il a huit ans. Il a les cheveux noirs, il est de taille moyenne pour son âge. Il porte un pullover rouge, une chemise bleue et un pantalon court.

*Agent*:  Il s'en va souvent comme ça?

*Mary*:  Ah non! Il reste toujours près de nous, surtout à l'étranger. Je ne comprends pas du tout.

*Agent*:  Et il n'est pas dans sa chambre, vous êtes sûre?

*Mary*:  Mais oui, j'en suis certaine.

*Agent*:  Il est absent depuis combien de temps?

*Mary*:  Une demi-heure, à peu près.

*John*:  Il faut faire quelque chose. Je vais chercher dans le quartier. Il est peut-être tout près de l'hôtel.

*Agent*:  Calmez-vous, monsieur, et asseyez-vous, je vous en prie. La police cherche déjà votre fils . . . Regardez! Voilà mon collègue qui arrive avec lui. Vous voyez?

*John*:  Dieu merci!

*Agent*:  Ce n'est pas difficile de se perdre dans une ville inconnue, surtout quand on est petit.


### 8.2 VOCABULARY

**(a) Dialogue 1**

**(i) Useful expressions**

| | |
|---|---|
| nous sommes quatre | there are four of us |
| nous sommes ici depuis quatre jours | we've been here for four days |
| encore quinze jours | another fortnight |
| dans le Midi | in the South of France |
| d'habitude | usually |
| ça dépend | it all depends |
| ou alors | or else |
| il y a tellement de choses à faire | there are so many things to do |
| je vous remercie | thank you |

**(ii) Nouns – Masc.**

| | |
|---|---|
| le sondage | public opinion poll |
| le tourisme | tourism |
| le prénom | Christian name |
| le nom de famille | surname |

**Nouns – Fem.**

| | |
|---|---|
| les vacances | holidays |
| la municipalité | municipality |
| la question | question |
| la fille | daughter |
| une intention | intention |
| une année | year |
| une excursion | excursion |
| une profession | profession |

| | | | |
|---|---|---|---|
| le camping | camping (site) | une école | school |
| le professeur | teacher | une impression | impression |
| le fils | son | | |
| les gens | people | | |
| un endroit | place | | |
| le vent | wind | | |
| le marché | market | | |
| le jour de marché | market day | | |

## (iii) Other words

| | | | |
|---|---|---|---|
| répondre à | to answer | je viens (venir) | I come |
| pressé | in a hurry | parler | to ask |
| demander | to ask | seul | alone |
| donc | then; therefore | loger | to stay; put up at |
| pendant | during | | |
| se promener | to go for a walk; to go for a ride | général(-e) | general |
| | | sur | on |
| | | tout à fait | completely |
| depuis | since | se lever | to get up |
| rentrer | to return home | satisfait(-e) | satisfied |
| | | à part | except for |
| secondaire | secondary | gris(-e) | grey |
| sûrement | surely | vieux (vieille) | old |
| chaque | each, every | | |

## (b) Dialogue 2
### (i) Useful expressions

| | | | |
|---|---|---|---|
| mon Dieu! | good heavens! | à l'étranger | abroad |
| il a quel âge? | how old is he? | j'en suis certain | I'm sure of it |
| il est de taille moyenne | he is of average height | tout près | very close |
| | | Dieu merci | thank God |
| comme ça | like this; like that | | |

### (ii) Nouns – Masc.

| | | Nouns – Fem. | |
|---|---|---|---|
| le salon | sitting room; lounge | la description | description |
| | | la police | police |

| | |
|---|---|
| un âge | age |
| un an | year |
| les cheveux | hair |
| le pantalon | trousers |
| le quartier | district |
| le collègue | colleague |

**(iii) Other words**

| | | | |
|---|---|---|---|
| enfin | at last | court(-e) | short |
| perdu(-e) | lost | s'en aller | to go away |
| inquiet(-iète) | worried; | souvent | often |
| | anxious | toujours | always |
| se calmer | to calm down | à peu près | about, approx- |
| comprendre | to | | imately |
| | understand | arriver | to arrive |
| sûr (sûre) | sure | se perdre | to lose oneself |
| certain(-e) | certain; sure | inconnu(-e) | unknown |
| absent(-e) | absent | | |

## 8.3 EXPLANATIONS

### (a) Reflexive Verbs *grammar ref 5.3*

This is the name given to verbs such as the English 'I wash myself', 'you dress yourself' and so on, where the action described by the verb is applied to the person making the statement. 'Myself', 'himself' and so on, are called reflexive pronouns. The infinitive of such verbs is expressed as 'to wash oneself', 'to dress oneself' and so on. The French equivalent is found in infinitives such as se perdre – 'to lose oneself'. Quite a few verbs are reflexive in French but not in English. For example, se lever is translated 'to get up', se promener is 'to go for a walk'.

When asking questions, reflexive verbs are used in the ways already described. For example, s'appeler means 'to be called' (literally 'to call oneself'). To ask someone what their name is you can say: Vous vous appelez comment? *or* Comment est-ce que vous vous appelez? or, if you decide to invert the verb, as the young lady does when asking John Smith, Comment vous appelez-vous? See para (c) (ii).

When giving commands (imperative), you will remember that French says allez!; apportez!, without using vous. With reflexive verbs, the imperative is formed in the same way, but includes the reflexive pronoun vous, for example:

calmez-vous! ('calm down');
levez-vous! ('get up');
asseyez-vous ('sit down').

When written, there is always a hyphen between the verb and vous.

## (b) More about prepositions

(i) En is always used with countries (except au is used for the few which are masculine), either to mean 'in', for example:

Je suis en France;

or to mean 'to', for example:

Je vais en Angleterre.

There are certain other expressions where en translates 'in', for example:

En ville − 'in town'.

(ii) À is always used with the names of towns, either to mean 'in', for example: il est à Caen; or to mean 'to', for example: je vais à Paris.

## (c) Questions *grammar ref 5.11*

(i) We have already met the adjective quel in exclamations such as:

Quel repas délicieux!; Quel plaisir de vous revoir!

Quel is also used in questions to mean 'what' or 'which' when these words refer directly to a following noun, for example: 'what is your job?', 'which flavour do you prefer?'. Quel varies in form according to whether it is masculine (quel), feminine (quelle) or either masculine or feminine plural (quels; quelles). As so often in French, these differences really matter only in the written language, and there is no difference in the pronunciation of these four words, except where the plural form is followed by a word beginning with a vowel, in which case there is a liaison of the s, for example:

quelles_églises?

You will remember that in Chapter 2 the waitress asked the question quel parfum?, and in this chapter there are further examples, for example:

Quelle est votre profession?

(ii) You have already been introduced to a number of ways of asking questions. There is a further possibility, which is to ask a question by inverting the verb and its subject, that is, instead of saying, Vous allez au château?, you say, Allez-vous au château? Similarly you can say, Vous voulez une glace?, or, Voulez-vous une glace? There is also, in this chapter, an example of inversion with a reflexive verb, that is, Comment vous appelez-vous? It is generally true to say that although inversion remains correct usage, and perhaps the best form for written

French, there is a tendency to avoid inversion in the contemporary spoken language, either by using the questioning intonation, or by forming the question with est-ce que ...? In Dialogue 2, John Smith says, Où est-elle? This is probably the neatest way of phrasing the question, but he could equally well have said, Où est-ce qu'elle est?, or, Elle est où?

**(d) Some notes on items of vocabulary**

(i) The use of on, meaning 'one', has already been mentioned, but it is worth pointing out that its use is very much more widespread in French than in English. It is, for example, very often used where English would use 'we'. In Dialogue 1, John Smith uses it in this way to say how the family spend their day:

On se lève tard, on se promène en ville, on visite les monuments.

(ii) The vocabulary gives two words for 'year', an and année. The difference is that an is simply a unit of time, for example: you might say, Je passe un an à Caen, or, Il a huit ans. Année refers more to what actually happens, to the events that fill the period of time. So you say, Je passe une année splendide à Caen when you are thinking not just of the period of time but of all that you are doing during that period. The same distinction is made with other expressions of time, for example: you say, Bonjour, when you greet someone, but, Bonne journée when you mean 'have a good day!'. Similarly un soir is 'an evening', but une soirée can mean 'a party'.

(iii) In this chapter you are introduced to the plural form of c'est, in the statement, Ce sont les vacances.

(iv) Il faut may be translated as 'it is necessary'. It is usually followed by the infinitive, for example:

Il faut faire quelque chose — 'it is necessary to do something'.

It is clear that in this example, English would be more likely to say 'we must do something', and il faut can be used to mean 'I must', 'you must', 'we must' and so on, according to context.

(v) Avoir. Note the use of avoir to express age, for example:

Il a quel âge? ('how old is he?'); Il a huit ans ('he is eight').

(vi) A further case where the definite article is used in French but not in English is with the names of countries or regions, for example:

Vous connaissez bien la Normandie?

This is true of all cases except after en (je viens souvent en France) and de (je viens d'Angleterre).

(vii) Some words are singular in one language and plural in another. Two examples in this chapter are les cheveux — 'hair' (un cheveu means one single hair), and le pantalon — 'trousers'.

(viii) The adjective vieux – 'old', precedes its noun and is irregular in form. (Un vieux marché; une vieille ville.)

## 8.4 EXERCISES

### Section A

**(a) Exercises 1**
You are required to answer a few questions in a sondage. Give answers based on those given by John Smith.
*Demoiselle*: Vous avez quelques minutes pour répondre à des questions?
*You*: (Gladly. You are in no hurry.)
*Demoiselle*: Vous êtes en vacances ici?
*You*: (Yes, it's your first visit to Caen.)
*Demoiselle*: Vous venez d'où, monsieur?
*You*: (From England.)
*Demoiselle*: Vous êtes au camping municipal?
*You*: (No, you're staying at a hotel.)
*Demoiselle*: Vous êtes seul ici?
*You*: (No, you are with your wife and two children.)
*Demoiselle*: Quelle est votre profession?
*You*: (Teacher, or something appropriate – see supplementary vocabulary on p.212.)
*Demoiselle*: Comment est-ce que vous passez votre temps ici?
*You*: (You go for walks in town, visit the public buildings, make excursions and so on.)
*Demoiselle*: Et quelles sont vos impressions sur la ville?
*You*: (You and your wife are delighted. You think the people are friendly and you like the town.)
*Demoiselle*: C'est tout, monsieur. Merci bien.
*You*: (Don't mention it.)

**(b) Exercise 2**
Below are a list of reflexive verbs in the infinitive form. Give a brief account of events during your day by linking the verbs up with an appropriate time from the list on the right. Example: je me lève à sept heures.

| | | |
|---|---|---|
| (i) | se réveiller (to wake up) | à midi |
| (ii) | se lever (to get up) | à huit heures du soir |
| (iii) | se laver (to wash oneself) | à neuf heures du matin |
| (iv) | déjeuner (to have breakfast) | à sept heures |

| (v) | se promener en ville | |
|---|---|---|
| | (to take a walk in town) | à dix heures du matin |
| (vi) | se reposer (to take a rest) | à sept heures et demie |
| (vii) | se coucher (to go to bed) | à dix heures du soir |

**(c) Exercise 3**
Using the verbs above, form questions which you can put to another person, following the model: Quand est-ce que vous vous levez?

**(d) Exercise 4**
Practise using the prepositions in the following groups of sentences.
  (i) Use of à. Answer the question, Où allez-vous? using the following destinations.
      Example: Je vais au château.
                    l'église
                    le jardin
                    le port
                    Caen
                    Syndicat d'Initiative
  (ii) Use of en. Still using the question. Où allez-vous?, give answers saying which countries you are going to: France; Normandie; Bretagne, Angleterre.
  (iii) Use of de. Answer the question, Vous venez d'où?
      Example: Je viens du port; Je viens d'Angleterre.
      France; le château; l'Hôtel de Ville; Normandie; l'école.

## Section B

**(e) Exercise 5**
Translate into French
  (i) Can you answer a few questions?
  (ii) Where do you come from?
  (iii) You really speak very good French.
  (iv) This is not your first visit to France?
  (v) I come to France every year if possible.
  (vi) We usually spend our holidays in Paris.
  (vii) There are so many things to do.
  (viii) We like to take a walk in town.
  (ix) Your wife is very anxious.
  (x) We must do something.

**(f) Exercise 6**
Make up as many descriptions as you can from the information given
below, and answering the questions:
  Il a quel âge?
  Il est de quelle taille? (How tall is he?)
  Qu'est-ce qu'il porte? (What is he wearing?)
     Âge: huit ans            Taille: de taille moyenne
          douze ans                   de grande taille (tall)
          trente ans                  de petite taille (short)
          cinquante ans
Vêtements: un pullover noir; un pantalon bleu; un anorak jaune;
           un imperméable rouge; une blouse blanche (a white
           blouse); une jupe verte (a green skirt).

# CHAPTER 9

# IS IT POSSIBLE?

# HAVE YOU GOT

# ALL WE NEED?

## 9.1 DIALOGUES 📼

**(a) Dialogue 1    Au téléphone    On the telephone**

Having decided to take a break for a few days at a camping site on the coast, John Smith rings up the proprietor to see if it is possible to hire equipment.

*Propriétaire*:    Allô, Camping de la Plage, j'écoute.

*John*:    Bonjour, monsieur. Je voudrais venir passer deux ou trois jours sur la côte avec ma famille, mais nous n'avons pas de matériel de camping. Est-ce qu'il est possible de louer une tente, et tout ce qu'il faut?

*Propriétaire*:    Oui, monsieur, j'ai du matériel à louer. Qu'est-ce qu'il vous faut exactement? Une tente pour combien de personnes?

*John*:    Nous sommes quatre personnes, deux adultes et deux enfants. Est-ce que vous avez aussi tout le nécessaire pour faire la cuisine?

*Propriétaire*:    Mais oui, il y a des casseroles, des couteaux, des fourchettes, des cuillères, enfin, tout le nécessaire, mais nous n'avons pas de sacs de couchage à louer.

*John*:    Ça ne fait rien. Nous avons nos propres sacs de couchage. Qu'est-ce qu'il y a aussi comme facilités dans le camping?

*Propriétaire*:    C'est un camping cinq étoiles, monsieur, alors, bien sûr il y a tout — une épicerie, une salle de télévision, une salle de jeux, une buanderie, des douches et des salles de bains — enfin tout, vous voyez.

*John*:    C'est parfait. Et vous êtes près de la mer?

*Propriétaire*:    La plage est à deux minutes. Il y a un escalier qui descend des falaises.

*John*:    Très bien, monsieur. Alors, j'aimerais réserver une tente et les ustensiles de cuisine pour trois jours, à partir de demain.

*La plage est à deux minutes ...*

Photograph: Roger-Viollet

*Propriétaire*: Bien, monsieur. C'est d'accord. C'est à quel nom, s'il vous plaît?
*John*: John Smith.
*Propriétaire*: Comment est-ce que vous écrivez ça, monsieur?
*John*: S-M-I-T-H.
*Propriétaire*: Alors, à demain, monsieur.

**(b) Dialogue 2  À l'épicerie  At the grocery**
They arrive safely the next day, find their tent erected and while the children go to play in the salle de jeux, Mary and John go to stock up at the camp grocers.
*Vendeuse*: Bonjour, madame, bonjour, monsieur. Vous désirez?
*Mary*: Bonjour, madame. Je voudrais du lait et du pain, s'il vous plaît.
*Vendeuse*: Oui, madame. Un litre de lait?
*Mary*: Oui, ça ira, merci.

*Vendeuse*: Et quelle sorte de pain?

*Mary*: Deux baguettes, s'il vous plaît.

*Vendeuse*: Voilà madame, un litre de lait et deux baguettes. C'est tout?

*Mary*: Non, je voudrais aussi du fromage, une livre de beurre et des pommes de terre.

*Vendeuse*: Voilà le beurre. Quel fromage voulez-vous?

*John*: Dans cette région, un camembert, bien sûr.

*Vendeuse*: Les camemberts sont là. Vous pouvez choisir. Et combien de pommes de terre?

*Mary*: Un kilo, s'il vous plaît. Comme charcuterie, qu'est-ce que vous avez?

*Vendeuse*: Il y a du jambon, du saucisson.

*Mary*: Je voudrais quatre tranches de jambon.

*John*: Et qu'est-ce que nous allons boire? Vous avez de la bière?

*Vendeuse*: Oui, monsieur, il y a de la bière, et il y a aussi du cidre de la région.

*John*: Alors, une bouteille de cidre. Et une bouteille de limonade pour les enfants.

*Vendeuse*: Voilà, monsieur.

*Mary*: Bon, alors c'est tout, je crois. Ça fait combien?

*Vendeuse*: Ça fait quarante-six francs trente (46F30) en tout, madame. Merci. Voilà votre monnaie.

*Mary*: Merci bien. Au revoir, madame.

*Vendeuse*: Au revoir, madame, au revoir, monsieur.

## 9.2 VOCABULARY

### (a) Dialogue 1

#### (i) Useful expressions

| | |
|---|---|
| tout ce qu'il faut <br> tout le nécessaire | } everything necessary |
| qu'est-ce qu'il vous faut? | what do you need? |
| bien sûr | of course |
| à deux minutes de la plage | two minutes from the beach |
| (c'est) d'accord | OK; that's agreed; all right |
| c'est à quel nom | what name shall I put? |
| à demain | see you tomorrow |

#### (ii) Nouns – Masc.

| | | Nouns – Fem. | |
|---|---|---|---|
| le matériel | equipment | la falaise | cliff |
| le couteau | knife | la côte | coast |

| le sac (de couchage) | (sleeping) bag | la tente | tent |
| le jeu | game | la personne | person |
| le bain | bath | la cuisine | kitchen; cooking |
| un escalier | staircase; steps | la facilité | facility |
| | | une étoile | star |
| | | une épicerie | grocery |
| | | la salle | room |
| | | la télévision | television |
| | | la buanderie | laundry |
| | | la douche | shower |
| | | une ustensile | utensil |

(iii) **Other words**

| écouter | to listen (to) |
| louer | to hire; to let |
| exactement | exactly |
| faire la cuisine | to cook |
| propre | own _ clean |
| parfait (-e) | perfect |
| descendre | to go down |
| réserver | to reserve |
| à partir de | as from; with effect from |
| demain | tomorrow |

**(b) Dialogue 2**

(i) **Useful expressions**

| ça ira | that will be fine | quelle sorte de ...? | what sort of |

(ii) **Nouns – Masc.**   **Nouns – Fem.**

| le lait | milk | la vendeuse | sales lady |
| le pain | bread | la sorte | sort; kind |
| le litre | litre | la baguette | long, French loaf |
| le beurre | butter | | |
| le kilo | kilo | la pomme | apple |
| le jambon | ham | la pomme de terre | potato |
| le saucisson | salami-type sausage | la tranche | slice |
| le cidre | cider | la bière | beer |
| | | la bouteille | bottle |
| | | la limonade | lemonade |

## 9.3 EXPLANATIONS

### (a) Partitive Article *grammar ref 1.3*

(i) It is unusual for a French noun ever to stand alone with no article preceding it. In English, if there is no definite or indefinite article, we can either say 'milk' or 'some milk'; 'bread' or 'some bread'. In French, a word equivalent to this use of 'some' must always be used. This is called the partitive article, and it varies according to the gender of the word that follows it:

*Masculine words*: du (or de l' if the word begins with a vowel), for example:
du pain; du lait; du fromage;

*Feminine words*: de la or de l', for example:
de la bière.

All words in the plural are preceded by des, for example: des cigarettes.

You will find lots of examples in the dialogues of these various uses.

(ii) There are two commonly occurring situations when the partitive article becomes simply de, whatever the gender of the word. The first of these cases is after a negative verb. Thus you say:

j'ai du pain, *but* je n'ai pas de pain;
je bois de la bière, *but* je ne bois pas de bière.

This applies also to the plural, for example:

Nous n'avons pas de sacs de couchage.

The second example of the use of de, is whenever there is an expression of quantity, or when some sort of container is mentioned ('bottle', 'box' and so on). For example, Mary Smith asks for une livre de beurre and quatre tranches de jambon. The sales lady gives her un litre de lait and une bouteille de cidre.

(iii) The question word needed to ask for quantities is combien de? For example:

combien de pommes de terre? − 'how many potatoes?';
combien de beurre? − 'how much butter?'.

The expression ça fait combien? means 'how much does that come to?' when asking the price.

### (b) Irregular plurals *grammar ref 2.2*

As was stated earlier, the great majority of French nouns form the plural by adding s. There are a few cases of irregular plurals, of which two examples occur in this chapter. All nouns ending in -eu, -eau and -au form the plural by adding x, for example:

un couteau − des couteaux; un jeu − des jeux.

## 9.4 EXERCISES

### Section A

#### (a) Exercise 1
You've jotted down the following items on your shopping list. Ask for them in the shop, using the correct form of the partitive article, and beginning, Je voudrais ...

| | | |
|---|---|---|
| beurre (1 livre) | pommes de terre (kilo) | saucisson (200 grammes) |
| fromage | limonade (1 bouteille) | lait |
| bière | jambon (4 tranches) | pain |

#### (b) Exercise 2
You are out of luck with milk, cheese and beer — all sold out. The shoplady says, Je regrette madame, je n'ai pas ...

#### (c) Exercise 3
Complete your part of the dialogue.
*Vendeuse*:  Bonjour, madame. Vous désirez?
*You*:  (Say you'd like 1lb of butter, a kilo of potatoes and some bread.)
*Vendeuse*:  Oui, madame. Combien de baguettes?
*You*:  (Two. Say you'd also like two bottles of milk and ask what sort of cold meats there are.)
*Vendeuse*:  Voilà le lait, madame. Nous avons du jambon et du saucisson.
*You*:  (You'll have five slices of ham. Ask her if she has any cider.)
*Vendeuse*:  Je suis desolée, madame. Nous avons de la bière mais nous n'avons pas de cidre.
*You*:  (No, you don't want beer. Say you'll take a bottle of lemonade for the children and ask how much it all comes to.)

#### (d) Exercise 4
Here is a list of items that you might want to shop for. Practise (i) making requests for items from the list, saying Je voudrais ... s'il vous plaît; (ii) replying to the question Vous voulez ... with the answer Non, merci, je ne veux pas ...

| Nouns – Masc. | | Feminine – Fem. | |
|---|---|---|---|
| le vin rouge | red wine | la farine | flour |
| le vin blanc | white wine | la viande | meat |
| le café | coffee | les cigarettes | cigarettes |
| le chocolat | chocolate | les allumettes | matches |

| le thé | tea | les aspirines | aspirins |
|--------|-----|---------------|----------|
| les fruits | fruit | | |
| les légumes | vegetables | **Quantities and Containers** | |
| les oeufs | eggs | une boîte de | a box/tin of |
| les croissants | croissants | une bouteille de | a bottle of |
| | | un paquet de | a packet of |
| | | un kilo de | a kilo of |
| | | une livre de | a pound of |
| | | beaucoup de | a lot of |
| | | peu de | few; not much of |

**Section B**

**(e) Exercise 5**

Translate into French

(i) I would like to come and spend a few days on the coast.

(ii) Is it possible to hire a tent?

(iii) It is difficult to answer your questions.

(iv) I would like to reserve saucepans, knives and forks.

(v) For how long?

(vi) For five days from tomorrow ... My name is ...

(vii) I'd like cheese, butter, bread and milk, please.

(viii) How much butter do you want?

(ix) How many loaves and how much cheese would you like?

(x) I'm sorry, I haven't any milk.

**(f) Exercise 6**

Below are three columns. The first column contains phrases that are always followed by an infinitive. The second column contains a list of infinitives. The third column contains a variety of words and phrases which can link up with appropriate infinitives. By taking items from each column, see how many sentences you can form.

Examples:  Il est difficile de faire la cuisine.
           Je veux écouter la radio.

| | | | |
|------|------------------|----------|---------------|
| (i) | Il est difficile de | acheter | la ville |
| (ii) | Il est possible de | aimer | à huit heures |
| (iii) | Il faut | aller | les enfants |
| (iv) | Je vais | arriver | l'escalier |
| (v) | Nous allons | boire | au château |
| (vi) | Je veux | chercher | la radio |

|        |               |           |               |
|--------|---------------|-----------|---------------|
| (vii)  | Nous voulons  | descendre | du jambon     |
| (viii) | Je peux       | écouter   | un apéritif   |
| (ix)   | Nous pouvons  | faire     | de la bière   |
|        |               | louer     | six jours     |
|        |               | prendre   | l'église      |
|        |               | rester    | à la côte     |
|        |               | venir     | la cuisine    |
|        |               | visiter   | une tente     |

# CHAPTER 10

# WHEN WILL YOU ARRIVE?

# WHAT WILL YOU SEE?

## 10.1 DIALOGUES 📼

### (a) Dialogue 1  Des projets de voyage  Plans for a journey

*Michel*:  Vous connaissez déjà bien Paris, mon cher John.

*John*:  C'est vrai, mais c'est toujours un plaisir d'y retourner.

*Nicole*:  Qu'est-ce que vous allez voir? Un jour, ce n'est pas long pour visiter Paris.

*John*:  On va prendre le turbotrain. C'est plus rapide que l'auto et nous n'aurons pas de problèmes pour garer la voiture. Le train arrive à Paris à neuf heures trente-trois (9h33). Ça fera quand même une bonne journée.

*Mary*:  Les enfants seront sûrement bien fatigués le soir, mais ça vaut la peine, je crois.

*John*:  Évidemment, on ne va pas visiter tous les musées et toutes les galeries. Mais le Sacré Coeur et l'Arc de Triomphe les intéresseront, j'espère. Il y aura tellement de choses à voir.

*Nicole*:  Et il y a le Centre Pompidou. Vous le connaissez déjà, peut-être.

*John*:  Non, pas encore, mais je vais y aller. Ça m'intéresse beaucoup de le voir.

*Michel*:  Et dans la cour devant le Centre vous verrez toutes sortes d'activités, des mimes, des jongleurs. Les enfants trouveront ça fascinant.

*Mary*:  Et puis, il y a la Tour Eiffel. Les enfants veulent la voir de près, bien sûr!

*Michel*:  Est-ce que vous aurez le temps de faire une excursion en bateau-mouche sur la Seine?

*John*:  J'espère bien. Nous aurons peut-être assez de temps l'après-midi. Mais ça sera bien assez pour la journée, j'espère. Ça donnera une première impression aux enfants, et ils reviendront sans doute quand ils seront plus âgés.

*Michel*: Vous allez traverser Paris à pied?

*John*: À pied, et aussi en autobus. J'aime bien les autobus parisiens. C'est aussi une bonne façon de voir la ville.

*Nicole*: Le métro est parfois plus rapide.

*John*: C'est sans doute vrai, mais je ne l'aime pas. On ne voit rien, et il y a toujours tellement de monde.

*Michel*: Et vers quelle heure est-ce que vous rentrerez le soir?

*John*: Les trains sont fréquents. On prendra le train de dix-huit heures vingt-trois (18h23), je crois, et on sera de retour à Caen à vingt heures vingt-trois (20h23).

*Champs Elysées*

Photograph: Roger-Viollet

*Michel*: Je viendrai vous chercher à la gare, si vous voulez.

*Mary*: C'est vraiment gentil. Ça ne vous dérange pas? Vous êtes sûr?

*Michel*: Non, ça ne me dérange pas du tout. Je serai à la gare à 20h23 alors.

*John*: Bon, et maintenant, au lit. Demain matin il va falloir partir de bonne heure.

*Michel*: Eh bien, au revoir, alors. Et bonne journée à Paris.

## (b) Readings

The following are edited extracts from John Smith's guide to Paris. Using the vocabulary on p.90, see how much you can understand. A full translation will be found on p.199.

### L'Avenue des Champs Elysées

**De la Concorde au Rond-Point**

Remonter vers l'Étoile par les allées de marronniers bordant l'avenue. C'est la partie la plus fréquentée de la promenade. Les enfants y sont nombreux, attirés par les petites boutiques, les balançoires.

**Du Rond-Point à l'Étoile**

Remonter l'avenue en flânant. On marchera sur le côté droit, le plus animé et le plus typique. Une rue, un café, un cinéma portent le nom de Colisée. On arrive Place de l'Etoile au pied de l'Arc grandiose.

### La Tour Eiffel

C'est le monument parisien le plus universellement connu.
Ascension: tous les jours de 10h45 à 18h (de 9h30 à 18h en juillet et août). La vue pour le visiteur qui monte au sommet peut porter jusqu'à soixante-sept kilomètres.

### La Basilique du Sacré Coeur

La haute silhouette blanche fait maintenant partie du paysage parisien. La montée au dôme (de 10h à 13h, et de 14h à 17h), fournit un panorama magnifique.

### Paris, vu de son fleuve

Il y a des services réguliers de bateaux-mouches tous les jours du premier avril au cinq octobre. En hiver, un service par jour, à 15h15. Embarcadère: pont de Solférino.

## 10.2 VOCABULARY

### (a) Dialogue 1

#### (i) Useful expressions

| | |
|---|---|
| quand même | all the same |
| ça vaut la peine | it's worth it |

| | |
|---|---|
| ça m'intéresse beaucoup | it interests me a good deal |
| ils veulent la voir de près | they want to see it from close up |
| j'espère bien | I hope so |
| ce sera bien assez | that will be quite enough |
| tellement de monde | so many people |
| on sera de retour | we shall get back |
| je viendrai vous chercher à la gare | I'll come to meet you at the station |
| ça ne vous dérange pas? | it's no trouble for you? |
| il va falloir . . . | we shall have to . . . |
| de bonne heure | early |

(ii) **Nouns – Masc.**

| | | **Nouns – Fem.** | |
|---|---|---|---|
| le train | train | une auto | car |
| le turbotrain | high-speed train | la peine | trouble; worry |
| le musée | museum | la galerie | gallery |
| le coeur | heart | la cour | courtyard |
| l'arc | arch | une activité | activity |
| le triomphe | triumph | la tour | tower |
| le centre | centre | la façon | method; way |
| le mime | mime | la gare | railway station |
| le jongleur | juggler | | |
| le bateau | boat | | |
| le bateau-mouche | pleasure steamer | | |
| le doute | doubt | | |
| le métro | underground train | | |
| le retour | return | | |

(iii) **Other words**

| | | | |
|---|---|---|---|
| cher/chère | dear | évidemment | evidently |
| retourner | to return | sacré(e) | holy |
| long/longue | long | intéresser | to interest |
| rapide | fast | fascinant(-e) | fascinating |
| garer | to park | espérer | to hope |
| fatigué(-e) | tired | donner | to give |
| revenir | to come back | tellement | so many; so much |
| âgé(-e) | old | | |
| parisien (-enne) | Parisian | fréquent(-e) | frequent |
| | | falloir | to be necessary |
| parfois | sometimes | partir | to leave |

**(b) Readings**

| Nouns – Masc. | | Nouns – Fem. | |
|---|---|---|---|
| le rond-point | roundabout | une allée | drive (usually lined with trees) |
| le marronnier | horse chestnut | | |
| le côté | side | | |
| le cinéma | cinema | la partie | part |
| le sommet | top; summit | la promenade | walk |
| le kilomètre | kilometre | la boutique | small shop |
| le paysage | landscape | la balançoire | swing |
| le dôme | dome | une ascension | climb; ascent |
| le panorama | panorama | la vue | view |
| le fleuve | river | la silhouette | silhouette |
| le pont | bridge | la montée | climb |
| un embarca-dère | landing-stage | | |

**(iii) Other words**

| | | | |
|---|---|---|---|
| remonter | to go up; walk up | grandiose | grand; grandiose |
| bordant | bordering; lining | universelle-ment | universally |
| fréquenter | to frequent | monter | to climb |
| nombreux(-se) | numerous | haut(-e) | high |
| attiré(-e) | attracted | fournir | to offer; provide |
| en flânant | strolling | | |
| marcher | to walk | magnifique | magnificent |
| animé(-e) | animated | vu de | seen from |
| typique | typical | régulier(-ière) | regular |

## 10.3 EXPLANATIONS

**(a) Future tense** *grammar ref 5.2 (c)*
We have already met one way of expressing the future in French, for example:

Nous allons visiter le château.

Je vais voir la musée.

This is equivalent to the English expressing, 'I am going to . . .' but it is now quite widely used in modern spoken French to indicate a range of future intentions. French also has a future tense equivalent to the English 'I shall visit . . .' As with other tenses in French, there is a distinction to be made between regular and irregular verbs.

### (i) **Future tense of regular verbs**

To form the future tense, French takes the infinitive of the verb, and adds to it the endings of the present tense of avoir, for example:

J'arriver*ai*; nous arriver*ons*; il trouver*a*; elles trouver*ont*.

(Complete lists are on *grammar ref.* p.225. Note that infinitives ending in -re are regular, but drop the final -e, when forming the future, for example: je prendrai.

### (ii) **Future tense of irregular verbs**

Some of the most common irregular futures occur in this chapter, for example:

| | | | |
|---|---|---|---|
| être | to be | je serai | I shall be |
| (*Note:* c'est | it is | ce sera | it will be) |
| avoir | to have | j'aurai | I shall have |
| faire | to do; make | je ferai | I shall do |
| voir | to see | je verrai | I shall see |
| venir | to come | je viendrai | I shall come |

One further point to note is that French is sometimes more precise about future meaning than English, especially after quand. English says, 'when the children are older . . .' French says, quand les enfants seront plus âgés . . . .

### (b) **Object Pronouns** *grammar ref 4.1 (a) (b)*

Pronouns are used to avoid the necessity of repeating a noun. If you are asked in English, 'Have you read this book?', you reply, 'Yes, I've read it', to avoid the need to repeat 'book'. The direct object of the verb 'to read' is 'the book', so the pronoun replacing the word is called the direct object pronoun. In French, the direct object pronouns are: me, te (familiar form), le, la ('it', depending on the gender of the word replaced), nous, vous, les. The following examples are found in the dialogue of this chapter:

Ça m'intéresse – 'that interests me'

Vous le connaissez déjà? – 'do you know it already?'

Je ne l'aime pas – 'I don't like it'

Je viendrai vous chercher – 'I shall come to fetch you'

Le Sacré Coeur et l'Arc de Triomphe les intéresseront – '. . . will interest them.'

From the above examples, you will note that the pronoun comes immediately in front of the verb, even in a negative sentence. Also, where the construction is a verb + following infinitive, the pronoun comes before the infinitive (Je viendrai vous chercher).

**(c) Notes on items of vocabulary**

(i) Connaître and savoir. We have already met savoir in the expression Je ne sais pas, meaning, 'I don't know', and in the question, Vous savez où est le port de Caen? French has two verbs which are both translated by the English 'to know'. Savoir is to know *about* something; it is often followed by où, as in the example above, or by que, for example:

Je sais que Paris est la capitale de la France — 'I know (that) Paris is the capital of France.

Connaître is used in the sense of being acquainted with a person or place, for example:

Vous connaissez déjà Paris?; Vous connaissez ma femme?

(ii) Revoir, 'to see again', is commonly met with in the parting phrase, au revoir. Adding re- to a verb in this way adds the notion of repetition, for example:

| | | | |
|---|---|---|---|
| connaître | to know | reconnaître | to recognise |
| tourner | to turn | retourner | to return |
| faire | to do | refaire | to do again |
| venir | to come | revenir | to come back |

(iii) Un jour, ce n'est pas long ... — 'one day isn't much ...'.

This is a characteristic form of expression in French, where the noun which is the subject of the verb is repeated as ce, or sometimes, ça. Note these examples:

Un voyage à Paris, ça vaut la peine.

Le turbotrain, c'est la meilleure façon d'aller à Paris.

(iv) Note the way in which bien is used in a variety of contexts to strengthen the verb, for example:

J'aime bien — 'I'm very fond of'; ça sera bien assez — 'that will certainly be enough'; j'espère bien — 'I certainly hope so'.

## 10.4 EXERCISES

### Section A

**(a) Exercise 1**

Below are a list of things you want to do in Paris. From this list make up statements in answer to the question, Qu'est-ce que vous ferez à Paris? Your answers should be in the future tense.

Example: Qu'est-ce que vous ferez à Paris? — Je visiterai le Louvre

(i) voir l'Arc de Triomphe

(ii) visiter la cathédrale de Notre Dame

(iii) faire une excursion en bateau-mouche

(iv) déjeuner dans un grand restaurant

(v) prendre le métro

**(b) Exercise 2**

Answer the questions in the following dialogue, using object pronouns where possible, for example:

Vous connaissez déjà Paris? – Oui, je le connais bien.

|  | *Question*: | Vous connaissez déjà Paris? |
|---|---|---|
| (i) | *Réponse*: | (Yes you know it well. Say you are hoping to see it again.) |
|  | *Question*: | Vos enfants connaissent déjà Paris? |
| (ii) | *Réponse*: | (No, say they don't know it yet.) |
|  | *Question*: | Vous prendrez le turbotrain? |
| (iii) | *Réponse*: | (Yes, you'll catch it at 7.20.) |
|  | *Question*: | Vous aimez les excursions en bateau-mouche? |
| (iv) | *Réponse*: | (Yes, you like them very much.) |
|  | *Question*: | Vous visiterez la galerie du Louvre? |
| (v) | *Réponse*: | (Yes, say you'll visit it in the afternoon.) |

**Section B**

**(c) Exercise 3**

Translate into French

  (i) It's always a pleasure to see you again.
 (ii) Obviously, we shan't visit all the museums.
(iii) You'll see all sorts of activities in the courtyard in front of the Centre Pompidou.
 (iv) Will you have enough time to take a trip in a pleasure boat?
  (v) We shall visit the Eiffel Tower. We want to see it from close up.
 (vi) The metro is faster than the bus, but I prefer the bus because you can see (on voit) the town.
(vii) I hate (je déteste) the metro. There are always so many people.
(viii) When will you return tomorrow evening?
 (ix) I'll come to fetch you at the station. I'll see you at 8.00 p.m.
  (x) We shall have to leave early.

**(d) Exercise 4**

Rewrite each of the following sentences replacing the word in italics by a direct object pronoun.

Example: Vous connaissez ma *femme*? – Vous la connaissez?

  (i) Les enfants ne connaissent pas *Paris*.
 (ii) Nous prendrons *le train*.
(iii) J'aime bien *les jongleurs*.
 (iv) Nous ferons *une excursion* en bateau-mouche.
  (v) Je n'aime pas *le métro*.

# CHAPTER 11

# MAY I?
# WHERE IS IT LOCATED?

## 11.1 DIALOGUES 📼

### (a) Dialogue 1  À la gare  At the station

*John*:   Deux adultes et deux enfants, aller-retour pour Paris, s'il vous plaît.

*Homme au guichet*:   Deux aller-retour et deux demi-tarif. Ça fait sept cent vingt francs, s'il vous plaît, monsieur.

*John*:   Merci. Il part de quelle voie, le train pour Paris, s'il vous plaît?

*Homme*:   Quai numéro trois, à sept heures trente-quatre (7h34).

### (b) Dialogue 2  Dans le train  On the train

The train is already filling up fast and the family have difficulty finding four seats together in the open car.

*John*:   Excusez-moi, madame. Est-ce que ces places sont libres?

*Dame*:   Mais oui, monsieur. Il n'y a personne là.

*John*:   Et à côté de vous, c'est libre aussi?

*Dame*:   Mais oui, monsieur.

*Mary*:   Bien, je m'assieds à côté de vous. Vous permettez? Et les enfants en face de moi.

*John*:   Et moi, je vais m'asseoir ici, tout près. Vous permettez monsieur?

*Monsieur*:   Certainement, monsieur.

*John*:   On est bien ici.

*Monsieur*:   Oui, ce turbotrain est très confortable. Et le voyage à Paris est très rapide. On n'a pas le temps de s'ennuyer.

*Dame*:   On va bientôt partir, sans doute. Vous avez l'heure, madame?

*Mary*:   Oui, il est sept heures et demie.

*Dame*:   Encore quatre minutes, alors. Vous faites souvent le voyage à Paris, madame?

| Numéro du train | | 3948 | 3316 | 3918 | 3950 | 3926 | 3354 | 3986 | 3958 | 3954 | 3360 | 136 | 3982 | 3956 | 3990 | 3902 | 3922 | 3984 | 3924 | 3326 |
|---|---|---|---|---|---|---|---|---|---|---|---|---|---|---|---|---|---|---|---|---|
| Notes à consulter | | 1 | 2 | 3 | 4 | 5 | 18 | 6 | 7 | 7 | 8 | 9 | 19 | 6 | 10 | 6 | 7 | 7 | 11 | 12 |
| Caen | D | 14.34 | 15.17 | 15.45 | 16.15 | 16.27 | 16.30 | | 17.24 | 17.33 | 17.55 | 18.42 | | 18.56 | | 19.25 | 19.40 | | 19.57 | 19.57 |
| Mézidon | D | | | | 16.32 | | | | | 17.51 | | | | | | | 19.57 | | 20.14 | |
| Lisieux | D | 15.04 | | 16.21 | 17.00 | | 16.57 | 17.49 | 17.58 | 18.13 | 18.21 | | 19.20 | 19.28 | 19.43 | 19.57 | 20.15 | 20.27 | 20.33 | |
| Bernay | D | | | | | | | | | 18.39 | 18.39 | | | 19.52 | | | | 20.54 | 20.56 | |
| Serquigny | D | | | 17.23 | 17.32 | | | | | | | | | 20.01 | | | | 21.03 | | |
| Conches | D | | | | 17.54 | | | | | 19.07 | | | | | | | | | | |
| Évreux | A | 15.52 | | 17.12 | 18.06 | | 17.39 | 18.39 | 18.50 | 19.19 | 19.05 | | | 20.27 | | | 21.30 | 21.27 | | |
| Bueil | A | | | | 18.28 | | | | | 19.40 | | | | | | | | | | |
| Paris St-Lazare | A | 17.00 | 17.10 | 18.18 | 19.23 | 18.39 | 18.36 | 19.50 | 19.59 | 20.37 | 20.00 | 20.37 | 21.23 | 21.41 | 21.31 | 21.57 | 22.03 | 22.47 | 22.41 | 21.56 |

Tous les trains offrent des places assises en 1re et 2e cl. sauf indication contraire dans les notes.

**Notes :**

1. Circule les ven.
2. Circule jusqu'au 26 juin et à partir du 14 sept. sauf les dim. et fêtes. Turbotrain.
3. Circule le 8 juin ; du 27 juin au 13 sept. circule tous les jours.
4. Circule tous les jours sauf les dim. et fêtes.
5. Circule les 31 mai, 7, 8, 14, 21 juin et 20 sept.
6. Circule les dim. et fêtes sauf les 7 juin, 12 juil et 15 août.
7. Circule les dim. et fêtes.
8. Circule tous les jours sauf les dim. et fêtes et sauf le 13 juil. Turbotrain.
9. Circule tous les jours sauf les dim. et fêtes. Conditions spéciales d'emprunt pour les militaires les ven. Turbotrain à supplement. [icon]
10. Circule du 27 juin au 12 sept. tous les jours sauf les dim. et fêtes.
11. Circule du 29 juin au 7 sept. les lun. et lendemains de fêtes sauf les 13 juil. et 16 août.
12. Circule les ven. Turbotrain.
13. Circule jusqu'au 25 juin et à partir du 14 sept. sf ven. dim. et fêtes ; du 27 juin au 13 juil. sf dim. et fêtes et les 29 juin, 3, 6 et 10 juil.; du 16 juil. au 12 sept. circule les mar., mer., jeu., sam. sf le 15 août.
14. Circule les ven. Turbotrain.
15. Circule tous les jours sauf dim. et fêtes. Turbotrain.
16. Circule les dim. et fêtes sauf les 7 juin et 15 août. Turbotrain.
17. Circule les dim. et fêtes. Turbotrain.
18. Circule jusqu'au 26 juin et à partir du 14 sept. sauf les dim. et fêtes. Turbotrain. [icon]

*By courtesy of SNCF*

# les différents services
# various station offices

SOME USEFUL PHRASES
TO HELP YOU FIND YOUR WAY IN A FRENCH STATION

Pour faciliter votre orientation, vous trouverez partout des symbols ou "pictogrammes" adoptés par la plupart des réseaux ferroviaires.

**For English speaking visitors**
To help you find your way around, the following symbols are widely used by most railway networks.

- **Where is the enquiry office?**
Où se trouve le bureau de renseignements?

- **Is there a train to Paris at about 6 o'clock?**
Y a-t-il un train pour Paris vers 6 heures?

- **Where does this train go to?**
Où va ce train?

- **Is there a connection at...?**
Y a-t-il une correspondance à...?

- **On which platform?**
Sur quel quai?

- **Where do I have to change?**
Où faudra-t-il changer?

- **I wish to register my luggage.**
Je désire enregistrer mes bagages.

| | | |
|---|---|---|
|  Information - Reservation / Information - Reservations |  Salle d'attente / Waiting-room |  Non fumeurs / Non smokers |
|  Billets / Tickets |  Facilités pour handicapés / Facilities for the handicapped | Eau potable / Drinking water |
| Bagages / Registered luggage | Bureau de poste / Post office |  Relais-toilettes (bains-douches) / Toilets and washroom (baths, showers) |
|  Consigne / Left luggage | Téléphone public / Public telephone |    Bureau des objets trouvés / Lost property |
|  Consigne automatique / Luggage lockers |   Bureau de change / Bureau de change | Entrée / Way in |
|  Chariot porte-bagages / Luggage trolleys | Bar (cafeteria) / Bar (cafeteria) | Sortie / Way out |
|  Train Auto Couchettes Motorail |  Buffet (restaurant) / Buffet (restaurant) |   Toilettes pour dames / Ladies toilet |
|  Point de rencontre / Meeting point |  Fumeurs / Smokers | Toilettes pour hommes / Gents toilet |

*By courtesy of SNCF*

*À la gare*

Photograph: Roger-Viollet

*Mary*:  Oh, non! Nous sommes anglais, et c'est notre première visite à Caen, alors c'est aussi la première fois que nous faisons ce voyage. Mais nous connaissons déjà Paris.

*Dame*:  Vous parlez bien français. Est-ce que les enfants le parlent aussi?

*Mary*:  Un peu, seulement. Mais ils vont l'apprendre à l'école, et nous viendrons probablement chaque année en France.

*Dame*:  C'est très bien. Ah, nous partons! Qu'est-ce que vous allez voir à Paris?

*Mary*:  On ira sans doute à la Tour Eiffel, au Sacré Coeur, etc. C'est surtout pour les enfants, cette visite. On ne va pas avoir le temps de tout voir, bien sûr, mais ça sera un début.

*Dame*:  Bien sûr!

**(c) Dialogue 3   À Paris   In Paris**

Among the various activities of the day the family manage to take a trip on the river. They are given a commentary over the loudspeaker.

*Guide:*   Alors, mesdames, messieurs, sur votre gauche vous voyez les Jardins des Tuileries. Un peu plus loin, ce grand bâtiment, c'est le Palais du Louvre. Maintenant, vous voyez devant vous, le Pont Neuf et les tours de la cathédrale Notre-Dame. Notre-Dame est située sur l'Île de la Cité. Sur cette île se situent les origines de la ville de Paris. Ce bâtiment sur votre gauche, et en face de Notre-Dame est la Préfecture de Police. Sur la droite, maintenant, le quai Saint-Michel, avec ces bouquinistes célèbres, et ce boulevard-là s'appelle le Boulevard Saint-Michel, célèbre pour ses cafés et pour ses étudiants, parce que c'est dans ce quartier de Paris que se trouve la Sorbonne, l'université ancienne de Paris. Cette deuxième île sur la gauche s'appelle l'Île Saint-Louis. Nous passons maintenant sous le Pont Sully, et à gauche, le Boulevard Henri Quatre mène à la Place de la Bastille. Un peu plus loin, à droite, ces arbres et ces espaces verts, c'est le Jardin des Plantes ...

**(d) Dialogue 4   Au café   At the café**

They take a break for refreshment. The cafés seem crowded, but the Smiths find a table on the terrasse, where one person is sitting alone.

*John:*   Excusez-moi, monsieur. Ces chaises ne sont pas prises?

*Monsieur:*   Non, monsieur. Il n'y a personne.

*John:*   Alors, vous permettez?

*Monsieur:*   Je vous en prie.

*John:*   Il y a tellement de monde, aujourd'hui.

*Monsieur:*   À Paris, en été, c'est toujours comme ça. Il y a tellement de touristes.

*John:*   Oui, tout le monde veut voir Paris. Mais ici, on est bien.

*Monsieur:*   Ce n'est pas mal. On a une belle vue sur la Seine et sur les jardins. Vous êtes ici pour longtemps?

*John:*   Oh non! Aujourd'hui, seulement. Nous passons un jour seulement à Paris.

*Serveuse:*   Bonjour, monsieur; bonjour, madame. Qu'est-ce que vous prenez?

*John:*   Une bière, un citron pressé et deux limonades, s'il vous plaît.

*Serveuse:*   Bien, monsieur.

*Monsieur:*   Vous avez une journée bien chargée, alors.

*John:*   On ne peut pas tout voir, évidemment. Nous reviendrons, et la prochaine fois nous resterons plus longtemps, j'espère.

*. . . a trip on the river*

Photograph: J. Allan Cash

## 11.2 VOCABULARY

### (a) Dialogue 1

| Nouns – Masc. | | Nouns – Fem. | |
|---|---|---|---|
| un aller-retour | return ticket | la voie | (railway) track |
| le guichet | ticket window | | |
| le demi-tarif | half-price ticket | | |
| le quai | platform | | |

**(b) Dialogue 2**

(i) **Useful expressions**

| | |
|---|---|
| vous permettez? | may?; may we? |
| tout près | close by |
| on est bien ici | this suits us fine |
| vous avez l'heure? | have you got the time? |

(ii) **Other words**

| | | | |
|---|---|---|---|
| personne | nobody | confortable | comfortable |
| à côté de | beside; next to | s'ennuyer | to get bored |
| | | apprendre | to learn |
| s'asseoir | to sit down | probablement | probably |
| en face de | opposite | le début | beginning |

**(c) Dialogue 3**

(i) **Nouns – Masc.** | | **Nouns – Fem.** | |
|---|---|---|---|
| le guide | guide | la cathédrale | cathedral |
| le bâtiment | building | une île | island |
| le palais | palace | la cité | city |
| le bouquiniste | bookseller | une origine | origin |
| le boulevard | boulevard | la préfecture | police HQ |
| un étudiant | student | une université | university |
| un arbre | tree | | |
| un espace | space | | |

(ii) **Other words**

| | | | |
|---|---|---|---|
| neuf (neuve) | (brand) new | se trouver | to be situated |
| situé(-e) | situated | deuxième | second |
| situer | to situate | sous | under |
| célèbre | famous | mener | to lead |
| ancien (-ienne) | ancient, old | | |

**(d) Dialogue 4**

(i) **Nouns – Masc.** | | **Noun – Fem.** | |
|---|---|---|---|
| le touriste | tourist | la chaise | chair |
| le citron | lemon | | |

(ii) **Other words**

| | |
|---|---|
| pris(-e) | taken; occupied |
| mal | bad |
| longtemps | a long time |
| pressé(-e) | squeezed (as in the drink, citron pressé) |

| | |
|---|---|
| chargé(-e) | loaded; full |
| prochain(-e) | next |

## 11.3 EXPLANATIONS

### (a) Demonstrative adjectives *grammar ref 3.6*

The demonstrative adjectives in English are 'this' and 'that'. French does not make such a sharp distinction, and the demonstrative adjectives, ce, cet, cette, ces, can often be used to translate either of the English forms. The usage is as follows:

Masculine nouns are preceded by ce, unless they begin with a vowel, in which case the form used is cet, for example:

ce bâtiment, ce train, cet agent.

Feminine nouns have the form cette, for example:

Cette île; cette visite.

All nouns in the plural take the form ces, regardless of gender, for example:

Ces îles vertes; ces bouquinistes célèbres.

If it is necessary to stress the idea of 'the one over there', French adds -là after the noun, for example:

Ce bâtiment-là ('that building over there'); ce boulevard-là.

### (b) Ordinal numbers

are those like 'first', 'second' and so on, which express the order in which things occur. The word for 'first' is irregular, premier/première. Other ordinal numbers are formed on the pattern of deuxième, which occurs in this chapter (cette deuxième île), that is, the ending -ième is added on to the number. *See grammar ref. 9.2(b).* Note that in the case of onze, douze, treize, the final -e is dropped before adding -ième, for example: douzième.

Ordinal numbers are used as in English with one or two notable exceptions. In the section where the guide is pointing out the sights of Paris, he refers to the boulevard Henri Quatre. This boulevard is named after the French king Henry the Fourth, and as you can see, the simple number is used with all names of kings, except the first (for example: Charles Premier). The same is true of expressing dates. In Chapter 10, the extract from the guide book giving details about the bateaux-mouches said: Service régulier tous les jours du premier avril au cinq octobre. Thus, all dates except the first of the month are expressed by using the simple numeral, and not by the ordinal.

### (c) Prepositions to express duration of time

So far in this book we have encountered sentences of the following two types: Nous sommes ici depuis quatre jours (Chapter 8) – 'We have been here for four days'; Vous êtes ici pour longtemps? (Chapter 11) – 'are you here for long?' In these two cases the English preposition 'for' is translated quite differently in French. Depuis is used (with a verb in the present tense), to express the idea that something has started sometime in the past and is still continuing. Look at these other examples:

Il est à l'école depuis trois ans – 'He has been at school for three years';

Elle est à Caen depuis quelques jours – 'She has been in Caen for a few days'.

Pour is used to express a period of time looking to the future, for example:

Je vais à Paris pour trois semaines – 'I'm going to Paris for three weeks'.

### (d) Some notes on items of vocabulary

(i) Note the use of the verb se trouver. It means 'to be situated' or 'to be located', but French often uses it where English would only use the verb 'to be', for example: Dans ce quartier se trouve la Sorbonne – 'In this district is the Sorbonne'.

(ii) A further example of the negative is introduced into this chapter, namely, ne ... personnne, for example; il n'y a personne là. Like other negatives introduced already, personne can stand alone with negative force, for example, in answer to the question, qui est là?, you could answer either: il n'y a personne; or, simply, personne!

### 11.4 EXERCISES

### Section A

### (a) Exercise 1

You've jotted down the following notes to remind yourself of the details for train tickets you are going to buy, and also information that you need. Make up the sentences that you would actually use on the basis of the information.

quatre adultes | départ quelle heure? | arrivée quelle heure?
aller-retour | départ quelle voie?
Paris

### (b) Exercise 2

From the plan of the Île de la Cité on p.105, describe what you can see using the verbs se trouver, or, est situé(e), and a suitable preposition from the list.

Example:  La Préfecture de Police se trouve en face de la Cathedrale.
   (i)  La Préfecture de Police                   à côté de
  (ii)  La Cathédrale Notre-Dame            en face de
 (iii)  Le Palais de Justice       se trouve   derrière
 (iv)  La Rue de la Cité         est situé(e)  devant
  (v)  Le Marché aux Fleurs              près de
 (vi)  La Place du Parvis Notre-Dame

**(c) Exercise 3**

Complete your part of this conversation on the terrasse of a café.

*You*:  (Ask if these seats are free.)

*Monsieur*:  Oui, monsieur, il n'y a personne.

*You*:  (Ask if you may sit there.)

*Monsieur*:  Je vous en prie, monsieur.

*You*:  (Say that there are so many people in town today.)

*Monsieur*:  En été, c'est toujours comme ça. Vous êtes là pour longtemps?

*You*:  (No, say that you are just spending the day in Paris with your family.)

*Monsieur*:  Qu'est-ce que vous allez voir pendant votre visite?

*You*:  (Tell him a few of the places you hope to visit.)

*Monsieur*:  Alors, bonne journée, monsieur.

**Section B**

**(d) Exercise 4**

Translate into French

   (i)  I'll sit here, close by, may I?
  (ii)  There's no time to get bored.
 (iii)  We'll soon be leaving. Have you got the time?
 (iv)  They are going to learn French at school.
  (v)  We shan't have time to see everything, of course.

**(e) Exercise 5**

Insert the correct form of the demonstrative pronoun in the gaps.

   (i)  Est-ce que − places sont libres?
  (ii)  − train est très confortable.
 (iii)  C'est pour les enfants, − visite.
 (iv)  − grand bâtiment − est le Louvre.
  (v)  − deuxième île s'appelle l'Île Saint-Louis.
 (vi)  − agent de police est devant la Préfecture.

# CHAPTER 12

# HAVE YOU HAD A GOOD DAY?

# WHAT DID YOU SEE?

## 12.1 DIALOGUES 📼

### (a) Dialogue 1

When the Smiths' train arrives back in Caen that evening, Michel Lebrun is waiting for them.

*John*: Ah, Michel. C'est gentil de venir nous chercher.

*Michel*: Mais je vous en prie. Ça me fait plaisir de vous rendre service. Vous avez passé une journée agréable?

*Mary*: Oui, vraiment formidable. On a eu de la chance avec le temps. Mais les enfants sont épuisés. Nous avons vu beaucoup de choses, et beaucoup marché.

*Michel*: Ah, c'est fatigant, Paris. Alors voilà la voiture. Montez. Vous n'avez pas de bagages?

*John*: Non, on n'a pris qu'un petit sac pour notre piquenique.

*Michel*: Vous avez mangé des sandwiches à midi?

*John*: Oui. Comme ça on a eu plus de temps pour visiter. Mais nous avons pu dîner dans le train pendant le voyage de retour.

### (b) Dialogue 2 *(suite)*

*Michel*: Alors, qu'est-ce que vous avez vu?

*Mary*: D'abord, on a pris l'autobus de la Gare Saint-Lazare à la Place de la Concorde. On a remonté les Champs Elysées jusqu'à l'Arc de Triomphe.

*Michel*: Mais dites donc! C'est assez loin, ça!

*John*: Oui, mais ça vaut la peine. Ça donne une impression générale de la ville.

*Mary*: Ensuite, on a pris un bus pour aller à la Tour Eiffel. Mais nous n'avons pas eu le temps d'y monter.

*John*: Non, pour ça il faut vraiment plus de temps.

*Michel*: Oui, sûrement. Tiens, nous voilà à votre hôtel.

*John*: Vous voulez bien entrer prendre quelque chose avec nous?

*Michel*: Avec plaisir, si ça ne vous dérange pas.

*John*: Mais non, au contraire.

**(c) Dialogue 3** *(suite)*

*Mary*: Je vais coucher les enfants. Je vous rejoins dans un quart d'heure.

*Michel*: Bien. Alors, bonne nuit, les enfants. Dormez bien ... Et après la Tour Eiffel alors, qu'est-ce que vous avez fait?

*John*: Nous avons mangé nos sandwiches tout près de la Tour Eiffel, nous avons marché encore un peu, et puis on a pris un bateau-mouche pour se reposer un peu, et pour voir la ville sous un autre angle. Nous avons vu l'Île de la Cité, et puis, après le bateau-mouche, on a pris quelque chose dans un café, et on a repris l'autobus pour aller vers Montmartre regarder l'église du Sacré Coeur.

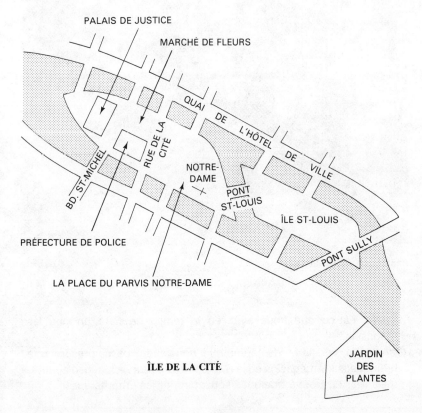

*... chez les bouquinistes*

Photograph: Roger-Viollet

*Michel*:  Est-ce que vous avez eu le temps de faire un peu les
   magasins?

*John*:   Oui, vers la fin de l'après-midi nous avons passé presque une
   heure dans les magasins de la Rue de Rivoli. Moi, je n'ai rien acheté,
   mais Mary a trouvé quelques souvenirs, et les enfants aussi.

**(d)** **Dialogue 4** *(suite)*

*John*: Voilà enfin Mary. Alors Michel, qu'est-ce que vous prenez?

*Michel*: Je prendrai bien un petit cognac, s'il vous plaît.

*John*: Moi aussi, je crois, et toi, Mary?

*Mary*: Moi, je vais prendre un jus de fruit. Jus d'orange, de préférence.

*John*: Garçon, deux cognacs et un jus d'orange, s'il vous plaît.

*Garçon*: Bien, monsieur.

*Michel*: Alors, les enfants sont au lit. Ils sont fatigués, sans doute.

*Mary*: Oui, c'est vrai, mais ils ont été ravis de cette journée. Demain matin, ils pourront faire la grasse matinée. Demain, on n'a rien de prévu.

*Michel*: Vous avez acheté des souvenirs de Paris?

*Mary*: Pas grand'chose. Les enfants ont acheté des cartes postales et quelques petits trucs. Moi j'ai acheté une écharpe et un chemisier. John n'a rien acheté.

*John*: Malheureusement, je n'ai pas eu le temps d'aller chercher des livres chez les bouquinistes. Pour ça, il me faut une journée à Paris sans les enfants.

*Michel*: C'est vrai. Bien, il est déjà dix heures passées. Il faut que je m'en aille maintenant.

*John*: Oui. Alors, merci encore, hein? C'était gentil de venir nous chercher.

*Michel*: Il n'y a vraiment pas de quoi. Reposez-vous bien. Au revoir.

## 12.2 VOCABULARY

**(a)** **Dialogue 1**

  **(i)** **Useful expression**

| | |
|---|---|
| Ça me fait plaisir de ... | It's a pleasure to ... |

  **(ii)** **Nouns – Masc.**

| | |
|---|---|
| les bagages | luggage |
| le piquenique | picnic |
| le sandwich | sandwich |
| le voyage | journey |

  **(iii)** **Other words**

| | |
|---|---|
| rendre service | to do a favour |
| agréable | pleasant; nice |
| formidable | terrific |
| épuisé(-e) | exhausted |
| fatigant(-e) | tiring |

108

## (b) Dialogue 2

### (i) Useful expressions

| | |
|---|---|
| dites donc! | An expression with a variety of meanings. Here it is an expression of surprise, for instance, 'good heavens!' But it is also used at the beginning of a statement to mean 'I say . . .' or 'Tell me . . .' |
| tiens! | well, well!; here we are! |
| au contraire | on the contrary |

### (ii) Nouns — Masc.

| | |
|---|---|
| le bus (same as autobus) | bus |
| le contraire | opposite |

### (iii) Other words

| | |
|---|---|
| d'abord | first of all |
| entrer | to come in; to go in |

## (c) Dialogue 3

### (i) Useful expressions

| | |
|---|---|
| sous un autre angle | from another point of view |
| faire les magasins | to 'do' the shops |

### (ii) Nouns — Masc. / Nouns — Fem.

| Nouns — Masc. | | Nouns — Fem. | |
|---|---|---|---|
| un angle | angle | la nuit | night |
| le magasin | shop | la fin | end |
| le souvenir | souvenir; memory | | |

### (iii) Other words

| | | | |
|---|---|---|---|
| coucher | to put to bed | puis | then |
| je rejoins (rejoindre) | I rejoin | autre | other |
| | | reprendre | to take again |
| dormir | to sleep | presque | almost |

## (d) Dialogue 4

### (i) Useful expressions

| | |
|---|---|
| de préférence | preferably |
| faire la grasse matinée | to have a long lie-in |
| rien de prévu | nothing in mind; no plans |
| il me faut . . . | I need |

| | | | |
|---|---|---|---|
| dix heures passées | | past ten o'clock | |
| il faut que je m'en aille | | I must be going | |
| c'était gentil ... | | it was kind | |
| il n'y a vraiment pas de quoi | | you really don't need to thank me | |

(ii) **Nouns – Masc.**  **Nouns – Fem.**

| | | | |
|---|---|---|---|
| le cognac | brandy | la préférence | preference |
| le truc | thing | la carte postale | postcard |
| le chemisier | shirt-blouse | une écharpe | scarf |

(iii) **Other words**

| | |
|---|---|
| prévu(e) | planned |
| gras (grasse) | fat |
| grand'chose | a lot |
| sans | without |
| hein? | (see Explanations (c) (iv)) |

## 12.3 EXPLANATIONS

### (a) The Perfect Tense *grammar ref 5.2 (f)*

(i) Both English and French have a number of different past tenses, that is to say, ways of expressing events which took place in a period of time in the past. In English, the various forms such as, 'I bought'; 'I have bought' are all types of past tense, each with a different shade of meaning. In spoken French, the perfect tense has to be used with two different functions, either with the sense of the English perfect, 'I have bought' or with the sense of the English past definite, that is, 'I bought'. Compare these two sentences and their translations:

J'ai acheté une écharpe à Paris l'année dernière – 'I bought a scarf in Paris last year'.

J'ai acheté une écharpe ce matin – 'I have bought a scarf this morning'.

### (ii) Formation

The perfect tense in French is formed rather like its English equivalent, by combining the auxiliary verb avoir ('to have') with the past participle of the verb. The past participle of regular verbs in English ends in '-ed' (for example: 'walked') Regular verbs in French form their past participles as follows:

-er verbs, for example: porter – porté
-ir verbs, for example: choisir – choisi
-re verbs, for example: attendre – attendu

Thus, the English expressions, 'I bought', and 'I have bought' are both rendered j'ai acheté.

(A small number of verbs take être as their auxiliary. These will be discussed in Chapter 13.)

(iii) **Irregular verbs**
Those verbs which have already shown themselves to be irregular in their present tense are also likely to have an irregular past participle, for example:

prendre – j'ai pris  avoir – j'ai eu   pouvoir – j'ai pu
voir – j'ai vu    être – j'ai été   faire – j'ai fait

A complete list of all parts of irregular verbs is given on pp. 226–8.

(iv) **Negatives** *grammar ref 5.10*
In forming negative verbs in the perfect tense, the two parts of the negative come before and after the auxiliary verb, for example:

Nous n'avons pas eu le temps d'y monter.

(v) Questions are formed in the same ways as already described, for example:

Vous avez mangé des sandwiches à midi?;
Qu'est-ce que vous avez vu?

(Note that this last example could be translated either, 'what did you see?', or 'what have you seen?', depending on context.)

(b) **Pour + infinitive; verbs of motion + infinitive** *grammar ref 5.7 (a)*
When the infinitive is preceded by pour, it usually has the force of 'in order to', even if English doesn't always translate this in full, for example:

Nous avons pris un bus pour aller à la Tour Eiffel (that is, 'to go ...', or 'in order to go ...').

When a verb of motion has a dependent infinitive, this follows directly, with no preposition intervening, for example:

Vous voulez bien entrer prendre quelque chose?;
Je n'ai pas eu le temps d'aller chercher les livres.

(c) **Some further points raised in this chapter**
(i) The negative formation, ne ... que, means 'only', for example:
On n'a pris qu'un petit sac – 'We only took a small bag'.
(ii) The present tense is sometimes used (as in English) with future meaning, for example: when Mary says, Je vous rejoins dans un quart d'heure. Another example occurred in Chapter 10, namely, Le train arrive à Paris à 9h33.

(iii) Un truc is a useful little word, since it can be used to mean almost anything of which you can't remember the actual name! Un petit truc therefore means 'a little thingamajig'; 'a little whatsit' or something of the kind.

(iv) Hein? is commonly heard with a rising intonation at the end of sentences. It is a way of inviting agreement, rather like the use of 'isn't it?' or 'don't you?' in English.

## 12.4 EXERCISES

### Section A

#### (a) Exercise 1
In the following exchange, respond to the questions as indicated, using the perfect tense and answering with the appropriate pronoun (je, elle, nous, on, ils). All the verbs are regular.

*Question*: Vous avez passé une bonne journée à Paris avec la famille?

*Réponse*: (Yes, say that you all spent a good day. All of you walked a lot.)

*Question*: Vous avez déjeuné au restaurant?

*Réponse*: (No, you ate sandwiches.)

*Question*: Qu'est-ce que vous avez acheté dans les magasins?

*Réponse*: (Say that you personally didn't buy anything, but your wife bought a scarf and the children bought some souvenirs.)

*Question*: Vous avez passé longtemps dans les magasins?

*Réponse*: (Say you spent about an hour there.)

#### (b) Exercise 2
In the columns below you will find, on the left, a list of pronouns and nouns; then the parts of the auxiliary verb avoir; then a selection of irregular past participles; then a further list. See how many sentences you can form by linking one item from each column.

Example: Ma femme a eu le temps de se reposer.

| | | | |
|---|---|---|---|
| (i) J' | ai | pris | la Tour Eiffel. |
| (ii) Ma femme | a | vu | le temps de se reposer. |
| (iii) Mon ami Michel | a | fait | souvent à Paris. |
| (iv) Nous | avons | eu | voir la cathédrale. |
| (v) Vous | avez | été | le bus. |
| (vi) Mes enfants | ont | pu | le train. |
| (vii) Les Lebrun | | repris | une visite à Paris. |

## (c) Exercise 3

Taking the same combinations you have worked out from Exercise 2, make them all negative with the addition of ne ... pas.

## Section B

## (d) Exercise 4

Translate into French.

   (i) We were lucky with the weather
  (ii) We only took a small bag for our picnic.
 (iii) We were able to have dinner on the train.
 (iv) What did you see?
  (v) We took a bus to go to the Eiffel Tower.
 (vi) We took the pleasure steamer in order to have a rest.
(vii) What did you do after the Eiffel Tower?
(viii) I didn't buy anything, but my wife found some souvenirs.
 (ix) The children bought postcards.
  (x) We spent a terrific day in Paris.

## (e) Exercise 5

Replace the infinitive in brackets with the correct form of the verb in the perfect tense.

  (i) Est-ce que vous (coucher) les enfants?
 (ii) Ils (dormir) pendant tout le voyage.
(iii) Est-ce que vous (goûter) les tripes à la mode de Caen?
(iv) Je (manger) des sandwiches et je (voir) les monuments.
 (v) Vous (visiter) la cathédrale?
(vi) Nous (oublier) d'acheter les billets.

# CHAPTER 13

# HAVE YOU SEEN HIM?

# WHAT CAN HAVE HAPPENED?

## 13.1 DIALOGUES 🔲

### (a) Dialogue 1

Mary and the children get up late and have a leisurely breakfast. John went out a little earlier for a walk, but Mary grows rather anxious when he fails to return. She asks the hotelier.

*Mary*: Excusez-moi, monsieur. Est-ce que vous avez vu mon mari? Il est sorti il y a une heure pour acheter un journal et pour se promener. Il n'est pas encore rentré, et ça m'étonne.

*Hôtelier*: Je l'ai vu sortir, madame. Mais il n'est pas rentré, j'en suis sûr.

*Mary*: Je suis inquiète pour lui. Qu'est-ce qui a pu arriver?

*Hôtelier*: Ne vous inquiétez pas, madame. Il fait beau ce matin, et il est allé se promener, sans doute.

*Mary*: Vous croyez? J'espère que vous avez raison, mais je suis inquiète quand même.

### (b) Dialogue 2

John's delay is caused by the fact that he has witnessed an accident, and the police are questioning passers-by.

*Agent*: Excusez-moi, monsieur. Vous voulez bien répondre à quelques questions? Vous avez été témoin de l'accident, non?

*John*: Oui, j'ai vu l'accident.

*Agent*: Comment vous appelez-vous, monsieur?

*John*: John Smith. Je suis anglais.

*Agent*: Quelle est votre adresse à Caen?

*John*: Hôtel Beau Rivage.

*Agent*: Bien alors, qu'est-ce qui s'est passé exactement?

*John*: Eh bien, quand je suis arrivé ici au passage clouté, j'ai attendu pour traverser. Tout d'un coup, j'ai entendu un choc violent. Une

*Une voiture a brûlé le feu rouge ...*

Photograph: Roger-Viollet

voiture a brûlé le feu rouge et est rentré dans une autre voiture en face.

*Agent*: À votre avis, alors, c'était bien la faute du chauffeur de la voiture rouge, la Citroën?

*John*: À mon avis, oui.

*Agent*: Eh bien, merci, monsieur. On aura peut-être besoin de vous contacter pendant votre séjour ici, s'il faut vérifier les faits. Quel est votre numéro de téléphone à l'hôtel?

*John*: C'est le soixante-quinze, quatre-vingt-douze, soixante-dix-neuf (75 92 79).

*Agent*: Merci, monsieur.

**(c) Dialogue 3**

John returns belatedly to his hotel.

*Hôtelier*: Ah! Monsieur Smith, vous voilà enfin. Votre femme est très inquiète pour vous.

*John*: Oui, je suis en retard à cause d'un accident de route. La police a voulu me poser des questions.

*. . . au passage clouté*

Photograph: Roger-Viollet

*Hôtelier*: Vous avez eu un accident?

*John*: Pas personnellement, mais j'ai été témoin d'un accident.

*Hôtelier*: Bon, je téléphone tout de suite à votre chambre pour prévenir votre femme. . . . Allô, Madame Smith . . . oui, il est là. Il vient d'arriver. . . . Elle descend immédiatement, monsieur, avec les enfants. Alors, vous avez été témoin d'un accident?

*John*: Oui, quelqu'un ne s'est pas arrêté au feu rouge. Ça s'est passé à un carrefour.

*Hôtelier*: C'est incroyable, ça. Et ça arrive! . . . mais voilà votre femme.

## 13.2 VOCABULARY

### (a) Dialogue 1

#### (i) Useful expressions

| | |
|---|---|
| je suis inquiète pour lui | I'm worried about him |
| qu'est-ce qui a pu arriver | what can have happened? |
| vous avez raison | you're right |

(ii) **Nouns – Masc.**

| le mari | husband |
| le journal | newspaper |

**Noun – Fem.**

| la raison | reason |

(iii) **Other words**

| sortir | to go out; come out |
| il y a | ago |
| étonner | to astonish |
| arriver | to arrive; to happen |
| avoir raison | to be right |

**(b) Dialogue 2**

(i) **Useful expressions**

| tout d'un coup | all of a sudden |
| c'était la faute de ... | it was the fault of ... |

(ii) **Nouns – Masc.**

| le témoin | witness |
| un accident | accident |
| le rivage | bank (of river) |
| le passage clouté | pedestrian crossing |
| le coup | blow |
| le choc | shock, collision |

**Noun – Fem.**

| une adresse | address |

(iii) **Other words**

| se passer | to happen |
| violent(-e) | violent |
| brûler | to burn; to jump the lights |
| rentrer dans | to collide into |
| avoir besoin de | to need |
| contacter | to contact |
| vérifier | to check |

**(c) Dialogue 3**

(i) **Useful expressions**

| je suis en retard | I am late |
| tout de suite | immediately |
| et ça arrive! | and to think that sort of thing can happen! |

| (ii) **Nouns – Masc.** | | **Noun – Fem.** | |
|---|---|---|---|
| le feu | fire; traffic light | la route | road |
| le carrefour | crossroads | | |

(iii) **Other words**

| | |
|---|---|
| à cause de | because of |
| poser (une question) | to put/ask (a question) |
| personnellement | personally |
| descendre | to go down |
| immédiatement | immediately |
| s'arrêter | to stop |
| incroyable | incredible |

### 13.3 EXPLANATIONS

**(a) Perfect Tense** *(continued) grammar ref 5.2 (f)*

**(i) Être as an auxiliary verb**

Although the great majority of French verbs form the perfect tense by a combination of the auxiliary verb avoir with the past participle, there are a number of verbs which use être as the auxiliary. Firstly, there is a group of verbs of motion (listed on p.230). Thus, in the dialogues we find: il est sorti; il n'est pas encore rentré; je suis arrivé; and so on. Secondly, all reflexive verbs take être as their auxiliary verb, for example:

Qu'est-ce qui s'est passé?

Quelqu'un ne s'est pas arrêté.

**(ii) Agreement of past participle**

When the verb takes être as an auxiliary, the past participle agrees with the subject, that is to say it changes, rather in the same way as an adjective, according to whether the subject is feminine or plural. For John Smith we say, il n'est pas rentré, but if we had been talking about his wife we would say, elle n'est pas rentrée; if we had been talking about the children, we should say, ils ne sont pas rentrés. As often happens with such agreements, they very often make no difference to the pronunciation, and are only of importance if you want to write correct French. Past participles are often used as adjectives, in French and English, and they then agree like any other adjectives, for example:

Une église connue – 'a well known church';

des enfants épuisés – 'exhausted children'.

**(iii) Position of object pronouns**

It will be clear from the examples given of reflexive verbs, that the object pronouns precede the auxiliary verb, for example, il s'est arrêté. The same is true of other object pronouns as well as reflexives, for example, je l'ai vu.

**(b) Some uses of verbs**
(i) Note that voir is followed directly by a dependent infinitive, as is the case with verbs of motion, for example:
je l'ai vu sortir; il est allé se promener
(see also explanations (b) in Chapter 12).
(ii) Note the use of avoir besoin de (to need) and avoir raison (to be right), for example:
Vous avez raison − 'You are right';
On aura peut-être besoin de vous − 'We shall perhaps need you'.
When avoir besoin de is followed by a pronoun referring to a person, the disjunctive pronoun is used, as in the example given. When the verb is followed by an object, the pronoun en is used. For example:
Est-ce que vous avez besoin d'une chaise? Oui, j'en ai besoin.
(iii) Note the use of que in the expression, j'espère que ... − 'I hope that ...' (compare, je sais que ... − 'I know that ...').
(iv) Venir de. One case where English uses a Perfect Tense but French has a present tense as in the expression, il vient d'arriver − 'he has just arrived'.

**(c) Translating 'because (of)'**
Earlier in the book we met parce que, meaning 'because' when followed by a clause, for example:
Parce qu'ils sont en grève.
We should note the difference between this usage and the English preposition 'because of ...' which is followed by a noun, for example:
à cause d'un accident − 'because of an accident'.

**(d)** In the last chapter it was pointed out that the word hein? may be added to a statement to invite the agreement of the listener, rather like the English use of 'isn't it?', 'don't you?' and so on. Another possibility in French is to finish a statement with non? and a rising (questioning) intonation, for example:
Vous avez été témoin de l'accident, non?

**(e)** French telephone numbers are normally grouped in pairs of figures and expressed accordingly, for example:
81 43 77 − quatre-vingt-un, quarante-trois, soixante-dix-sept.

**(f)** Note the use of il y a to mean 'ago', for example: il y a une heure − 'an hour ago'.

## 13.4 EXERCISES

### Section A

#### (a) Exercise 1
You are asked to give an account of your movements yesterday
morning, in answer to the question, Qu'est-ce qui s'est passé hier
matin? – 'What happened yesterday morning?' Make up the
sequence of events using the following verbs in the perfect tense:
sortir de l'hôtel; se promener dans la rue; aller acheter un journal;
rentrer; arriver à l'hôtel vers 9h30.

#### (b) Exercise 2
Find a path through the 'flow chart' shown below. Starting with
leaving the hotel, you can take your choice as long as you follow an
arrow. You are talking about what happened in the past, so each verb
in a box should be expressed in the perfect tense. Some of the verbs
take être, and some take avoir.

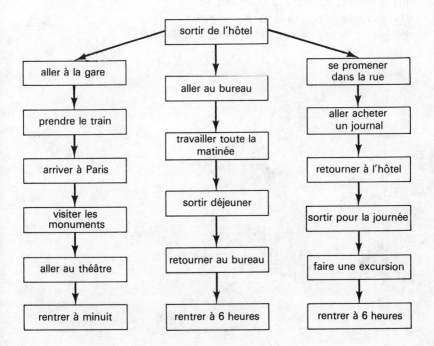

**Section B**

**(c) Exercise 3**

Translate into French.

  (i) He went out an hour ago to buy a paper.

 (ii) I saw him go out, but he has not come back.

(iii) I hope that you are right. I am worried about him.

(iv) We shall need to contact you. What is your telephone number?

 (v) I'm late because of a road accident.

(vi) Someone didn't stop at the traffic lights.

(vii) I have just arrived in Paris, and I hope that you have a room.

(viii) We went out to have lunch and we saw an accident.

(ix) Have you see him? I saw him three weeks ago.

 (x) What has happened? Have you let my wife know? (use prévenir).

**(d) Exercise 4**

Replace the words in italics by the correct form of the object pronoun.

Example: J'ai acheté *le journal* – Je l'ai acheté.

 (i) J'ai vu *votre mari* en ville.

(ii) Nous avons visité *les monuments* à Paris.

(iii) Il n'a pas entendu *le choc violent.*

(iv) J'ai besoin d'*un kilo de pommes.*

 (v) J'ai prévenu *votre mari* et j'ai appelé *Michel.*

# CHAPTER 14

# HOW SHALL WE SPEND THE DAY? WHAT HAVE YOU GOT PLANNED?

## 14.1 DIALOGUES 🔲

**(a) Dialogue 1**

The Smiths' friends from the south of France, Pierre and Anne-Marie Jacquier, are touring in Normandy, and have called in to see them. After a meal at the hotel they make plans for an excursion together.

*Pierre*: Alors, qu'est-ce que vous nous proposez pour cette excursion? Vous avez déjà des idées?

*John*: Pas vraiment. Il'y a plusieurs possibilités, et c'est difficile à décider. Nous n'avons pas encore visité Bayeux. Il faut absolument voir la tapisserie.

*Pierre*: Oui, d'accord. Et Bayeux n'est pas loin de la mer. On pourra se baigner en route.

*Mary*: Oui, ça plaira aux enfants, et les plages de cette côte sont tellement belles.

*Anne-Marie*: Et à Bayeux on pourra aussi visiter la cathédrale. Vous n'y êtes pas encore allés?

*John*: Non, on a été jusqu'à Arromanches, mais on n'a pas eu le temps de visiter Bayeux ce jour-là.

*Pierre*: J'y suis allé il y a bien des années, mais j'y retournerai avec plaisir.

*John*: Alors, vous voulez aller directement à Bayeux? Ou est-ce qu'on va à la plage d'abord?

*Anne-Marie*: Je crois que ça va dépendre un peu du temps. Quelle est la météo pour demain?

*Pierre*: Regardons le journal. 'Temps ensoleillé sur les côtes du Calvados. Possibilité d'orages vers la fin de l'après-midi'. Alors, je crois qu'on commence par la plage.

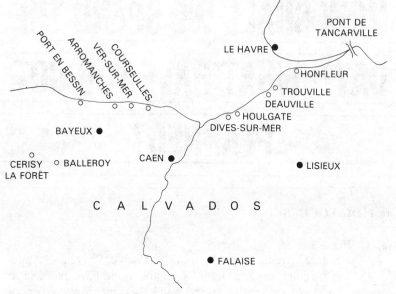

*John*: Et puis, ensuite Bayeux. Et pour manger, qu'est-ce qu'on va faire?

*Pierre*: Il y a un petit restaurant à Bayeux qu'un ami m'a recommandé. Il paraît qu'il n'est pas cher du tout, et qu'on y mange bien.

*Mary*: L'après-midi il faudra peut-être se détendre un peu et trouver un peu d'espace où les enfants pourront courir.

*Pierre*: Vers le sud de Bayeux il y a la forêt de Balleroy qui est très jolie, paraît-il. On pourra s'y arrêter pour jouer ou pour se promener, comme on voudra.

*John*: C'est une bonne idée. Et il y a aussi le château de Balleroy qui mérite une visite, paraît-il. Écoutez, j'ai ici le guide de la région, je vais vous lire un petit extrait; 'Le château de Balleroy, construit de seize cent vingt-six (1626) à seize cent trente-six (1636) par François Mansart, appartient depuis trois siècles aux marquis de Balleroy. . . . Cette construction d'une grande sobriété, s'élève majestueusement dans l'unique rue du village . . .' etc.

*Pierre*: Bien, bien, John. On sait bien qu'il vous faut un château par jour pour vous satisfaire pendant les vacances!

*Anne-Marie*: De toute façon, il y a quelque chose pour tout le monde pendant cette journée. Je crois qu'on va bien s'amuser.

*Bayeux Cathedral*

Photograph: Roger-Viollet

## (b) Dialogue 2

They decide to set out in two cars for their excursion.

*John*: Alors, tout est prêt pour le départ. On y va dans deux voitures, je suppose.

*Pierre*: Oui, je crois qu'on est trop nombreux pour une seule. Où est-ce qu'on se retrouve si on se perd en route? C'est bien la route de Courseulles qu'on prend, non?

*John*: Oui, et après il faut prendre la route de la côte et on se retrouvera à Ver sur Mer. Là on va pouvoir nager, et nous ne serons qu'à quelques kilomètres de Bayeux.

*La tapisserie de Bayeux*

Photograph: The Mansell Collection

*Pierre*: Bien. Mais ne roulez pas trop vite. Notre voiture est assez chargée.

### (c) Dialogue 3

After a couple of hours on the beach they decide to move on.

*Mary*: Quel temps magnifique. On est si bien ici, mais il va falloir qu'on s'en aille bientôt, je crois. Autrement on n'aura pas le temps de déjeuner et de tout voir.

*Pierre*: Que c'est bon, le soleil! Mais vous avez raison. Je vais dire aux enfants de s'habiller.

*Anne-Marie*: J'ai le temps d'écrire encore une carte postale?

*Mary*: Mais bien sûr. Moi aussi, j'ai des cartes à mettre à la poste.

*John*: On achètera des timbres à la poste de Bayeux.

. . . . . .

*John*: Bonjour, madame. Combien est-ce que ça coûte pour envoyer une carte postale en Angleterre?

*Dame au guichet*: Pour une carte postale ça coûte un franc vingt (1F20) et pour une lettre, un franc soixante-dix (1F70).

*John*: Alors, donnez-moi quatre timbres à 1F20, s'il vous plaît, et un timbre à 1F70.

### (d) Dialogue 4   Dans la forêt   In the forest

After lunch in the restaurant, and a visit to the cathedral and tapestry, they drive out to the forest and relax.

*John*: C'est tellement varié, le paysage normand. Il y a la côte, la plaine autour de Caen, toute cette verdure des prés, des pommiers et des bois, et ici il y a la forêt.

*Pierre*: Oui, c'est vrai — et ce n'est pas tout. Le paysage change encore si on va vers Rouen et de l'autre côté de la Seine. C'est très différent de chez nous dans le Midi. Mais pour vous autres Anglais, le paysage ressemble beaucoup à certaines parties de l'Angleterre, non?

*Mary*: C'est vrai que ces pâturages, ces vaches, ces pommiers, tout cela ressemble à certains paysages du sud de l'Angleterre; dans le Somerset ou dans le Devon, par exemple.

*John*: Remarquez que le département du Calvados est même jumelé avec le Devon. Mais il ne faut pas oublier quand même que Caen est une ville industrielle très importante. Et il y a le Havre, qui est le deuxième port de France, et Rouen avec sa zone industrielle. La Normandie n'est pas seulement un pays de vaches, de pommes et de fromages.

*Anne-Marie*: Vous avez bien raison, mais la culture reste quand même très importante pour l'économie de la région.

*John*: C'est certainement très varié; et puis il y a le côté historique, comme la tapisserie de Bayeux, ces belles églises et ces châteaux.

*Mary*: Trois semaines de vacances, ce n'est certainement pas assez pour tout voir. Mais c'est un début.

*John*: Oui, c'est sûr. Et maintenant, je crois qu'il est temps de partir. J'ai l'impression qu'il se prépare un de ces orages prévus pour la fin de l'après-midi.


## 14.2 VOCABULARY

### (a) Dialogue 1

#### (i) Useful expressions

| | |
|---|---|
| en route (pour) | on the way (to) |
| pas cher du tout | not at all expensive |
| de toute façon | in any case |

#### (ii) Nouns – Masc.

| | | Nouns – Fem. | |
|---|---|---|---|
| un orage | (thunder) storm | une idée | idea |
| le sud | south | la possibilité | possibility |
| un extrait | extract | la tapisserie | tapestry |
| le siècle | century | la météo | weather forecast |
| le marquis | marquis | la forêt | forest |

| le village | village | la construc-tion | building |
| la sobriété | restraint, sobriety |

(iii) **Other words**

| proposer | to suggest | il paraît | it seems |
| plusieurs | several | se détendre | to relax |
| difficile | difficult | courir | to run |
| décider | to decide | jouer | to play |
| absolument | absolutely | mériter | to deserve |
| d'accord | I agree | lire | to read |
| se baigner | to bathe, swim | construit(-e) | built |
| | | appartenir à | to belong to |
| bien des | a lot of | s'élever | to rise |
| directement | directly, straight | majestueuse-ment | majestically |
| dépendre de | to depend on | unique | only |
| ensoleillé(-e) | sunny | satisfaire à | to satisfy |
| commencer par | to begin with | s'amuser | to enjoy oneself; to have a good time |
| recommander | to recommend | | |
| cher (chère) | expensive | | |

(b) **Dialogue 2**

| le départ | departure | se retrouver | to meet up |
| supposer | to suppose | rouler | to drive; travel (by car) |
| nager | to swim | | |
| seul | single; one only | chargé(-e) | loaded |

(c) **Dialogue 3**
  (i) **Useful expressions**
  combien est-ce que ça coûte     how much does it cost?
  quatre timbres à 1F20           four stamps at 1F20

  (ii) **Nouns – Masc.**                **Nouns – Fem.**

| le soleil | sun | la poste | post office |
| le timbre (-poste) | (postage) stamp | la lettre | letter |

  (iii) **Other words**
  autrement                        otherwise

| s'habiller | to get dressed |
| écrire | to write |
| mettre | to put |
| mettre à la poste | to post (a letter) |
| coûter | to cost |
| envoyer | to send |

### (d) Dialogue 4

#### (i) Useful expressions

| de l'autre côté de ... | on the other side of ... |
| vous autres Anglais | you English |
| il se prépare un orage | a storm is brewing |

#### (ii) Nouns – Masc.

| le pré | meadow |
| le pommier | apple tree |
| le bois | meadow |
| le pâturage | pasture |
| un exemple | example |
| le département | department |
| le pays | country |

**Nouns – Fem.**

| la plaine | plain |
| la verdure | green(ness) |
| la vache | cow |
| la zone | zone |
| la culture | farming; agriculture |
| une économie | economy |

#### (iii) Other words

| varié(-e) | varied |
| autour de | around |
| changer | to change |
| différent (de) | different (from) |
| ressembler à | to resemble |

| remarquer | to notice |
| jumelé(-e) | twinned |
| industriel(-elle) | industrial |
| historique | historical |

## 14.3 EXPLANATIONS

### (a) Relative Pronoun *grammar ref 4.2*

The relative pronoun is rendered in English by the words 'which', 'who' or 'where' in sentences such as the following: 'the forest which is very pretty'; 'a restaurant which a friend recommended'; 'a space where the children can play'; 'a friend who lives in the Midi'. In French, no distinction is made between 'who' and 'which'; they can both be translated by qui or que depending on the function they perform in the sentence. It is important to stress this point, as a good deal of confusion can be caused by the fact that, as a question, the word qui? means 'who?' As a relative pronoun, qui can mean 'who' or 'which'. Study these examples:

un ami qui habite dans le Midi − 'a friend who lives in the Midi'
la forêt qui est très jolie − 'the forest which is very pretty'
In each of these cases the word qui is the subject of the relative clause,
that is to say, that in each sentence, qui stands for the word which is
the subject of the verb, such as ami, or forêt. Now look at these
examples:

un restaurant qu'un ami a recommandé − 'a restaurant which a
friend recommended'
un ami que je connais depuis longtemps − 'a friend whom I have
known for a long time.'

In each of these cases qu' (standing for que in front of the vowel) or,
que, is the *object* of the relative clause. This means that the relative
pronoun stands for the word which is the object of the verb, such as
restaurant, or, ami. Note that qui is never shortened, even in front of a
vowel. Note also that the relative pronoun may *not* be omitted in
French, as is often possible in English (for example, 'a friend I have
known'). The use of où, as a relative pronoun, offers no problems,
since French and English usage are identical, for example:

un espace où les enfants pourront jouer − 'a space where the
children will be able to play'.

## (b) Indirect object pronouns *grammar ref 4.1*

In Chapter 10 the direct object pronouns were introduced, for
example: je la vois − 'I see her'. Some verbs take an indirect object,
that is to say that in English the preposition 'to' is either present, or
understood, even when it does not actually appear − for example:
'give the wine to her', where 'wine' is the direct object and 'to her' is
the indirect object. This might also be expressed 'Give her the wine'
and 'her' is still the indirect object. In French, the preposition which
indicates an indirect object is à, and it occurs with a noun used as
indirect object, but not with the pronoun. For example: Je donne le
vin à mon ami, where à mon ami is the indirect object. Substituting a
pronoun this would be, Je lui donne le vin. There are numbers of
French verbs which take an indirect object where a direct object is
normal in English − for instance, plaire à, means 'to please', and is
commonly used as a way of expressing liking for something, for
example:

Est-ce que ça lui plaît? − 'does he like it?'
Note these further examples:
Son fils lui ressemble − 'his son is like him' (ressembler à)

Je lui propose une promenade − 'I suggest to him (or to her) that
we take a walk' (proposer à)
You will notice that lui means 'to him' or 'to her'. All other indirect
object pronouns, except leur − 'to them' are the same as the direct
object pronouns. In the dialogues you will find, for example:
   qu'est-ce que vous nous proposez (that is, 'to us')
   il vous faut un château par jour − you need ... (literally 'it is
   necessary to you ...').

### (c) Use of y
Y is a pronoun which has already been used in previous dialogues, and
especially in the phrase, il y a. The usual way of translating y is 'there',
and it precedes the verb (or the auxiliary verb, in the perfect tense), for
example:
   J'y suis allé − 'I went there';
   On y mange bien − 'one eats well there';
   On pourra s'y arrêter − 'we shall be able to stop there'.

**(d)** It has already been explained that expressions of quantity are
normally followed by de, for example: beaucoup de pain. There are a
small number of exceptions to this rule, two of which occur in this
chapter, that is:
   il y a bien des années − 'many years ago'
   plusieurs possibilités − 'several possibilities'

### (e) Position of adjectives
Certain adjectives change their meaning according to whether they
come in front of the noun or after it. Three of these adjectives occur in
this chapter, namely, cher, certain, seul. A complete list of such
adjectives and their meanings is given in *grammar ref. 3.3 (d)*.

**(f)** The way in which the numerals for a particular year are expressed
(for example, 1626) is explained in *grammar ref. 9.2 (c) (ii)*.

**(g)** In the course of this book, various characters have referred to la
Normandie. In fact, la Normandie, like la Bretagne, l'Aquitaine and
so on are the names of the ancient provinces of France, which have
not existed as administrative units since the Revolution, but of which
the names are still freely used. The administrative units into which
France is divided, that is, the equivalent of English counties, are called

départements. Caen is the principal town (le chef-lieu) of the département of Calvados, which is one of a number of départements which go to make up the old province of la Normandie.

## 14.4 EXERCISES

### Section A

**(a) Exercise 1**

Imagine you are asked a question, for example: Vous connaissez la tapisserie? You don't know which tapestry is being referred to, so you ask, in return. Quelle tapisserie? You are then given an explanation which uses a relative pronoun, for example: La tapisserie qui est à Bayeux. Try giving the final explanation in each of these cases below, where qui is required; use the words in brackets as a clue for what to say:

   (i) Vous connaissez la cathédrale? Quelle cathédrale? ...... (à Bayeux)
   (ii) Vous connaissez la forêt? Quelle forêt ...... (au sud de Bayeux)

In the following two examples, que is required:

  (iii) Vous avez le timbre? Quel timbre? (the stamp which you bought)
   (iv) Vous avez l'argent? Quel argent? (the money which you lost)

Now do the following sentences on the same model, and see if you can use qui or que correctly:

   (v) Vous connaissez mon ami? Quel ami? (he lives in the Midi)
   (vi) Vous avez le sac? Quel sac? (the bag you put (placer) in the car)
  (vii) Vous voyez ces vaches? Quelles vaches? (the cows in the meadow)
 (viii) Vous avez visité le château? Quel château? (the castle in the forest)

**(b) Exercise 2**

In the following sentences, you are asked to carry out an action, for example:

Donnez cette lettre à Madame Lebrun, s'il vous plaît. You reply that you have already done so, changing the indirect object for a pronoun, for example: Je lui ai déjà donné la lettre.

   (i) Donnez cette bouteille à Monsieur Smith, s v p.
   (ii) Écrivez cette carte postale à votre ami, s v p.
  (iii) Présentez ce paquet à l'hôtelier, s v p.

(iv) Proposez une excursion à vos amis.

(v) Téléphonez aux enfants, s v p.

## (c) Exercise 3

(i) Using the expression, il me faut (I need), make up a list of things you need when you go shopping, using any vocabulary learned so far, for example: Il me faut du pain; il me faut une bouteille de vin, and so on.

(ii) Then try doing the same thing, but this time asking someone else whether they need these items, for example: Il vous faut du pain? and so on.

## Section B

## (d) Exercise 4

Translate into French

(i) We absolutely must visit Bayeux. I have never seen the tapestry.

(ii) Yes, I agree. We'll take the children. They will like that. (Use plaire à.)

(iii) I went there many years ago. I hope the weather will be fine.

(iv) There is a little restaurant, which my friend recommended to me.

(v) They say that (on dit que) the castle deserves a visit.

(vi) There are too many of us for just one car. Where shall we meet up?

(vii) The landscape here is so varied. We shan't have time to see everything.

(viii) I prefer the landscape which lies (se trouve) on the other side of the Seine.

(ix) I have given them the money. They have gone to buy a souvenir.

# CHAPTER 15

# WHAT WERE THINGS LIKE WHEN YOU WERE YOUNGER?

## 15.1 DIALOGUE 📼

As their holiday draws to a close, the Smiths spend a pleasant evening together with the Lebruns and the Jacquiers. After a meal they chat about a variety of topics.

*Pierre*: Dites-moi, John, est-ce que vous vous êtes toujours intéressé à l'étude des langues?

*John*: Oui, même quand j'étais jeune, les langues m'intéressaient. Il y avait certaines difficultés pour moi à l'école. Ma famille n'était pas riche et nous habitions à la campagne. Alors, tous les jours je devais faire deux kilomètres à pied pour aller prendre l'autobus de l'école.

*Pierre*: Mais vous ne regrettez pas ces efforts?

*John*: Bien sûr que non. Mes parents étaient si fiers quand j'ai passé l'équivalent anglais du baccalauréat. Et évidemment il y a beaucoup de satisfaction à poursuivre ses études. Mais vous aussi Pierre, vous aviez des difficultés à cette époque-là.

*Pierre*: Oui, surtout parce que j'étais à l'école dans la période de l'après-guerre, et il y avait beaucoup de problèmes à résoudre à l'époque. Et puis, j'étais aussi à la campagne comme vous, et on avait des problèmes de transport. Vous êtes caennais, Michel, ce n'était pas pareil pour vous en ville.

*Michel*: Non, ce n'etait pas pareil. Surtout que je suis plus âgé que vous. J'étais à l'école primaire déjà en mil neuf cent quarante-quatre (1944), et on nous a évacués à la campagne avant l'invasion. Quand nous sommes revenus à Caen après les bombardements, c'était le chaos. Peu à peu on a commencé à rebâtir, mais pour les enfants c'était une période difficile. J'ai quitté l'école à l'âge de quinze ans pour commencer à travailler dans l'entreprise où je me trouve à présent.

*John*: Vous êtes resté plus de vingt ans dans la même compagnie?

*Michel*: Oui, j'y étais très bien, alors, pourquoi changer? C'était la

*Arromanches*

Photograph: Roger-Viollet

période de la reconstruction de Caen, parce que la ville était en
ruines après les bombardements. Autrefois Caen était une ville de
trente mille habitants, mais depuis la guerre Caen est devenu peu à
peu un des centres régionaux les plus importants de France, avec
plus de cent mille habitants. La vie ici a beaucoup changé − mais
c'est pareil aussi chez vous dans le Midi.

*Anne-Marie*:  Oui, c'est certainement pareil dans les grandes villes et
près des zones industrielles. Mais à la campagne, chez nous,
beaucoup de choses ne changent pas vite. La vie est aussi paisible
qu'avant, aussi lente que quand on était petit.

*Mary*:  Pour moi, c'est le charme du Midi; on retrouve toujours le
même rythme de vie qu'autrefois. J'y suis allée la première fois
quand j'étais écolière et nous avons fait un échange scolaire. Je me
rappelle que tout était plus calme, plus décontracté que chez nous.

*Pierre*:  C'est peut-être à cause du soleil. A mon avis, on a besoin de
conserver son énergie quand il fait tellement chaud.

*John*:  C'est vrai que la chaleur du Midi, c'est peut-être l'impression
la plus frappante d'un jeune Anglais qui visite la région pour la
première fois.

*Michel*:  Et c'est peut-être aussi à cause du climat du nord que les Normands etaient si énergiques dans le temps. Rappelez-vous que c'était la race la plus aventureuse de l'époque. On les retrouvait partout, en Angleterre, en Italie . . .

*Mary*:  Oui, mais il faut peut-être se méfier de trop généraliser. Regardez les Romains; eux venaient d'un pays chaud, après tout.

*Nicole*:  L'influence du climat sur l'histoire, c'est peut-être le sujet le plus difficile à résoudre. Ça ressemble aux discussions sur les caractéristiques nationales. On n'en finit jamais.

*Pierre*:  C'est vrai. Mais il faut quand même admettre que les Anglais et les Normands ont beaucoup de traits communs. Ils sont tous les deux plus flegmatiques que les gens du Midi . . ., il faut bien le reconnaître!

*John*:  Vous êtes contestataire, mon vieux Pierre. Vous savez bien qu'il y a des gens du Midi qui sont excessivement flegmatiques et des Normands qui sont même fougueux!

*Nicole*:  Vous voyez, c'est exactement ce que je vous disais. On n'en sortira pas!

## 15.2 VOCABULARY

### (i) Useful expressions

| | |
|---|---|
| bien sûr que non | certainly not |
| ce n'était pas pareil | it wasn't the same |
| peu à peu | little by little |
| dans le temps | in the old days |
| il faut se méfier de généraliser | one must be careful not to generalise |
| on n'en sortira pas | there's no end to it |

### (ii) Nouns – Masc.

| | |
|---|---|
| un effort | effort |
| un équivalent | equivalent |
| le transport | transport |
| le bombarde-ment | bombing |
| le chaos | chaos |
| un habitant | inhabitant |
| le rhythme | rhythm |
| un écolier | schoolboy |
| un échange | exchange |
| le nord | north |
| le Romain | Roman |
| le sujet | subject |

### Nouns – Fem.

| | |
|---|---|
| une étude | study |
| la langue | language; tongue |
| la difficulté | difficulty |
| la campagne | country |
| la satisfaction | satisfaction |
| une époque | period, era |
| la période | period |
| une écolière | schoolgirl |
| la guerre | war |
| une invasion | invasion |
| une entreprise | firm, company |

| le trait | feature | la compagnie | company |
|---|---|---|---|
| | | la reconstruction | rebuilding |
| | | la ruine | ruin |
| | | la vie | life |
| | | l'énergie | energy |
| | | la race | race (of people) |
| | | une influence | influence |
| | | l'histoire | history; story |
| | | la discussion | discussion |
| | | la caractéristique | characteristic |

## (iii) Other words

| s'intéresser à | to be interested in | rebâtir | to rebuild |
|---|---|---|---|
| jeune | young | quitter | to leave |
| riche | rich | travailler | to work |
| habiter | to live | à present | now; at present |
| je devais | I had to | | |
| fier (fière) | proud | autrefois | in the old days |
| passer (un examen) | to take an exam | devenir | to become |
| poursuivre | to pursue | régional(-e) | regional |
| résoudre | to resolve; solve | paisible | peaceful |
| | | lent(-e) | slow |
| caennais(-e) | a native of Caen | toujours | still |
| | | scolaire | educational |
| pareil(-lle) | similar | se rappeler | to remember |
| primaire | primary | calme | quiet; calm |
| évacuer | to evacuate | finir | to finish |
| décontracté (-e) | relaxed | admettre | to admit |
| | | commun(-e) | common, in common |
| conserver | to preserve; conserve | | |
| | | aventureux (-se) | adventurous |
| énergique | energetic | partout | everywhere |
| flegmatique | phlegmatic | se méfier de | to beware of ...; to take care not to ... |
| contestataire | argumentative | | |
| excessivement | excessively | | |
| fougueux (-euse) | fiery; impetuous | national(-e) | national |

## 15.3 EXPLANATIONS

**(a) The Imperfect Tense** *grammar ref 5.2 (b)*
This tense is used to describe past events and scenes in the following cases:

(i) Where the action described is habitual or often repeated, for example:

Nous habitions à la campagne — 'We used to live in the country';
J'allais tous les jours à l'école — 'I used to go every day to school'.

(ii) Where the action described is continuous, and the beginning and end of it are not indicated, for example:

J'allais à l'école quand j'ai vu mon ami Jean — 'I was going to school when I saw my friend Jean'.

The second verb here (j'ai vu) recounts a single event occurring at a certain moment. The verb, j'allais, describes an ongoing action, and draws attention to the fact that the action was continuous (the same meaning attaches to the English continuous past tense, 'I was going', as opposed to the past definite, 'I went').

(iii) Where a description is given of a landscape, or a state of mind, or a state of affairs in the past, for example:

Ma famille n'était pas riche
La ville était tout en ruines
Mes parents étaient si fiers.

It is quite usual, as in the dialogue of this chapter, for perfect and imperfect tenses to occur together in the same passage, and in the same sentence, depending on the meaning implied. You will find in this dialogue perfect tenses such as, j'ai quitté l'école; nous sommes revenues à Caen; je suis allée la première fois, and so on. In all the examples the action described happened at a single point of time in the past. In cases using the imperfect, such as the examples already given, the verb describes events and so on, in the past, which are not so clearly delineated in time. The formation of the imperfect tense is explained in *grammar ref 5.2 (b)*.

**(b) Comparative and superlative of adjectives** *grammar ref. 3.4*
Chapter 6 described the ways in which French forms the comparative and superlative of adjectives. This chapter gives a number of further examples, such as:

le sujet le plus difficile à résoudre — 'the most difficult subject to resolve'.

Note in addition, a further way in which adjectives are compared.

La vie est aussi paisible qu'avant — 'life is as peaceful as before';
La vie est aussi lente que quand on était petit — 'life is as slow as when one was small'.

**(c) Notes on vocabulary**

(i) The baccalauréat is the French equivalent of the Advanced level of the General Certificate of Education. A pass in the bac (as it is called) gives right of entry to most university courses.

(ii) The adjective caennais is used to describe someone who is a native of Caen, in the same way that parisien is used for someone from Paris.

(iii) Note that adjectives of nationality have a small initial letter, for example:

romain, normand, français.

When the adjective is used to refer to the people of the country, a capital letter is used, for example:

les Romains, un Normand, les Français.

## 15.4 EXERCISES

**Section A**

**(a) Exercise 1**

Below are some notes jotted down to describe a few details of the life of some imaginary person. Using this information, tell the life story as if it were your own. Watch out for examples of the perfect tense (for example, starting school), and use the imperfect tense to describe things you used to do, or to describe conditions.

| | |
|---|---|
| jeune | commencer à travailler dans un |
| habiter à la campagne | bureau |
| mes parents − pas riches | il y a des difficultés à cette |
| commencer l'école à l'âge de | époque-là |
| cinq ans | venir à la ville plus tard |
| habiter loin de l'école | changer de travail |
| prendre le bus tous les jours | la ville − petite à cette époque- |
| quitter l'école − 14 ans | là |
| | la ville − devenir plus grande |

**(b) Exercise 2**

Using this information and any other vocabulary you have already learned, make notes about your own life in this way, and then imagine telling someone about yourself, about your schooldays, your work and so on.

**(c) Exercise 3**

In the left-hand column below are a number of words and expressions which you would expect to be followed by the imperfect tense, because they introduce descriptions of past events. Combine elements from the four columns to make meaningful sentences, and use the verbs given in column 3 in the imperfect. (Make adjectives agree if necessary.)

| | | | |
|---|---|---|---|
| autrefois | les villages | prendre | petit |
| à cette époque-là | la ville | être | à la campagne |
| dans le temps | les langues | intéresser à | plus paisible |
| quand j'étais jeune | mes parents | habiter | à l'école |
| tous les jours | la campagne | aller | plus calme |
| | la vie | | John |
| | Pierre | | l'autobus |
| | | | en ville |

**Section B**

**(d) Exercise 4**
Translate into French
   (i) I have always been interested in languages.
  (ii) We used to live in the country but three years ago we came to Caen.
 (iii) There were a lot of problems at that time in the town.
  (iv) Yes, it wasn't like that in the country. Life was calm when we were little.
   (v) Caen gradually became one of the most important regional centres.
  (vi) I remember that everything in the south was more peaceful and relaxed.
 (vii) It is so hot in the Midi that one needs to conserve one's energy.
(viii) We used to go every day to the beach, but now we no longer have time.
  (ix) You must admit that the English and the Normans have many features in common.
   (x) I was working in my office when he arrived.

# CHAPTER 16

# AS YOU KNOW...;

# I HAVE TO START

# WORK AGAIN...

## 16.1 NARRATIVES

### (a) Narrative 1

John Smith writes a letter to friends they had hoped to visit during their stay.

Chers amis,

Comme vous le savez, nous avions l'intention de vous rendre visite pendant notre séjour en France. Maintenant que ces trois semaines touchent à leur fin, il est évident que nous n'aurons pas assez de temps pour faire le voyage. Nous le regrettons beaucoup, mais de toute façon nous allons nous revoir en automne quand vous viendrez passer quelques jours chez nous en Angleterre. Avec les enfants, les longs voyages ne sont pas faciles, et il y avait beaucoup à faire dans cette région. Pendant les premiers jours de notre visite il faisait mauvais. Il y avait beaucoup d'averses et nous avons même dû acheter des anoraks et des imperméables! Heureusement nous y sommes habitués, et nous avons pu nous amuser quand même. Nous avons découvert la ville de Caen, ce qui était un vrai plaisir. Bien qu'une grande partie de la ville soit tout à fait nouvelle, à cause des bombardements de la guerre, il reste beaucoup de choses historiques à voir, et même les bâtiments modernes ne sont pas laids. Mardi dernier nous avons fait une excursion d'une journée à Paris. Ce n'était pas très long, mais les enfants étaient contents de pouvoir y aller, et Mary et moi, nous étions ravis de revoir cette belle ville. Heureusement nous avons eu du soleil pour cette visite à Paris, et depuis, on n'a eu que quelques petits orages. Nous avons pu profiter des plages et de la campagne. Nous avons passé deux jours dans un camping tout près de la mer, et nous avons fait plusieurs excursions. J'ai du mal à croire que nous sommes ici depuis déjà trois semaines; le temps a passé si vite. Mais lundi prochain je dois recommencer mon

Postman

travail et les enfants aussi doivent rentrer à l'école. J'ai dû vous dire déjà que Mary a repris son travail, et elle aussi recommence dans quelques jours. Demain, c'est le premier septembre, et nous avons passé presque tout le mois d'août en France.

Nous attendons avec plaisir de vous revoir en octobre.

Bien amicalement,

John

*Caen, modern precinct*

Photograph: Roger-Viollet

**(b) Narrative 2**

John receives a letter from the police relating to his witnessing the accident some days before.

Monsieur,

J'ai l'honneur de vous envoyer une copie d'un document rédigé à la suite de votre déclaration du 23 août concernant un accident de la route qui a eu lieu Place Gambetta. Veuillez signer ce document et le renvoyer au commissariat de police. Ceci fait, nous n'aurons plus à vous déranger à ce sujet. Veuillez aussi remplir la section au bas du document afin de nous fournir quelques détails personnels.

Je vous prie d'agréer, cher Monsieur, l'expression de mes sentiments dévoués.

*Déclaration de John Smith*

Je me promenais le long du Boulevard Bertrand en direction de la Place Gambetta peu après neuf heures le matin du 23 août, mil neuf cent quatre-vingt-deux (1982). Je me suis arrêté à un passage clouté pour attendre un feu rouge. Soudain une voiture rouge a brûlé le feu rouge à pleine vitesse et est allée emboutir une voiture qui traversait la place.

. . . . . . . . . . . . . . . . . . . . . . .(signature)

*Nom* . . . John Smith
*Date de Naissance* . . . le 30 mai, mil neuf cent quarante-trois (1943)

*Nationalité* ... anglaise
*Domicile* ... Angleterre
*Raison de Séjour à Caen* ... vacances
*Adresse à Caen* ... Hôtel Beau Rivage
*Date de Départ* ... le 2 septembre 1982

**(c) Narrative 3**
John Smith's reply
Monsieur,

Je vous renvoie le document que vous m'avez prié de remplir. Les détails me paraissent être corrects. Je dois vous signaler que je rentre en Angleterre après-demain, le deux septembre, et je ne serai donc plus en mesure de vous aider.

Je vous prie de croire, Monsieur, à l'expression de mes sentiments distingués.

John Smith

## 16.2 VOCABULARY

**(a) Narrative 1**
  **(i) Useful expressions**
    j'ai du mal à croire que ...  I find it difficult to believe that ...

  **(ii) Nouns – Masc.**

| | | **Noun – Fem.** | |
|---|---|---|---|
| l'automne | autumn | une averse | shower of rain |
| le travail | work | | |
| le mois | month | | |

  **(iii) Other words**

| | | | |
|---|---|---|---|
| rendre visite à | to pay a visit to | il reste ... | there remains ... |
| toucher à la fin | to draw to a close | moderne | modern |
| | | laid(-e) | ugly |
| évident(-e) | evident; obvious | mardi | Tuesday |
| | | profiter de | to take advantage of |
| facile | easy | | |
| être habitué à | to be accustomed to | lundi | Monday |
| nouveau (nouvelle) | new | recommencer | to begin again |
| | | amicalement | friendly |

**(b) Narrative 2**

  **(i) Useful expressions**

| | |
|---|---|
| à la suite de | in consequence of |
| ceci fait | when this has been done |
| nous n'aurons plus à . . . | we shall have no further need to . . . |
| veuillez | be so good as to |
| à pleine vitesse | at full speed |

  **(ii) Nouns – Masc.**

| | | | |
|---|---|---|---|
| l'honneur | honour | la copie | copy |
| le document | document | la suite | sequel; result |
| le commis-sariat | police-station | la déclaration | statement |
| | | la section | section |
| le détail | detail | une expres-sion | expression |
| le sentiment | feeling | | |
| | | la vitesse | speed |
| le domicile | dwelling | la date | date |
| le départ | departure | la naissance | birth |
| | | la nationalité | nationality |

  **(iii) Other words**

| | | | |
|---|---|---|---|
| rédiger | to draw up | signer | to sign |
| concernant | concerning | renvoyer | to send back |
| avoir lieu | to take place | remplir | to fill up |
| au bas de | at the bottom of | dévoué(-e) | devoted |
| | | soudain | suddenly |
| afin de | in order to | plein(-e) | full |
| personnel(elle) | personal | emboutir | to bump into |
| agréer | to receive favourably | | |

**(c) Narrative 3**

| | | | |
|---|---|---|---|
| prier | to request | en mesure de | in a position to |
| paraître | to appear; seem | aider | to help |
| correct(-e) | correct | distingué(-e) | distinguished |
| signaler | to point out | | |
| après-demain | the day after tomorrow | | |

## 16.3 EXPLANATIONS

### (a) Writing letters

Letters are probably the most likely way in which students in the early stages of language learning may be required to write the language. This chapter contains an informal letter to friends and two more formal letters. The rules for letter writing may be briefly summarised as follows:

(i) Formal letters begin Monsieur, or, Madame. If the person addressed has a title, that may be included, for example: Monsieur le Directeur. Such letters may be ended in a number of ways, all of which sound rather long-winded to English ears, as an alternative to 'Yours faithfully'. Two such endings are given in the chapter, and other possibilities are:

Veuillez agréer, Monsieur, l'expression de mes sentiments dévoués;
Je vous prie d'agréer, Monsieur, l'expression de mon respectueux dévouement.

In such endings, the title (Monsieur, Madame, and so on) is always written in full.

(ii) Informal letters to friends begin, Cher Jean; Chère Marie; they end, Amicalement; Amitiés; Nous vous envoyons toutes nos amitiés; Je vous envoie l'amical souvenir de toute la famille; Meilleurs sentiments; and so on.

(iii) In French, as in English, there are certain formulas of expression which crop up frequently in letters. Note the following for formal letters:

J'ai l'honneur de vous rendre compte — I beg to inform you . . .
Je vous serais très obligé de
Je vous serais très reconnaissant de } I should be grateful if . . .
J'ai le regret de vous informer — I regret to inform you
J'ai le plaisir de vous informer — I have pleasure in informing you
In informal letters you might find:
J'ai bien reçu votre lettre du . . . — I received your letter of . . .
Je vous remercie de votre lettre du . . . — Many thanks for your letter of . . .
Votre lettre du . . . m'est bien arrivée — Your letter of . . . arrived safely
Je suis heureux de savoir que . . . — I'm glad to know that . . .

### (b) Use of the verb devoir *grammar ref 5.8 (b)*

We have already met two ways of expressing compulsion or necessity in French, that is, il faut, *or* il est nécessaire de. Another possibility is to use the verb devoir in much the same way as English uses 'must' or 'have to'. In the present tense we find, Je dois recommencer mon travail — 'I must start work again'; Les enfants doivent rentrer à l'école — 'the children must go back to school'. English only uses the word 'must' in the present tense, and in all other tenses uses 'have to', for example: 'I shall have to', 'I had to' and so on. If the examples above were expressed in the future, for instance: 'I shall have to start work again', the French rendering would be, Je devrai recommencer mon travail, that is, the future tense of devoir is used. The use of the past tense is slightly more complicated because of the distinction made between imperfect and perfect. Compare the following two sentences, the first from Chapter 15 and the second from Chapter 16:

Je devais faire deux kilomètres à pied.

Nous avons dû acheter des anoraks.

Both these statements would be rendered in English by 'had to', but French makes a distinction, because the first one tells of something that had to take place habitually, every day (therefore, imperfect of devoir), whereas the second one tells of an action which took place on one occasion only (therefore, perfect of devoir).

One other point which should be mentioned here is that English has another form of the past tense, namely, 'must have'. French does not distinguish between the two forms 'had to' and 'must have', but only, again, between imperfect or perfect, for example:

J'ai dû vous dire que Mary a repris son travail — I must have told you that Mary has started work again (perfect — one event in the past);

Il devait être trois heures quand il est venu — It must have been three o'clock when he came (imperfect, since this is the tense used to give the time in the past, cf Il était trois heures).

### (c) Subjunctive *grammar ref 5.5*

The subjunctive mood is a form of the verb with which we shall not be much concerned in this book, since the use of this form is very restricted in spoken French. The forms of the subjunctive are set out in *grammar ref 5.5* and it will be sufficient to say that there are certain forms of speech where you may expect to hear the subjunctive, for example, after: il faut que ... and, bien que ....

The expression, il faut que je m'en aille — 'I must be going', is commonly used, and was introduced in Chapter 12. Bien que, meaning 'although' is often heard, followed by the subjunctive of the verb être, for example:

Bien qu'une grande partie de la ville soit nouvelle — 'although a large part of the town is new'.

**(d) Relative Pronoun** *(cont) grammar ref 4.3*

Consider these two English sentences:

'You will perhaps be interested to know what we have been doing.'

'We have got to know the town of Caen, which has been a real pleasure.'

In each of these cases the words 'what' and 'which' are relative pronouns, however they do not refer to a single noun, but to the whole of the preceding idea. In the second sentence it is not Caen which is referred to by 'which', but the fact of getting to know the town. In such examples as these French uses a fuller form of the relative pronoun, ce qui, or ce que, according to whether the relative pronoun is subject or object in the clause, for example:

Ça vous intéressera de savoir ce que nous avons fait;

Nous avons fait la connaissance de la ville de Caen, ce qui était un vrai plaisir.

**(e) Notes on vocabulary**

(i) Afin de + infinitive means 'in order to' and therefore has much the same meaning as pour + infinitive. It is little more specific than pour, and might be rendered, 'with a view to' or 'with the purpose of'.

(ii) An object pronoun is sometimes used with a verb in French where English does not require one, for example:

Comme vous le savez bien ... − 'as you well know ...';

nous le regrettons beaucoup, mais ... − 'we are very sorry, but ...'.

**16.4 EXERCISES**

**Section A**

**(a) Exercise 1**

'What have you got to do today?' − Qu'est-ce que vous devez faire aujourd'hui?. Reply to the question using the notes below, and using the verb devoir to express what you have to do:

| 9h | se lever | 12h30 déjeuner | 16h rentrer |
|----|----------|----------------|-------------|
| 10h | bureau | 14h45 faire des courses | 19h30 dîner |
| | | | 22h30 au lit |

**(b) Exercise 2**

Can you now answer the question, Qu'est-ce que vous avez dû faire? − 'What did you have to do?' and reply in the perfect tense, using the same information as above.

**(c) Exercise 3**

Here is a letter written to a hotel to reserve rooms:

Monsieur,

Votre hôtel m'a été recommandé par un ami. Je vous écris pour réserver deux chambres avec salle de bains pour la période du 12 au 27 juillet. Nous serons quatre personnes, ma femme, mes deux enfants et moi-même. Pourriez-vous me renseigner sur vos tarifs et me dire s'il faut vous envoyer des arrhes? Je voudrais savoir aussi si l'hôtel est près de la plage, et s'il y a des possibilités de divertissements pour les enfants.

Je vous prie d'agréer, Monsieur, l'expression de mes sentiments les plus distingués.

(*Note:* le tarif − scale of charges
les arrhes (*f.pl.*) − deposit)

Using this as a model, write another letter, changing as many elements in the original letter as you like, for example: number of rooms, number of people, with or without bathroom, proximity to town centre, and so on.

## Section B

**(d) Exercise 4**

Translate into French

Dear John,

Now that our holidays are coming to an end, we must write to tell you what we have been doing here in Normandy. At first the weather was bad, and we had a lot of showers. Luckily there was a lot to do, and many places to visit. We got to know the town of Caen, which was a great pleasure. We were able to spend a day in Paris, which was very interesting for the children. We shall have to return with them to Paris, as one day is not very long. We had sunshine during that excursion, and since that day it has been fine. We were able to take advantage of the lovely beaches in this region. The time has passed so quickly, that it is difficult to believe that we shall have to leave tomorrow.

Yours sincerely

**(e) Exercise 5**

Replace the infinitive form of devoir with the correct tense of the verb, and write out a translation into English of each sentence.

(i) Jeudi dernier je (devoir) quitter mon bureau de bonne heure.

(ii) Quand j'étais jeune mon père (devoir) commencer son travail à 7 heures.

(iii) Les enfants (devoir) rentrer à l'école aujourd'hui.

(iv) Mardi prochain vous (devoir) venir me rendre visite.

# CHAPTER 17

# I AM WORRIED ABOUT . . . ;

# WHAT ARE THE SYMPTOMS?

# WHAT DID HE SAY?

## 17.1 DIALOGUES 📼

**(a) Dialogue 1   Une visite chez le médecin   A visit to the doctor**

Both the children are feeling unwell. Mary decides to take them along to see the doctor.

*Mary*:   Bonjour, Docteur. Je viens pour les enfants. Ils ont tous les deux mal à la gorge et ils ont toussé toute la nuit. Ce n'est peut-être qu'un rhume, ou une grippe, mais je préfère en être sûre.

*Médecin*:   Mais bien sûr, madame. Quel âge ont-ils?

*Mary*:   Le garçon a huit ans et la fillette en a six.

*Médecin*:   Eh bien, fais voir ta gorge, mon petit . . . oui, comme ça c'est bien; tire ta langue. Oui, et toi aussi, ma petite. Bon. Et maintenant, mets le thermomètre dans la bouche comme ça. Oui, et toi aussi. Bien, attendez quelques secondes. Est-ce qu'il y a d'autres symptômes, madame?

*Mary*:   Ils n'ont pas faim et ils ont mal à la tête.

*Médecin*:   Oui, bien sûr, ils ont un peu de fièvre, mais rien de sérieux. Vous leur avez donné des médicaments déjà?

*Mary*:   Je leur ai donné de l'aspirine pendant la nuit.

*Médecin*:   Ils sont tous les deux un peu enrhumés, mais ce n'est pas grave. Vous n'avez aucune raison de vous inquiéter. Je vais vous faire une ordonnance pour des comprimés et pour un sirop qui soulagera la toux. Donnez-leur les comprimés trois fois par jour, après les repas, et ne les laissez pas aller dans l'eau.

*Mary*:   Non, sûrement pas. Ce n'est vraiment pas de chance que ça nous arrive, juste à la fin de nos vacances. Il ne nous reste qu'un jour à Caen.

*Médecin*:   Ce n'est qu'un rhume, madame. On peut attraper un rhume n'importe quand.

*Mary*: Mais on s'y attend davantage en hiver ou au printemps, pas en été.

*Médecin*: Il fait quelquefois frais le soir. De toute façon, ça ne durera que deux ou trois jours. N'oubliez pas de leur donner les médicaments, et tout ira bien.

*Mary*: Merci beaucoup, docteur. Combien est-ce que je vous dois?

*Médecin*: Le prix de la consultation est 56 francs madame. Pour les médicaments, vous les paierez chez le pharmacien.

*Mary*: Merci beaucoup, docteur.

*Médecin*: Au revoir, madame. Au revoir, les enfants.

. . . *chez le pharmicien*

Photograph: Roger-Viollet

**(b) Dialogue 2  Au supermarché  In the supermarket**

The children are taken back to the hotel to rest, and while John looks after them, Mary goes to meet up with Nicole Lebrun to do the last-minute shopping for the return journey.

*Nicole*:  Alors, comment vont les enfants?

*Mary*:  Ce n'est qu'un rhume, mais ils ne se sentent pas bien en ce moment. John est resté à l'hôtel avec eux. Je leur ai donné des médicaments, et j'espère qu'ils seront remis bien vite.

*Nicole*:  Et le docteur, qu'est-ce qu'il a dit?

*Mary*:  Il m'a dit que ce n'était pas grave et que ça sera vite passé.

*Nicole*:  Il n'a pas dit qu'il fallait les garder au lit?

*Mary*:  Non, il a dit qu'il n'y avait vraiment aucune raison de s'inquiéter et qu'ils pourront faire le voyage demain.

*Nicole*:  Les pauvres petits! Alors, qu'est-ce qu'il vous reste à acheter? Votre panier est déjà plein.

*Mary*:  Oui, il est assez lourd. J'ai déjà acheté pas mal de choses pour

*Au supermarché*

Photograph: Roger-Viollet

le piquenique pendant le voyage. Est-ce que je peux mettre ça dans votre voiture?

*Nicole*: Bien sûr, laissez-le là, sur le siège arrière. J'ai mon sac et un autre panier vide, si vous en avez besoin.

*Mary*: Il me faut encore des provisions pour le voyage, et John veut aussi que j'achète du vin.

*Nicole*: Allons au supermarché, alors. Il y a plus de choix . . . voilà, qu'est-ce qu'il veut comme vin, alors?

*Mary*: Nous avons droit à trois litres chacun pour passer à la douane anglaise. Si je prenais trois bouteilles de blanc et trois de rouge?

*Nicole*: Celui-ci est très bon, c'est un Bourgogne rouge que je peux vous recommander.

*Mary*: Et celui-ci, vous connaissez?

*Nicole*: C'est un blanc assez doux. Celui-là est plus sec, ça dépend des goûts.

*Mary*: Nous préférons le blanc sec en général, alors je vais prendre deux bouteilles de celui-là, et une bouteille de vin doux pour le dessert.

*Nicole*: Et qu'est-ce qu'il vous faut encore?

*Mary*: Nous voulons emporter des fromages de la région.

*Nicole*: Gardez-les au frais, alors, jusqu'à votre départ. Ne les laissez pas au chaud, ou alors les autres passagers sur le bateau vont se plaindre!

*Mary*: Et puis, je voudrais aussi des petits pains pour le voyage.

*Nicole*: Eh bien, voilà le rayon de la boulangerie.

*Mary*: John m'a aussi demandé de lui acheter un journal, mais pour ça il faut aller ailleurs, je suppose.

*Nicole*: Oui, payons d'abord tout ça à la caisse, et puis on va chercher un marchand de journaux.


## 17.2 VOCABULARY

### (a) Dialogue 1

#### (i) Useful expressions

| | |
|---|---|
| ils ont mal à la tête | they've got a head-ache |
| ils ont mal à la gorge | they have a sore throat |
| fais voir . . . | show me . . . |
| aucune raison | no reason at all |
| ce n'est vraiment pas de chance | we're really out of luck |
| n'importe quand | any time at all |

**Useful Expressions** *continued*
tout ira bien                    everything will be fine

(ii) **Nouns – Masc.**           **Nouns – Fem.**

| le médecin | doctor | la gorge | throat |
| le docteur | doctor | la grippe | 'flu |
| le mal | ache; pain | la langue | tongue |
| le rhume | cold | la bouche | mouth |
| le thermo-mètre | thermometer | la seconde | second |
|  |  | la tête | head |
| le symptôme | symptom | la fièvre | fever |
| le médic-ament | medicine | une ordon-nance | prescription |
| le comprimé | tablet | la toux | cough |
| le sirop | cough medicine | la consult-ation | consultation |
| l'hiver | winter |  |  |
| le printemps | spring |  |  |
| le prix | price |  |  |
| le pharmacien | chemist |  |  |

(iii) **Other words**

| tousser | to cough | laisser | to let; to permit |
| tirer | to pull; to put out (tongue) | juste | just |
|  |  | attraper | to catch |
| mettre | to put | davantage | more |
| sérieux(-se) | serious | frais (fraîche) | cool; fresh |
| enrhumé(-e) | with a cold | durer | to last |
| aucun(-e) | not a single one | je dois (devoir) | I owe |
| soulager | to relieve; comfort |  |  |

(b) **Dialogue 2**

(i) **Useful expressions**

comment vont les enfants?     how are the children?
ça sera vite passé            it will soon be over
qu'est-ce qu'il vous reste à acheter   what have you got left to buy?
pas mal de                    quite a few

(ii) **Nouns – Masc.**

| le super-marché | supermarket |
| le panier | basket |
| le siège | seat |
| le siège arrière | back-seat |
| le choix | choice |
| le droit | right |
| le Bourgogne | Burgundy (the wine) |
| le goût | taste |
| le frais | cool (place) |
| le chaud | warm (place) |
| le passager | passenger |
| le petit pain | bread roll |
| le marchand | merchant; shopkeeper |

**Nouns – Fem.**

| la provision | provision |
| la douane | customs |
| la boulangerie | bakery |
| la Bourgogne | Burgundy (the province) |

(iii) **Other words**

| se sentir | to feel |
| garder | to keep |
| pauvre | poor |
| lourd(-e) | heavy |
| vide | empty |
| avoir droit à | to have a right to |

| chacun | each one |
| doux (douce) | sweet |
| sec (sèche) | dry |
| emporter | take away |
| se plaindre | to complain |
| ailleurs | elsewhere |

## 17.3 EXPLANATIONS

### (a) Reported speech

When reporting the statements of others, French usage is the same as English, for example:

Il a dit qu'il n'y avait aucun danger – 'He said that there was no danger';

Il m'a dit que ce n'était pas grave 'He told me that it wasn't serious'.

French uses dire to translate either 'to say' or 'to tell'. Dire is then followed by a clause beginning with que, and the verb is expressed in the imperfect tense, as in the examples above.

**(b) Order of object pronouns in the imperative** *grammar ref 4.1 (c)*
When the imperative is used in the negative, the order of object
pronouns is as usual, before the verb, for example:
   Ne les laissez pas aller dans l'eau.
However, when the imperative is affirmative, the object pronouns
follow the verb, for example:
   Donnez des comprimés aux enfants, *becomes,* Donnez-leur des
   comprimés.
Similarly, when Nicole tells Mary to keep the cheese in a cool place,
she says, gardez-les au frais. When the object pronouns follow the
imperative in this way, they are linked to the verb by a hyphen.

**(c) Demonstrative pronoun** *grammar ref 4.4*
The demonstrative pronoun in English is expressed by 'this one', 'that
one', for example: 'You take that bottle and I'll have this one'. In
French the equivalent sentence would be expressed.
   Prenez cette bouteille, et moi, je prends celle-ci.
In the second dialogue of this chapter, Nicole refers to the wine by
saying, Celui-ci est très bon; later on she says, Celui-là est plus sec. It
is clear, therefore, that the demonstrative pronoun in French is celui,
for masculine words, and celle for feminine words. To indicate
whether 'this one' or 'that one' is intended, celui and celle can be
followed by -ci or -là. In the plural, the masculine forms are ceux-ci
and ceux-là; the feminine forms are celles-ci and celles-là.

**(d) Negatives** *grammar ref 5.10*
 (i) Rien may be followed by de + adjective to render the English
form, 'nothing serious', 'nothing good', and so on for example:
   rien de sérieux; rien de bon.
(ii) Ne ... aucun expresses a stronger level of negation than a simple
ne ... pas. For example, Vous n'avez pas de raison de vous inquiéter,
is not as strong as, Vous n'avez aucune raison de vous inquiéter ('no
reason at all').

**(e) En** *grammar ref 4.1 (d)*
En has already been used on a number of occasions, particularly with
numerals, for example:
   Il y en a six − 'There are six (of them)'.
En is the pronoun used when a verb does not take a direct object but is
followed by de + noun, for example:
   Je suis sûr de l'heure du départ;
   J'ai besoin d'une cuillère.

If these sentences are expressed with a pronoun instead of the noun they become:

Ｊ'en suis sûr; J'en ai besoin.

### (f) Some notes on items of vocabulary

(i) Laisser, meaning 'to let', 'to permit', is used with a direct infinitive, for example:

Laissez-le sortir;

Ne les laissez pas aller dans l'eau.

(ii) Masculine nouns ending in -al have an irregular plural form ending in -aux, for example: le journal, les journaux.

(iii) The preposition used with three of the seasons of the year is en, for example: en hiver – 'in winter'. The one exception is 'in spring' which is au printemps.

(iv) Devoir was introduced in Chapter 16 in the sense of 'must'. When not used in that way, devoir means 'to owe', for example:

Combien est-ce que je vous dois? – 'How much do I owe you?'

(v) Parts of the body are often, but by no means always, referred to by the definite article, for example: ils ont mal à la gorge; ils ont mal à la tête. But when the doctor addresses the children directly he says:

Fais voir ta gorge ... tire ta langue – 'show me your throat, put your tongue out'.

## 17.4 EXERCISES

### Section A

#### (a) Exercise 1

You take your child to the doctor's and he makes the comments listed below. You meet up with your friend who asks what he said. Report the doctor's comments, beginning each statement Il a dit que ...

ce n'est pas grave,

vous n'avez aucune raison de vous inquiéter,

l'enfant est un peu enrhumé,

il a un peu de fièvre,

il ne doit pas sortir,

il faut lui donner deux comprimés par jour,

il faut le laisser dormir, si possible.

#### (b) Exercise 2

Here are a list of items, each with two adjectives to describe them. Offer these items to a friend using demonstrative pronouns, for example: Voilà deux bouteilles de vin; celui-ci est rouge, celui-là est blanc.

|       |                       |       |          |
|-------|-----------------------|-------|----------|
| (i)   | deux bouteilles de vin | sec   | doux     |
| (ii)  | deux sacs             | plein | vide     |
| (iii) | deux paniers          | lourd | léger    |
| (iv)  | deux voitures         | rouge | blanche  |
| (v)   | deux routes           | bonne | mauvaise |

## Section B

### (c) Exercise 3
Translate into French

(i) I've got a headache and a sore throat. What can you give me?

(ii) You need some tablets and some cough medicine. Take this prescription to the chemist.

(iii) Give them these tablets three times a day and do not let them go into the water.

(iv) You have caught a cold, but it isn't serious. You have no reason to be worried.

(v) What sort of wine does he like? This one is dry.

(vi) I think he will probably prefer this one; or perhaps that one over there is better.

(vii) Here are your cheeses. Keep them in a cool place until you leave.

(viii) Did he say that we had to wait here? Are you sure?

(ix) I have bought some bread rolls, but we don't need them now.

(x) In spring we shall have to return to France.

# CHAPTER 18

# IF YOU HAD MORE TIME!
# IT'S BEST TO BE SURE

## 18.1 DIALOGUES 📼

### (a) Menu

Nicole has asked the Smiths and Jacquiers to come and have a meal on the last evening of the holiday. This is the menu she has prepared, with some notes from her cookery book.

Soupe à l'oignon

(1 ½ litres de bouillon, 250g d'oignons, 60g de beurre, 80g de farine, sel, poivre).

Soufflé de poisson

(200g de poisson cuit, 50g de beurre, 70g de farine, 3dl de lait, 4 oeufs).

Poulet sauté chasseur

(1 poulet, 1dl de bouillon, 2dl de vin blanc, 1dl de cognac, 50g de beurre, 50g de farine, 125g de tomates fraîches, sel, poivre, estragon, cerfeuil, 40g d'échalotes. Avant de mouiller avec le vin blanc, mettre le cognac et faire flamber. Ajouter le bouillon. Saler. Poivrer. Couvrir. Laisser cuire 30 minutes. Incorporer alors les tomates. Cuire encore 10 minutes. Terminer la sauce avec ½ cuillère à café d'estragon et de cerfeuil hâchés finement. 30g de beurre fin. Bien mélanger sans faire bouillir).

Fromages: Camembert, Livarot, Pont l'Évêque.

Dessert: Bavaroise au chocolat

( ½ litre de lait, 250g de crème, 150g de chocolat, 5 oeufs, 100g de sucre, 20g de feuilles de gélatine, 3 cuillerées d'eau froide).

### (b) Dialogue 1   Une dernière rencontre   A final get-together

After the meal, the friends sit and talk, before the Smiths have to go back to their hotel.

*Michel*: Alors, les vacances se terminent. Mais il y a encore beaucoup à voir, vous savez! Si vous aviez plus de temps vous pourriez visiter la vallée de la Seine, les montagnes de la Suisse Normande, ou même aller jusqu'au Mont St-Michel.

*John*: Ah oui, si on avait le temps ... Mais il y a vraiment un embarras de richesses dans cette région, et comme vous savez, il faut bien gagner sa vie.

*Anne-Marie*: C'est bien vrai, ce que vous dites; nous aussi, nous allons bientôt partir et la semaine prochaine on recommence le travail.

*Mary*: Ces vacances étaient vraiment réussies. On a passé un excellent séjour. Mais nous espérons beacoup vous revoir chez nous en Angleterre. Vous avez bien notre adresse?

*John*: Et le numéro de téléphone aussi, je vous l'ai donné, Michel, non?

*Michel*: Oui, oui, vous me l'avez donné, et je vous assure qu'on va faire notre possible pour vous rendre visite. Merci beaucoup pour l'invitation.

*John*: C'est nous qui vous remercions pour votre accueil.

*Nicole*: Mais c'est normal, voyons. Si nous étions en Angleterre, vous feriez la même chose pour nous sans doute.

*Mary*: C'est sûr. Et Anne-Marie et Pierre savent bien où nous trouver aussi.

*John*: Alors, à votre santé, tout le monde, et à la prochaine fois.

*Tout*: À la vôtre, et à la prochaine fois.


**(c) Dialogue 2   Départ de l'hôtel   Leaving the hotel**

*Hôtelier*: Alors, Monsieur Smith, c'est déjà le départ. Voilà votre note.

*John*: Merci. C'est tous compris, taxes et service aussi?

*Hôtelier*: Oui, monsieur. Taxes et service sont compris.

*John*: Excusez-moi, monsieur, mais il y a peut-être une petite erreur ici. Les boissons pour le 24 août, je ne m'en souviens pas bien.

*Hôtelier*: Faites voir, monsieur. Oui, c'est le soir où vous êtes rentré avec votre ami, après le voyage à Paris.

*John*: Mais, oui, bien sûr. Excusez-moi, j'avais oublié. Alors, c'est correct. Voilà, et merci.

*Hôtelier*: C'est moi qui vous remercie, monsieur. J'espère que vous êtes satisfait de votre séjour.

*John*: Oui, très satisfait. S'il ne fallait pas recommencer le travail, nous aimerions rester encore quelques jours.

*Hôtelier*: Alors, bon voyage, monsieur. Bon retour chez vous et au plaisir de vous revoir.

*John*: Merci, monsieur, et au revoir.

**(d) Dialogue 3   Au garage   At the garage**

*John*: Le plein, s'il vous plaît.

*Garagiste*: Oui, monsieur, super ou ordinaire?

*John*: Super. Et vous voulez bien vérifier le niveau d'huile et la pression des pneus aussi? Je ne veux pas tomber en panne.

*Garagiste*: Vous êtes en route pour le Havre?

*John*: Oui, mais nous ne sommes pas pressés. Nous allons prendre le bateau de nuit, alors nous aurons le temps de nous arrêter un peu en route.

*Les garagistes*

Photograph: Roger-Viollet

*Garagiste*: Il vous faut pas mal d'huile, monsieur.

*John*: Ça m'étonne un peu.

*Garagiste*: Et regardez les bougies. Celle-ci est sale et huileuse.

*John*: Ah, mon Dieu! Qu'est-ce que cela veut dire?

*Garagiste*: Je ne crois pas que ça soit grave. Mais il vaut mieux être sûr. Autrement, vous allez certainement tomber en panne. Est-ce que vous pouvez nous laisser la voiture pour une demi-heure?

*John*: Mais oui; heureusement on a le temps. Nous allons nous promener en attendant.

......

*Garagiste*: Voilà, monsieur. Tout est en ordre maintenant. Nous avons trouvé une petite fuite d'huile. Rien de grave, mais il vaut mieux que ça soit réparé.

*John*: Oui, alors. Combien est-ce que je vous dois?

*Garagiste*: 120F pour trente litres de super; 42F pour deux litres d'huile, et 84F pour la réparation. Ça fait 246F en tout monsieur. Merci, et bonne route.

*John*: C'est moi qui vous remercie. Au revoir.

## 18.2 VOCABULARY

### (a) Menu

#### (i) Nouns – Masc.

| | | Nouns – Fem. | |
|---|---|---|---|
| un oignon | onion | la rencontre | meeting |
| le bouillon | stock | la soupe | soup |
| le sel | salt | la tomate | tomato |
| le soufflé | soufflé | une échalote | shallot |
| le poisson | fish | la sauce | sauce; gravy |
| le chasseur | hunter | la cuillère à | coffee-spoon |
| le poulet | chicken | café | |
| l'estragon | tarragon | la feuille | leaf |
| le cerfeuil | chervil | la gélatine | gelatine |
| le sucre | sugar | la cuillerée | spoonful |

#### (ii) Other words

| | | | |
|---|---|---|---|
| souffler | to blow; breathe; puff | incorporer | to mix in |
| | | alors | then |
| sauter | to jump; to fry and toss | terminer | to finish |
| | | hâcher | to chop up |

| | | | |
|---|---|---|---|
| mouiller | to wet; to soak | fin(-e) | fine; refined; best quality |
| flamber | to set light to | | |
| ajouter | to add | mélanger | to blend; mix |
| saler | to add salt | faire bouillir | to bring to the boil |
| poivrer | to add pepper | bavarois(-e) | Bavarian |
| couvrir | to cover | froid(-e) | cold |

## (b) Dialogue 1

### (i) Useful expressions

| | |
|---|---|
| un embarras de richesses | too much to choose from |
| gagner sa vie | to earn one's living |
| nous allons faire notre possible | we shall do everything possible |
| voyons! | come now! |
| à la vôtre | cheers!; good health! |

### (ii) Nouns – Masc.

| | | Nouns – Fem. | |
|---|---|---|---|
| le mont | mount | la vallée | valley |
| un embarras | hindrance; an embarrassing quantity | la montagne | mountain; hill |
| | | la Suisse | Switzerland |
| | | la richesse | wealth |
| un accueil | welcome | une invitation | invitation |
| | | la santé | health |

### (iii) Other words

| | | | |
|---|---|---|---|
| se terminer | to come to an end | assurer | to assure |
| gagner | to earn; to win | normal(-e) | normal |
| réussi(-e) | successful | | |

## (c) Dialogue 2

### (i) Useful expressions

| | |
|---|---|
| j'avais oublié | I had forgotten |
| bon retour chez vous | safe journey home |
| au plaisir (de vous revoir) | I hope we shall meet again |

### (ii)

| Nouns – Fem. | |
|---|---|
| la note | bill, check |
| la taxe | tax |
| une erreur | mistake |

(iii) **Other words**

| | |
|---|---|
| se souvenir de | to remember |

**(d) Dialogue 3**

(i) **Useful expressions**

| | |
|---|---|
| le plein, s'il vous plaît | fill her up, please |
| tomber en panne | to break down |
| qu'est-ce que cela veut dire? | what does that mean? |
| il vaut mieux être sûr | it's better to be sure |
| en attendant | while waiting |
| en ordre | in order |
| bonne route | have a good drive |

(ii) **Nouns – Masc.**

| | | **Nouns – Fem.** | |
|---|---|---|---|
| le garage | garage | (l'essence) ordinaire | low-grade petrol |
| le super | 4-star petrol | l'huile | oil |
| le niveau | level | la pression | pressure |
| le pneu | tyre | la panne | breakdown |
| | | la bougie | sparking plug; candle |
| | | la fuite | leak |
| | | la réparation | repair |

(iii) **Other words**

| | |
|---|---|
| ordinaire | ordinary |
| tomber | to fall |
| sale | dirty |
| huileux(-se) | oily |
| vouloir dire | to mean |
| laisser | to leave |
| réparer | to repair |

## 18.3 EXPLANATIONS

**(a) Conditional sentences** *grammar ref 5.2 (d)*

The word si – 'if' – introduces a condition into a sentence, for example:

'If you come to Caen, you will visit the castle' – Si vous venez à Caen, vous visiterez le château.

In these sentences, both languages have a present tense in the 'if' clause, followed by a future tense in the second part of the sentence. Although this type of sentence is introduced by 'if', the tenses show that it really indicates a near certainty. When there is an element of doubt and uncertainty, the sequence of tenses is different, for example: 'if you came to Caen, you would see the castle'. The tense expressed in English by 'would see' is the conditional. In French, the conditional is formed by adding the endings of the imperfect onto the infinitive (see p.225), that is to say, its form is rather similar to that of the future tense, and the irregular forms of the future are also irregular in the conditional for example: (je viendrais – 'I would come'). In French, the tense sequence in conditional sentences is always the imperfect in the si clause, followed by the conditional, for example:

Si vous veniez à Caen, vous verriez le château.

Consider these examples from the dialogues:

Si vous aviez plus de temps, vous pourriez visiter ... – 'If you had more time you would be able to visit ...'

Si nous étions en Angleterre, vous feriez la même chose ... – 'If we were in England, you would do the same thing ...'.

### (b) Use of the infinitive in instructions

Although the usual way of giving instructions and commands is by using the imperative, one often finds the infinitive used when instructions are given in books (as in the extracts from a cookery-book in the Menu section) or in public notices, for example: Ajouter le bouillon; terminer la sauce, and so on.

### (c) Subjunctive (cont.) grammar ref 5.5

This chapter contains two further examples of the use of the subjunctive,

(i) In a clause beginning with que, and following a negative statement, for example,

Je ne crois pas que ça soit grave.

(ii) In a clause beginning with que, and following the expression il vaut mieux, for example:

Il vaut mieux que ça soit réparé – 'it's better to have it repaired'.

### (d) Use of c'est for emphasis

In English, considerable use is made of the voice to stress particular words in a sentence. In French it is not so easy to stress individual words with the voice in this way, and a more usual way of indicating emphasis is to place the stressed word at the beginning of the sentence and preceded by c'est. For example, if Nous vous remercions, does not sound sufficiently emphatic, you can say, C'est nous qui vous remercions. If the garage attendant were to say, 'you need to change the *plug*', his voice would lay the emphasis on the word plug. The French garagiste would say, C'est la bougie qu'il faut changer.

**(e) Notes on items of vocabulary**
  (i) Note that pneu does not form its plural like most words ending in -eu. The plural of pneu, is pneus.
 (ii) Laisser was introduced in Chapter 17 with the meaning 'to let', 'to permit'. It can also mean 'to leave (behind)', as when the garagiste says, Vous pouvez nous laisser la voiture pour une demi-heure?
(iii) In expressions such as 'the evening when . . .'; 'the morning, when . . ., French says, le soir où . . .; le matin où . . . .
(iv) Avant de is followed by the infinitive in French, for example: avant de partir — 'before leaving'.
 (v) Vouloir dire is a combination of verbs equivalent to English 'to mean'. Therefore, Qu'est-ce que ça veut dire? can be used to refer to a word ('What does it mean?') or to a situation.
(vi) Voyons! is a difficult expression to render in English. It has a note of reproach about it, as when it is used by mothers scolding their children (Mais ne fais pas ça, voyons!).


## 18.4 EXERCISES

**Section A**

**(a) Exercise 1**
You can always dream! What if you won a large sum on the Loterie Nationale! Make up sentences beginning, Si je gagnais, and complete them, using the verbs given, in the conditional. If you don't like these suggestions, make up some of your own.

Si je gagnais, je . . .

faire le tour du monde
acheter un château sur la Côte
   d'Azur
manger dans les meilleurs
   restaurants
habiter à la campagne
avoir une grande voiture
aller souvent au théâtre
venir tous les ans en France
passer l'hiver dans le Midi

**(b) Exercise 2**
What if you had to prepare poulet sauté chasseur? On the right-hand side are your instructions from the cookery-book. Begin each sentence with, Si je devais préparer ce poulet, and complete the sentence with a verb in the conditional.

Si je devais préparer ce poulet,    mettre le cognac
    je . . .                            faire flamber
                                        ajouter le bouillon
                                        laisser cuire 30 minutes
                                        terminer la sauce
                                        mélanger bien

## Section B

**(c) Exercise 3**
Translate into French
   (i) If we had more time we would stay longer, but one has to earn one's living.
  (ii) Before leaving you must visit the valley of the Seine.
 (iii) We shall do everything possible to pay you a visit.
  (iv) What does that mean? I don't understand.
   (v) You know where to find us. We hope to see you again soon.
  (vi) If I didn't have to earn my living, I'd like to stay a few more days.
 (vii) Will you check the oil and the tyre pressures, please?
(viii) If you break down on the way to Le Havre you will have difficulty in finding a garage.
  (ix) It's better to repair this straight away. I don't think it is serious.
   (x) The plugs are dirty and oily. Do you know what that means?

# CHAPTER 19

# SUCH HAPPY MEMORIES;
# THE ADVANTAGES OF LEARNING
# A FOREIGN LANGUAGE

## 19.1 LETTERS

**(a) Letter 1**
John Smith writes to thank the Lebruns for their help during their stay in Caen.

Chers amis,

Ça fait déjà trois jours que nous sommes rentrés et les vacances paraissent déjà loin. Nous avons de si bons souvenirs de cette visite et nous vous sommes très reconnaissants de tout ce que vous avez fait pour nous accueillir. Le contact avec vous nous a aidés à mieux connaître la ville et la région.

Notre voyage de retour n'a pas été une réussite. Heureusement les enfants allaient mieux et n'étaient plus très enrhumés. Alors nous étions partis de bonne heure, et nous pensions que ce serait un voyage sans problèmes, mais nous avons d'abord eu des problèmes avec la voiture, puis nous avons pris du retard à cause de la circulation. Nous avions pensé que les petites routes ne seraient pas encombrées, mais c'était une erreur! Mais nous sommes enfin arrivés au Havre et nous avons eu le temps de prendre un snack avant d'embarquer. La traversée était calme, et nous n'avons pas eu de problèmes à la douane anglaise. Nous voilà de retour, les enfants sont rentrés à l'école, et pour Mary et moi, le travail a recommencé aussi. Mais nous gardons un très bon souvenir de notre visite en Normandie, et nous attendons avec plaisir de vous recevoir chez nous.

En vous remerciant encore, nous vous envoyons toutes nos amitiés.

**(b) Letter 2**
Some articles have been left behind ... John writes to the hotel.

Monsieur,

En quittant l'hôtel jeudi dernier, nous avons dû oublier plusieurs articles. Si vous avez trouvé ces articles, je vous prie de bien vouloir nous les renvoyer, et je vous rembourserai, bien sûr, les frais du port. Ma femme a oublié une écharpe de soie blanche et les enfants ont laissé quelques jouets et une balle noire.

Je vous remercie à l'avance et je vous prie d'accepter l'expression de mes sentiments les meilleurs.

## (c) Letter 3

To the Jacquiers

Chers amis,

Quel plaisir de vous revoir en Normandie! Nous sommes heureux d'avoir pu vous rencontrer lors de votre passage. Nous espérons que votre voyage de retour s'est bien passé. En passant, je peux vous dire que le nôtre n'a pas été une réussite! Mais je ne vais pas vous ennuyer avec les détails. L'important, c'est que nous sommes maintenant bien rentrés chez nous et qu'il y a beaucoup à faire dans la maison et dans le jardin. En travaillant pendant tous nos moments libres, nous arriverons peut-être à y remettre de l'ordre, mais ça sera difficile. Quant au travail, le mien a déjà commencé avec la rentrée des classes hier, et Mary va retourner demain à son bureau. Les enfants se font un plaisir de raconter à tous leurs amis tout ce qu'ils ont fait, et même de prononcer quelques mots français. La prochaine fois nous devrions peut-être essayer de les faire parler davantage. Mon français s'est certainement amélioré pendant la visite. On a toujours besoin de parler une langue étrangère, et la seule façon c'est de visiter le pays. Et puis, comme vous le savez bien, apprendre une langue c'est aussi se familiariser avec toute une nouvelle culture. Étant anglais de naissance, je ne pense pas être jamais capable de me sentir tout à fait français, mais il est possible quand même de partager un peu de la culture et de la façon de vivre des Français, et il est certain que cela représente un élément d'enrichissement personnel. C'est pour cette raison que je suis tellement en faveur des jumelages entre communes françaises et anglaises. La nôtre va bientôt signer une charte de jumelage avec un village français et cela va créer des possibilités de contacts personnels qui révèlent, non seulement les différences entre les pays et les peuples mais aussi les similarités. Le grand avantage de ces jumelages, c'est qu'ils offrent la possibilité d'entrer directement dans un foyer français, de connaître les gens chez eux, et c'est ce contact humain qui manque quelquefois si on visite un pays comme touriste seulement. Mais le tourisme est aussi un élément important dans l'entente cordiale, alors, ne le critiquons pas.

Vous m'excuserez la longueur de cette lettre. Étant rentré chez moi, je réfléchis, comme ça m'arrive quelquefois, aux avantages de connaître une langue étrangère.

En attendant le plaisir de vous lire, et de vous revoir tous, je vous envoie l'amical souvenir de toute la famille.

## 19.2 VOCABULARY

### (a) Letter 1

#### (i) Useful expressions

| | |
|---|---|
| ça fait déjà trois jours que... | it's already three days since... |
| les enfants allaient mieux | the children felt better |
| nous avons pris du retard | we were held up |
| nous voilà de retour | here we are, back again |

#### (ii) Nouns – Masc.

| | | | | |
|---|---|---|---|---|
| le contact | contact | la réussite | success |
| le snack | snack | la circulation | traffic |
| | | une amitié | friendship |

**Nouns – Fem.**

#### (iii) Other words

| | |
|---|---|
| reconnaissant de | grateful for |
| accueillir | to welcome |
| encombré(-e) | crowded |
| embarquer | to go on board |
| recevoir | to receive |

### (b) Letter 2

#### (i) Useful expression

| | |
|---|---|
| je vous prie de bien vouloir... | would you please be so kind as to.../ |

#### (ii) Nouns – Masc.      Nouns – Fem.

| | | | |
|---|---|---|---|
| un article | article | la soie | silk |
| les frais | expenses | la balle | ball |
| le port | postage | | |
| le jouet | toy | | |

#### (iii) Other words

| | |
|---|---|
| rembourser | to reimburse |
| noir(-e) | black |

### (c) Letter 3

#### (i) Useful expressions

| | |
|---|---|
| nous arriverons à ... | we shall manage to ... |
| ils se font un plaisir de ... | they take a delight in ... |

| | | | |
|---|---|---|---|
| étant anglais de naissance | | being English by birth | |
| non seulement ... mais aussi | | not only ... but also | |

(ii) **Nouns – Masc.**      **Nouns – Fem.**

| | | | |
|---|---|---|---|
| le mot | word | la réussite | success |
| un élément | element | la maison | house |
| un enrichis-sement | enrichment | la rentrée | return; start of term |
| le jumelage | twinning | la classe | class |
| le peuple | people | la culture | culture |
| un avantage | advantage | la faveur | favour |
| le foyer | home | la commune | commune; parish |
| | | la charte | charter |
| | | la différence | difference |
| | | la similarité | similarity |
| | | une entente | understanding |
| | | la longueur | length |

(iii) **Other words**

| | | | |
|---|---|---|---|
| rencontrer | to meet | se sentir | to feel |
| lors de | at the time of | partager | to share |
| ennuyer | to bore | vivre | to live |
| remettre | to bring back; to put back | représenter | to represent |
| | | signer | to sign |
| | | créer | to create |
| quant à ... | as for ... | révéler | to reveal |
| raconter | to relate | offrir | to offer |
| prononcer | to pronounce | humain(-e) | human |
| s'améliorer | to improve | manquer | to be missing |
| étranger(-ère) | foreign | cordial(-e) | cordial |
| se familiariser | to get acquainted with | critiquer | to criticise |
| | | réfléchir | to reflect |
| | | lire | to read |
| capable | capable; able | amical(-e) | friendly |

## 19.3 EXPLANATIONS

**(a) Pluperfect Tense** *grammar ref 5.2 (f) (i) and (iii)*
The pluperfect tense expresses an action or event which took place a stage further back in the past than the ordinary perfect. In English this is expressed with the auxiliary 'had', for example: 'We had already left, when he arrived'; 'We had thought that the roads would not be crowded'. The pluperfect in French is formed by using the imperfect tense of the auxiliary verbs être or avoir with the past participle. The

auxiliary verbs are the same as those used with the perfect tense, for example, the two examples given above would be:

Nous étions déjà partis quand il est arrivé.

Nous avions pensé que les routes ne seraient pas encombrées.

The rules for the agreement of the past participle are the same as those given for the perfect tense. There is one such rule for agreement which has not yet been introduced. So far we have said that verbs taking être agree with the subject if necessary, and verbs taking avoir never agree with the subject. This is true, but there is one case where avoir does agree, and that is where there is a direct object preceding the verb, and that direct object is plural or feminine. In the first letter of this chapter, John Smith writes:

Le contact avec vous nous a aidés . . .

The past participle agrees with the plural direct object nous. In most cases, this is a rule which is only of importance when writing French, since the difference cannot be heard with most participles.

### (b) Conditional of devoir *grammar ref 5.8 (b)*
In Chapter 16 an explanation was given of the uses of the tenses of devoir to express compulsion, necessity. There is one further tense to add to that explanation. The conditional of devoir is used with the sense of 'ought to'; for example:

La prochaine fois nous devrions essayer . . . − 'next time we ought to try'.

### (c) Present Participle *grammar ref 5.8 (e)*
In the grammar reference section you will see that one of the principal parts of the verbs is the present participle, that is to say the part of the verb equivalent to the English verb form ending in '-ing', for example: 'reading', 'writing'. The present participle is not so widely used in French as in English, and is never used as a noun. It is found in a number of common expressions such as en passant − 'in passing'; en attendant − 'while waiting'. It is also used when two actions are going on simultaneously, for example:

En vous remerciant, nous vous envoyons nos amitiés.

En quittant l'hôtel il a oublié quelques articles.

The present participle can be combined with the past participle to give the form equivalent to English 'having returned', for example: étant rentré.

### (d) Order of object pronouns
When more than one pronoun precedes the verb, there is an accepted order in which they are placed, for example: in Letter 2 John Smith writes, Je vous prie de . . . nous les renvoyer − 'would you be so

good as to send them back to us'. The rules for the order of object pronouns will be found in *grammar ref 4.1 (b) and (c)*.

### (e) Possessive Pronouns

In Chapter 1 the possessive adjective was introduced, that is, 'my children'; 'your holidays' and so on. There are occasions when the possessive appears without the noun, in which case the possessive pronoun is used, for example:

'We hope you had a good journey; ours (that is, our journey) was not a success'.

'As far as work is concerned, mine (that is, my work) has already begun'.

Both these examples are to be found in the third letter of this chapter, as follows:

Nous espérons que votre voyage de retour s'est bien passé; le nôtre n'a pas été une réussite.

Quant au travail, le mien a déjà commencé.

More about the forms and uses of the possessive pronouns will be found in *grammar ref 4.5*.

### (f) Uses of the infinitive

(i) English sometimes uses an infinitive in a statement such as:

'to learn a language is to get to know another culture';

the same idea might be expressed by using the English present participle, for example:

'Learning a language means getting to know another culture'.

However the idea is expressed in English, French always uses the infinitive without any preposition preceding it, for example:

Apprendre une langue, c'est aussi se familiariser avec une autre culture.

(ii) Faire + infinitive are used to express the notion of 'to have something done', or 'to make someone do something'; for example:

Nous devrions essayer de les faire parler — 'We ought to try to make them speak'.

(iii) There is a form of the verb in both English and French called the past infinitive. In English this is expressed as 'to have' + past participle, for example: 'to have seen'; 'to have been able. In French the same pattern is followed, for example: avoir vu; avoir pu; être parti. In Letter 3 John Smith writes:

Nous sommes heureux d'avoir pu vous rencontrer — 'we are happy to have been able to meet you'.

The past infinitive is most usually found in French after the

preposition après, when used with a verb, for example:
après être rentré − 'after returning';
après avoir vu − 'after seeing'.

**(g) Some notes on other items of vocabulary**
(i) The relative pronoun after tout is always ce qui, or ce que, for example:
tout ce qu'ils ont fait − 'all that they have done'.
(ii) Vivre means 'to live' in the sense of 'to exist', whereas habiter (*or,* demeurer) is used in the sense of 'to dwell'.
(iii) Peuple refers to 'a people' in the sense of 'a nation' or 'race'. Gens is used for people in the more everyday use meaning 'a group of individuals'.
(iv) Note the use of manquer, for example:
(i) c'est ce contact qui manque − 'it's this contact which is lacking;
(ii) mon ami me manque beaucoup − 'I miss my friend very much';
(iii) Ne manquez pas de me rendre visite − 'Don't miss paying me a visit'.

## 19.4 EXERCISES

**Section A**

**(a) Exercise 1**
The activities described below are grouped in pairs, with the verbs in the infinitive. Write out a full sentence linking these activities, so that the first appears in the pluperfect tense and the second in the perfect tense. Add the words déjà, and quand, so that your final sentence should look like this: Il était déjà parti, quand j'ai rencontré sa femme.

| (i) | Nous | prendre du retard | nous | arriver au port |
|---|---|---|---|---|
| (ii) | Elle | arriver à la gare | nous | aller la chercher |
| (iii) | il | recommencer le travail | sa femme | retourner au bureau |
| (iv) | L'hôtelier | renvoyer les articles | je | lui écrire |
| (v) | Mon ami | apprendre la langue | il | visiter le pays |

**(b) Exercise 2**
Compose a letter of thanks to friends in France, taking the first letter of the chapter as a guide and using the following outline.

174

Dear . . .

(Tell your friend that it is already more than a week since you returned home. Time goes so quickly. You have a lot of happy memories of your time with them in France. Tell them you are grateful for their welcome. Your return journey was not a success. You had to wait at a garage, then you broke down on the way and finally got held up in the traffic. But you found time for a snack before going on board the boat. Now the holidays are over and you are going to start work again. Tell your friends you are looking forward to a visit from them, and finish by thanking them again and sending your best wishes.)

## Section B

### (c) Exercise 3
Translate into French
  (i) After leaving the hotel I met my friend Pierre on the way to his office.
 (ii) We had already left for Le Havre when the car broke down.
(iii) If you wrote next week I should receive the letter soon after.
 (iv) I hope that you had a good journey. Ours was not a success.
  (v) He gets bored because his work isn't interesting, but mine is fascinating (fascinant).
 (vi) Getting to know another culture is an advantage when you learn a foreign language.
(vii) Sometimes the human contact is missing when you visit a country as a tourist.
(viii) Here we are back again, but we have happy memories of our visit.
 (ix) It's a pity that the car has broken down. We'll go for a walk while we are waiting.
  (x) I had already read that book when he bought it for me.

# CHAPTER 20

# REVISION EXERCISES

## 20.1 SUPPLEMENTARY EXERCISES FOR CHAPTERS 1–3

### (a) Exercise 1
Introduce members of your family to a French acquaintance; for example: Je vous présente ma femme.
  (i) mon mari
 (ii) mes enfants, Catherine et Robert
(iii) mon ami Jean
 (iv) mon père
  (v) ma mère
Imagine that these people are being introduced to you, and practise your replies, for instance, Très heureux; Très heureux de faire votre connaissance; Enchanté; Enchanté de faire votre connaissance.

### (b) Exercise 2
The following questions are formed by allowing the voice to rise at the end of the sentence. How would you form the same questions using Est-ce que?
Example: Vous êtes Monsieur Lebrun? Est-ce que vous êtes Monsieur Lebrun?
  (i) Vous êtes Madame Smith?
 (ii) Vous êtes Catherine?
(iii) Vous êtes libres ce soir?
 (iv) Vous pouvez dîner chez nous?
  (v) Vous restez en France?

### (c) Exercise 3
Using the plan, place yourself in front of the Hôtel de Ville, then answer the question Qu'est-ce que c'est by pointing to the places listed and answering C'est .... Then, in answer to the question C'est

loin d'ici? answer Oui or Non and give an approximate distance followed by the word environ (approximately).

Qu'est-ce que c'est?       C'est le château
                              le port
                              le Jardin des Plantes
                              l'église Saint-Pierre
                              la gare
                              l'université

C'est loin d'ici? Oui/Non    à deux cents mètres
                              à deux kilomètres
                              à cinquante mètres       environ
                              à cinq cents mètres
                              à un kilomètre

## 20.2 SUPPLEMENTARY EXERCISES FOR MAJOR GRAMMATICAL POINTS

### (a) Reflexive Verbs (Chapter 8)

Choose an appropriate verb from the list given below and write out each sentence in full with the chosen verb in its correct form.

  (i) Quand les enfants sont fatigués ils ...... vite.

 (ii) Les Smith sont en retard pour le train. Il faut qu'ils ......

(iii) Les enfants jouent. Ils ...... et leurs parents les cherchent.

(iv) L'église Saint-Étienne ...... près de l'Hôtel de Ville.

 (v) Je ...... de bonne heure quand il faut prendre le train.

(vi) En vacances on a le temps de ...... et on ...... à la campagne.

se trouver; se dépêcher; s'endormir; se cacher; se lever; se promener; se reposer.

### (b) Partitive Article and Object Pronouns (Chapter 9)

Example: Je donne[1]    champignons[1]    à mon ami[3]
          Je donne des champignons à mon ami.
          Je lui en donne.

Each of the sentence below has three elements, like the example given above. You are asked, firstly to write out the sentence using the correct form of the partitive article with the item in the second column; then to write out the sentence a second time replacing both items 2 and 3 with pronouns (as in the example).

| | | | |
|---|---|---|---|
| (i) | Vous envoyez | cerises | à votre père. |
| (ii) | Mary achète | crème | dans la laiterie. |
| (iii) | John présente | cadeaux | à ses enfants. |
| (iv) | Nous avons acheté | timbres | dans le tabac. |

| (v) | La Normandie offre | fromage | aux touristes. |
|---|---|---|---|
| (vi) | Comme piquenique, l'hôtel fournit | pain et charcuterie | à la famille. |
| (vii) | Elle explique | problèmes | à sa fille. |
| (viii) | Ils achètent | crayons | dans la papeterie. |
| (ix) | Les enfants dépensent | argent | dans les boutiques |

## (c) Future Tense (Chapter 10)
Replace the infinitives in brackets with the correct form of the verb in the future tense.
 (i) L'année prochaine nous (revenir) en France.
 (ii) Demain nous (discuter) des projets d'excursion.
 (iii) Malheureusement il (être) impossible de rester plus longtemps.
 (iv) Les amis (aller) en Angleterre pour la première fois.
 (v) Je vous (envoyer) une lettre avec tous les détails.

## (d) Perfect and Imperfect Tenses (Chapters 12, 13 and 15)
Translate into French
 (i) I saw the accident, of course. I was walking towards the crossroads when I saw a car jump the lights and it crashed into another car.
 (ii) Your wife was very worried about you. She asked me to telephone her in her room.
 (iii) He left the hotel half an hour ago but he hasn't returned yet. When I last saw him he was buying a newspaper at the kiosk.
 (iv) She was looking at the landscape when her son fell.
 (v) They were at home when a friend telephoned.

## (e) Use of Modal Auxiliaries: pouvoir (Chapter 2), vouloir (Chapter 4), devoir (Chapters 16 and 19)
From the four lists of language items below, make up as many meaningful sentences as you can, for example:
 Les parents veulent accompagner les enfants; Les parents doivent accompagner les enfants and so on.

| Les parents | | se dépêcher | écouter la musique |
|---|---|---|---|
| Les enfants | pouvoir | acheter | les enfants |
| L'hôtelier | devoir | chanter | la situation |
| La famille | vouloir | accompagner | des fruits |
| La femme de chambre | | occuper | une chanson populaire |
| John | | frapper | les heures de loisir |
| | | expliquer | pour prendre le train |
| | | | à la poste |

**(f) Conditional (Chapter 18), pluperfect (Chapter 19) and forms of verbs after prepositions (Chapter 19)**
Write out the following sentences using the correct forms of the verbs.
 (i) Après (arriver) il s'est assis.
 (ii) Avant de (partir) il m'a dit 'au revoir'.
 (iii) En (travailler) il pense à ses vacances.
*Pluperfect Tense*
 (iv) Elle (trouver) déjà son écharpe, quand il a commencé à la chercher.
 (v) Nous (rentrer) déjà, quand notre ami nous a téléphoné.
*Conditional*
 (vi) Si vous (venir) me chercher à la gare, il (être) plus facile pour moi.
(vii) Si je (gagner) la Loterie Nationale, je (partir) en vacances.

## 20.3 VOCABULARIES FOR REVISION EXERCISES

20.1

**(a) Exercise 1**

| Nouns – Masc. | | Nouns – Fem. | |
|---|---|---|---|
| le père | father | la mère | mother |
| un homme | man | | |

20.2

**(a)**

**Other words**

| | |
|---|---|
| se cacher | to hide oneself |
| s'endormir | to go to sleep |
| se dépêcher | to hurry |

20.2

**(b)**

| (i) Nouns – Masc. | | Nouns – Fem. | |
|---|---|---|---|
| le cadeau | present | la cerise | cherry |
| le crayon | pencil | la papeterie | stationer's |
| le tabac | tobacco; *also* a tobacco shop which sells stamps, confectionery etc. | | |

(ii) **Other word**
dépenser                          to spend

20.2

**(c)**

**Other words**
discuter                          to discuss
malheureusement                   unfortunately

20.2

**(d)**

**Noun – Masc.**
le kiosk                          newspaper stand, kiosk

20.2

**(e)**

(i) **Noun – Masc.**          **Nouns – Fem.**
le loisir        leisure      la chanson    song
                              la laiterie   dairy
                              la musique    music

(ii) **Other words**
chanter          to sing
expliquer        to explain
frapper          to knock
occuper          to occupy

# II REFERENCE MATERIAL

# TRANSLATIONS
# OF DIALOGUES IN
# CHAPTERS 1-5

## 1.1

**(a)**

*Policeman*:  Good morning, sir. Your passport, please.
*John Smith*:  Good morning. Here's my passport.
*Policeman*:  Thank you, sir. Are you John Smith?
*John*:  Yes, that's right. And this is my wife and my two children.
*Policeman*:  Good morning, madame.
*Mary*:  Good morning.
*Policeman*:  How long are you staying in France?
*John*:  Three weeks.
*Policeman*:  Right, sir. Here's your passport. Goodbye and have a nice trip.
*John*:  Thanks. Goodbye.

**(b)**

*John*:  Good afternoon. I'm Mr Smith. You have a room for my family.
*Hotelier*:  Ah yes! Good afternoon, Mr Smith; good afternoon, Mrs Smith.
*Mary*:  Good afternoon. And here are our two children, Catherine and Robert.
*Hotelier*:  Hello, children. Now, Mr Smith, you are staying three weeks, that's right, isn't it?
*John*:  Yes, that's right.
*Hotelier*:  Good, well it's room number five. Here is your key.
*John*:  Thank you.
*Hotelier*:  Goodbye, sir, goodbye, madame.

**(c)**

*John*:  Excuse me, is Mr Lebrun in please? My name is John Smith.
*Secretary*:  Ah, yes, you're Mr Smith. Mr Lebrun is in. Just a moment, please.
*Lebrun*:  Good afternoon, Mr Smith. I'm very pleased to meet you.
*John*:  Good afternoon, Mr Lebrun. May I introduce my wife, Mary, and our two children, Catherine and Robert.
*Lebrun*:  Delighted to meet you, Mrs Smith. Hello, children. Well, are you free this evening? Can you have dinner with us?
*John*:  We'd be delighted.

*Mary*: That's very kind of you.

*Lebrun*: Right, then. We'll see you at seven o'clock this evening.

*John*: Many thanks and goodbye.

*Lebrun*: Goodbye, Mr Smith. Goodbye, Mrs Smith. Goodbye, children. See you later.

**(d)**

*Lebrun*: Good evening, Mr Smith. Good evening, Mrs Smith. How are you?

*John*: Very well, thank you. And you?

*Lebrun*: I'm very well, thanks. Do come in, please. Nicole, Mr and Mrs Smith and the children are here.

*Madame L:* Good evening, Mr Smith. Good evening, Mrs Smith.

*John*: How do you do, Madame Lebrun. And these are our two children, Catherine and Robert.

*Madame L:* Good evening, children.

## 2.1

**(a)**

*Bank employee*: Good morning, sir. Can I help you?

*John*: Good morning. Can I change fifty pounds into francs, please?

*Employee*: Certainly, sir. You can change a cheque, or cash. Which would you prefer?

*John*: Can I change an English cheque?

*Employee*: Of course, sir. With the eurocheque system you can change an English cheque if you present your bank card.

*John*: Good. Well, here's my card and here's a cheque for £50.

*Employee*: Thank you, sir. May I see your passport, please?

*John*: Here is my passport.

*Employee*: Thank you, sir. That's fine, will you step along to the cash-desk, please?

**(b)**

*Waitress*: Good morning, sir. What would you like?

*John*: I'd like white coffee.

*Mary*: And I'd like black coffee. And two oranginas for the children.

*Waitress*: So that's one white coffee, one black coffee and two oranginas. Will that be all?

*John*: Will you also bring two ices for the children, please?

*Waitress*: Yes, sir. Which flavour? There is vanilla, strawberry or chocolate.

*Mary*: Chocolate, please.

*Waitress*: Certainly, madame.

*John*: Miss, the bill, please.

*Waitress*: Yes, sir. That's two coffees, three francs sixty; two oranginas, eight francs, and two ices, four francs. That comes to fifteen francs sixty altogether.

*John*: Is the service included?

*Waitress*: Yes, sir. Service is included.

*John*: There you are. Thank you.

*Waitress*: Thank you, sir. Goodbye, sir. Goodbye, madame.

**(c)**

*John*:  Excuse me. Can I have the key to room number five, please?

*Hotelier*:  Here you are, sir. I am sorry, but there is a small problem.

*John*:  Why?

*Hotelier*:  Because your room is not quite ready. The chambermaid is making the beds.

*John*:  It doesn't matter. Can we have lunch?

*Hotelier*:  I'm very sorry, sir. Lunch is not quite ready.

*John*:  But why? It is already half-past twelve.

*Hotelier*:  Because there is a problem with the staff, sir. It's not serious. It's a strike.

*John*:  A strike! Why?

*Hotelier*:  It is really not at all important, sir. Everything is settled now. You can have lunch in ten minutes.

*John*:  Good.

## 3.1

**(a)**

*John*:  Good morning. We are in Caen for the first time. Have you any information on the town, please?

*Lady*:  Certainly, sir. Here is a town plan and here is the official guide. Would you like information about the main sights?

*John*:  Yes, please.

*Lady*:  Well, on the plan you can see the castle here. In front of the main entrance to the castle you can see the church of St Pierre.

*Mary*:  Is that the church with the tall spire?

*Lady*:  That's right, madame. Well now, follow St Pierre Street and Écuyère Street, cross over Fontette Square and St Étienne church is on the left.

*John*:  Oh yes, that's very well-known. And near the church, what's that?

*Lady*:  That's the Town Hall. You can also visit the Port of Caen.

*Mary*:  Is there a port here at Caen?

*Lady*:  Yes, madame, there is a very important port. The Botanical Gardens are also very interesting.

*John*:  Good, thank you very much.

*Lady*:  You're welcome, sir. Have a nice stay in Caen.

**(b)**

*John*:  Excuse me. How do I get to St Étienne church, please?

*Passer-by*:  St Étienne church, well, you go straight on, cross over Fontette Square, take the first street on the right and the church is on your left.

*John*:  Is it far from here?

*Passer-by*:  Oh no. Ten minutes on foot, that's all.

*John*:  Thanks very much.

*Passer-by*:  Don't mention it.

**(c)**

*John*:  Excuse me, how do I get to the castle please?

*Passer-by*:  The castle. It's quite a long way.

*John*:  Oh, really?

*Passer-by*:   Yes, on foot you'll need half an hour, at least, especially with the children. Take the bus.

*John*:   That's a good idea. Where is the bus stop?

*Passer-by*:   Over there, in front of the Town Hall.

*John*:   Many thanks. That's very kind of you.

*Passer-by*:   You're welcome.

**(d)**

*John*:   Two adults and two children, please.

*Driver*:   Where are you going?

*John*:   To the castle.

*Driver*:   That'll be eight francs forty. Thank you. Don't forget to stamp your tickets. Here is your change.

*John*:   Thank you.

**(e)**

*John*:   Excuse me. Do you know where the port is?

*Passer-by*:   I'm sorry, sir. I don't know. I'm a stranger here.

*John*:   Excuse me, how do I get to the port, please?

*Lady*:   Go straight on, cross over Courtonne Square and the St Pierre docks are on your right.

*John*:   Thank you. Is it far from here?

*Lady*:   No, not at all. About two hundred metres away.

*John*:   Thank you.

*Lady*:   You're welcome.

## 4.1

**(a)**

*Man on the 'phone*:   Hello, this is the municipal swimming pool, Caen.

*John*:   Good morning. When is the swimming pool open?

*Man*:   This morning the pool is open from 9 o'clock until midday.

*John*:   Is it open in the afternoon as well?

*Man*:   Yes, in the afternoon the pool is open from 2 till 6.

*John*:   Are the times of opening the same every day?

*Man*:   The times are the same from Monday to Friday. On Saturdays the pool is open until 9 pm and on Sundays from 9.45 until 5.30.

*John*:   Thank you very much.

**(b)**

*John*:   Hello, is that the Museum of the Landings?

*Man*:   Hello, yes, this is the D Day Landings Museum at Arromanches.

*John*:   I'd like to know when the museum is open.

*Man*:   The museum is open every day from 9 till midday and from 2 pm until 7 pm.

*John*:   Thank you.

**(c)**

*Lady on the 'phone*:   Hello, Information Bureau, Lisieux.

*John*:   Good morning. I am coming to Lisieux with my family and I'd like to know if there is a guided visit to the Basilica of St Teresa.

*Lady*: Yes, sir, there are guided tours every day from 9 until midday and from 2 pm until 4.30 pm.

*John*: Good. And when is the Son et Lumière performance at the Basilica?

*Lady*: The Son et Lumière performance is presented every evening except Friday, at 9.30 pm.

*John*: Thank you.

*Lady*: You're welcome.

**(d)**

*Mary*: Good morning. Have you got two seats for the Tuesday evening performance?

*Lady at the cash-desk*: I'm sorry, madame. We're full up on Tuesday.

*Mary*: What a pity! How about Wednesday?

*Lady*: Wednesday as well. I'm sorry but we're fully booked. There are seats available on Thursday evening. Here are two seats at 20 francs.

*Mary*: Good. When does the performance begin?

*Lady*: At 7.15, madame. There is an interval at 8.45.

*Mary*: Right, here are 40 francs. Thank you.

## 5.1

**(a)**

*Lebrun*: Good morning, everybody. Enjoy your meal. How are things?

*John*: Good morning, Michel. How nice to see you again. We are fine, thanks. How are you?

*Lebrun*: I'm very well too. How is your stay in Caen going?

*Mary*: Very well. We're delighted with our visit.

*Lebrun*: Good. Well, forgive me for disturbing your breakfast, but what have you got planned for today?

*John*: This morning we are going to do some shopping.

*Mary*: Yes, this morning we want to buy some clothes for the children. After that, we don't know yet.

*Lebrun*: If you are free at midday I would like to invite you to join my wife and me for lunch in a restaurant.

*John*: We'd be delighted. How kind of you. The children as well?

*Lebrun*: Of course. Right then, we'll have lunch at the 'Cultivateurs' near the Avenue of 6 June. Do you know the street?

*John*: Yes I know the street, but where is the restaurant?

*Lebrun*: Well, you go down the street in the direction of the river and the restaurant is on the right on the Quai de Juillet. When would you like to eat?

*John*: We are at your disposal.

*Lebrun*: Right then, come at about half past twelve. Goodbye, see you later.

*John*: Goodbye and thank you.

**(b)**

*Hotelier*: Do you like this weather sir?

*John*: Certainly not! We are out of luck. It's raining again. Isn't it ever fine in Caen?

*Hotelier*: Oh yes! Usually it's fine in summer. Sometimes it's even very warm. But the sea isn't very far away, you know. We have a maritime climate like you in England, and it rains from time to time.

*John*:   Do you think it will be fine later on?

*Hotelier*:   That's possible. The weather changes quickly here. Look! You can already see a bit of blue sky. It's going to be sunny, perhaps. You never know.

*John*:   You're an optimist. But I think we shall go and buy anoraks for the children all the same. You never know, that's quite right.

*Hotelier*:   Good luck, all the same. Enjoy yourselves.

# KEY TO EXERCISES

**Chapter 1**

**Section A**

**(a) Exercise 1**

John Smith's rôle should be as follows.
- (i) Bonjour, monsieur. Voilà mon passeport.
  Oui, monsieur. C'est bien ça.
  Trois semaines.
  Merci, monsieur. Au revoir.
- (ii) Oui, c'est ça.
  Merci, monsieur.
- (iii) Je vous présente ma femme, Mary.
  Avec plaisir.
  Au revoir, monsieur.
- (iv) Enchanté, madame. *Or,* Très heureux de faire votre connaissance, madame.

**(b) Exercise 2**

- (i) Vous êtes Mary Smith? *Or,* Est-ce que vous êtes Mary Smith?
- (ii) Vous pouvez dîner chez nous ce soir? *Or,* Est-ce que vous pouvez dîner chez nous ce soir?
- (iii) Comment allez-vous?
- (iv) Monsieur Lebrun est là? *Or,* Est-ce que Monsieur Lebrun est là?
- (v) Vous avez une chambre pour ma famille? *Or,* Est-ce que vous avez une chambre pour ma famille?

**Section B**

**(c) Exercise 3**

- (i) Je m'appelle John Smith.
- (ii) Voilà mon passeport.
- (iii) Vous avez une chambre pour ma famille?
- (iv) Vous restez combien de temps en France?

    (v) Je vous présente ma femme. Très heureux (*or* enchanté) de faire votre connaissance.

   (vi) Est-ce que vous pouvez dîner chez nous ce soir?

 (vii) C'est la chambre numéro cinq. Voilà votre clef.

(viii) Vous êtes très gentil. À bientôt.

## (d) Exercise 4

     (i) Oui, c'est ma femme.

    (ii) Oui, c'est ma clef.

   (iii) Oui, c'est ma chambre.

   (iv) Oui, c'est mon enfant.

    (v) Oui, c'est notre chambre.

   (vi) Oui, c'est notre passeport.

 (vii) Oui, c'est notre enfant.

(viii) Oui, c'est notre hôtel.

## Chapter 2

## Section A

## (a) Exercise 1

    (i) Oui, est-ce que je peux changer un chèque en francs?

   (ii) Oui, est-ce que je peux voir votre passeport?

 (iii) Oui, est-ce que je peux avoir la clef?

 (iv) Oui, est-ce que je peux déjeuner?

## (b) Exercise 2

    Je voudrais un café crème, un café noir et deux oranginas.
    Je voudrais aussi deux glaces pour les enfants, s'il vous plaît.
    Alors, chocolat, s'il vous plaît.

## (c) Exercise 3

    (i) Je préfère changer un chèque. *Or*, Je préfère changer de l'argent liquide.

   (ii) Je préfère un thé. *Or*, Je préfère un café.

 (iii) Je préfère fraise. *Or* Je préfère chocolat.

 (iv) Parce que je voudrais un café.

   (v) Parce que je voudrais déjeuner.

 (vi) Parce qu'il y a un petit problème.

## Section B

## (d) Exercise 4

    (i) Est-ce que je peux changer dix livres en francs, s'il vous plaît?

   (ii) Certainement, monsieur. Est-ce que vous préférez changer un chèque ou de l'argent liquide?

 (iii) Est-ce que je peux voir votre passeport, s'il vous plaît?

 (iv) Je voudrais un café crème et un café noir, s'il vous plaît.

(v) Est-ce que je peux avoir la clef de la chambre numéro cinq, s'il vous plaît?

(vi) Je regrette beaucoup, monsieur, votre chambre n'est pas tout à fait prête.

(vii) Pourquoi est-ce que la chambre n'est pas prête?

(viii) Parce qu'il y a un petit problème.

(ix) Vous pouvez déjeuner dans dix minutes.

## (b) Exercise 5

(i) Est-ce que je peux changer un chèque?
Est-ce que je peux présenter ma femme?
Est-ce que je peux payer l'addition?
Est-ce que je peux apporter le café?
Est-ce que je peux rester une semaine?
Est-ce que je peux dîner ce soir?
Est-ce que je peux voir le menu?
Est-ce que je peux déjeuner chez vous?

(ii) Oui, vous pouvez changer un chèque.
Oui, vous pouvez présenter votre femme.
Oui, vous pouvez payer l'addition.
Oui, vous pouvez apporter le café.
Oui, vous pouvez rester une semaine.
Oui, vous pouvez dîner ce soir.
Oui, vous pouvez voir le menu.
Oui, vous pouvez déjeuner chez nous.

## Chapter 3

## Section A

## (a) Exercise 1

(i) Pardon, monsieur, le château, s'il vous plaît?
Pardon, monsieur, où est le château, s'il vous plaît?
Pardon, monsieur, pour aller au château, s'il vous plaît?

(ii) Pardon, monsieur, le Jardin des Plantes, s'il vous plaît?
Pardon, monsieur, où est le Jardin des Plantes, s'il vous plaît?
Pardon, monsieur, pour aller au Jardin des Plantes, s'il vous plaît?

(iii) Pardon, monsieur, le Port de Caen, s'il vous plaît?
Pardon, monsieur, où est le Port de Caen, s'il vous plaît?
Pardon, monsieur, pour aller au Port de Caen s'il vous plaît?

(iv) Pardon, monsieur, l'église Saint-Étienne, s'il vous plaît.
Pardon, monsieur, où est l'église Saint-Étienne, s'il vous plaît?
Pardon, monsieur, pour aller à l'église Saint-Étienne, s'il vous plaît?

(v) Pardon, monsieur, l'église Saint-Pierre, s'il vous plaît?
Pardon, monsieur, où est l'église Saint-Pierre, s'il vous plaît?
Pardon, monsieur, pour aller à l'église Saint-Pierre, s'il vous plaît?

(vi) Pardon, monsieur, l'Hôtel de Ville, s'il vous plaît?
Pardon, monsieur, où est l'Hôtel de Ville, s'il vous plaît?
Pardon, monsieur, pour aller à l'Hôtel de Ville, s'il vous plaît?

**(b) Exercise 2**

   (i)   La Tour Guillaume le Roy.

  (ii)   Le Bassin Saint-Pierre.

 (iii)   Le château.

 (iv)   L'église Saint-Étienne.

**(c) Exercise 3**

   Pardon, monsieur, pour aller au château, s'il vous plaît?

   Oui, à pied.

   C'est loin d'ici?

   Est-ce qu'il y a un autobus?

   Où est l'arrêt d'autobus?

   Merci, monsieur. Vous êtes très aimable.

## Section B

**(d) Exercise 4**

   (i)   Oui, c'est un port important.

  (ii)   Oui, c'est une église intéressante.

 (iii)   Oui, c'est un guide officiel.

 (iv)   Oui, c'est l'entrée principale.

**(e) Exercise 5**

    (i)   Pardon, monsieur/madame. Pour aller au château, s'il vous plaît?

   (ii)   Je vais au port et à l'église Saint-Étienne.

  (iii)   Je vais au Syndicat d'Initiative. C'est loin d'ici?

  (iv)   Non, c'est assez près. À deux cents mètres environ.

   (v)   Devant l'entrée principale du château il y a une église.

  (vi)   Sur votre droite est une église connue.

 (vii)   Où est le port? Je ne sais pas. Je suis étranger ici.

(viii)   Je suis ici pour la première fois.

## Chapter 4

## Section A

**(a) Exercise 1**

   Le château est ouvert de neuf heures à midi, et de quatorze heures à seize heures trente.

   La piscine est ouverte de neuf heures et quart à midi et demi, et de deux heures moins le quart à six heures et quart.

   Le musée est ouvert de neuf heures et demie à une heure, et de deux heures et demie à cinq heures et quart.

   La Basilique est ouverte de neuf heures quarante-cinq à midi et quart, et de quatorze heures quarante-cinq à dix-sept heures trente.

   L'église est ouverte de huit heures et demie à onze heures et quart et de deux heures et quart à sept heures moins le quart.

## (b) Exercise 2

  (i)  trois heures cinq
 (ii)  sept heures moins cinq
(iii)  dix heures moins le quart
 (iv)  une heure vingt-cinq
  (v)  huit heures vingt

## (c) Exercise 3

   (i)  Quand est-ce que la piscine est ouverte?
  (ii)  Ce matin la piscine est ouverte de neuf heures à midi.
 (iii)  Le musée est ouvert tous les jours de neuf heures et demie jusqu'à cinq heures.
 (iv)  Je voudrais savoir s'il y a un musée à Caen.
  (v)  Est-ce que vous avez deux places pour la représentation de jeudi soir?
 (vi)  Je regrette beaucoup. La représentation de jeudi est complète.
(vii)  Quel dommage! Quand est-ce que la représentation commence vendredi?
(viii)  À sept heures et quart. Il y a un entr'acte à neuf heures moins le quart.

## (d) Exercise 4

   (i)  Je viens à Caen.
  (ii)  Je suis John Smith.
 (iii)  La représentation commence à sept heures.
 (iv)  La femme de chambre fait les lits.
  (v)  Nous préférons le café noir.
 (vi)  Quand est-ce que vous commencez le déjeuner?.
(vii)  Vous pouvez visiter le château.
(viii)  Les enfants sont là.

# Chapter 5

## Section A

## (a) Exercise 1

| Je vais / Nous allons | acheter des vêtements. |
| Je vais / Nous allons | visiter le musée. |
| Je vais / Nous allons | voir le château. |
| Je vais / Nous allons | manger une glace. |
| Je vais / Nous allons | changer un chèque. |
| Je vais / Nous allons | déjeuner au restaurant. |

A number of other combinations are also possible, for example: je vais acheter une glace, and so on.

**(b) Exercise 2**

As above, but substitute je veux, or nous voulons instead of je vais/nous allons.

**(c) Exercise 3**

Je vais voir le château à neuf heures et demie.
Je vais voir l'église Saint-Pierre à dix heures et demie.
Je vais voir le port vers onze heures.
Je vais voir l'Hôtel de Ville à deux heures de l'après-midi (quatorze heures).
Je vais voir le musée vers trois heures et quart.
Je vais voir le Jardin des Plantes vers quatre heures et demie.

Quand est-ce que vous allez visiter ...?

## Section B

**(d) Exercise 4**

Lundi nous allons visiter le port.
Mardi nous allons visiter le château et le musée.
Mercredi nous allons visiter la Basilique de Lisieux et mercredi soir nous allons visiter le théâtre.
Jeudi matin nous allons visiter le Musée du Débarquement et jeudi après-midi nous allons visiter la Tapisserie de Bayeux.
Vendredi matin nous allons faire des courses et nous allons déjeuner au restaurant.
Samedi matin nous allons visiter la piscine et samedi après-midi nous allons visiter la plage.
Dimanche nous allons visiter l'église Saint-Pierre.

**(e) Exercise 5**

(i) Je vais déjeuner à midi et demi.
(ii) Je veux visiter le port vers deux heures moins le quart.
(iii) Si vous êtes libre* à midi, venez au restaurant.
(iv) Excusez-moi de déranger votre déjeuner.
(v) Je crois qu'il va faire beau plus tard.
(vi) Est-ce qu'il ne fait jamais beau ici?
(vii) Le temps change vite ici. Il va y avoir du soleil, peut-être.
(viii) On ne sait jamais. Je crois que nous allons acheter des anoraks quand même.

*Note that vous might be addressing one person or a number of people. If more than one person is addressed libre would have to end with a plural -s, that is, libres.

## Chapter 6

## Section A

**(a) Exercise 1**

Answers to this exercise can vary according to individual reactions. The answers below are a selection of possible reactions.

(i) Non, je n'aime pas le sport.

   (ii)  Non, je n'aime pas le tennis.
  (iii)  Oui, j'aime beaucoup le beau temps.
   (iv)  Ça dépend.
    (v)  Comme ci comme ça.
   (vi)  Oui, j'aime visiter les musées.
  (vii)  Oui, j'adore ça.
 (viii)  Oui, j'aime beaucoup aller au théâtre.
   (ix)  Ça dépend.
    (x)  Oui, j'aime aller à la piscine.

## (b) Exercise 2

Oui, il fait encore mauvais. Est-ce qu'il va faire beau plus tard?
Oui, bien entendu. Il pleut beaucoup en Angleterre, parce qu'il y a un climat maritime. On n'a pas de chance, mais il va y avoir du soleil plus tard, peut-être.
Non, on ne sait jamais. Je crois que nous allons visiter un musée aujourd'hui.
Merci bien, monsieur. Au revoir.

## (c) Exercise 3

    (i)  Oui, c'est pour elle.
   (ii)  Oui, c'est pour elle.
  (iii)  Oui, c'est pour lui.
   (iv)  Mais si, c'est pour lui.
    (v)  Oui, ils sont avec lui.
   (vi)  Oui, il est avec eux.
  (vii)  Oui, il est avec elle.
 (viii)  Oui, elle est avec eux.

## (d) Exercise 4

    (i)  J'aime beaucoup la région, mais il pleut beaucoup.
   (ii)  Je crois qu'il va faire beau plus tard.
  (iii)  C'est possible. On ne sait jamais. Qu'est-ce que vous prévoyez pour aujourd'hui?
   (iv)  Nous allons faire des courses ce matin.
    (v)  À midi nous allons déjeuner dans un restaurant (*or* au restaurant).
   (vi)  Vous avez de la chance! Amusez-vous bien!
  (vii)  L'anorak de Catherine est trop petit.
 (viii)  Nous avons des anoraks de toutes les tailles. Est-ce que vous voulez un anorak bleu ou rouge pour elle?
   (ix)  Elle préfère l'anorak rouge, je crois. Oui, c'est la taille exacte pour elle.
    (x)  Bien, et je voudrais un imperméable pour moi.

## (e) Exercise 5

    (i)  Le pullover de Monsieur Lebrun.
   (ii)  Le port de Caen.
  (iii)  L'entrée du château.
   (iv)  La voiture du monsieur.
    (v)  La clef de la porte.
   (vi)  Le numéro de la chambre.

(vii) La piscine de la ville.
(viii) Les vêtements des hommes.
(ix) L'imperméable de l'enfant.

## Chapter 7

## Section A

### (a) Exercise 1

The actual menu selected will clearly depend on personal preferences. The following is just one suggestion.

Je voudrais un martini, s'il vous plaît, et je voudrais voir le menu.
Comme hors d'oeuvre, je voudrais le pâté. Comme plat principal je vais prendre l'escalope normande, puis le plateau de fromages et comme dessert une glace.
Comme boisson je voudrais une carafe de vin rouge.
Garçon, l'addition s'il vous plaît. Le service est compris?

### (b) Exercise 2

Once again, these are possible answers, but you should aim to express your personal preferences using these answers as models to be followed.

  (i) Oui, s'il vous plaît, j'aime beaucoup ça.
 (ii) Non merci, je n'aime pas ça.
(iii) Non merci, je n'aime pas beaucoup les escargots.
 (iv) Avec plaisir, j'adore le canard.
  (v) Non merci, je déteste le coq au vin.
 (vi) Non merci, je n'aime pas ça.

### (c) Exercise 3

  (i) Le climat français est meilleur que le climat anglais.
 (ii) Le Jardin des Plantes est plus intéressant que le port.
(iii) La couleur rouge est plus chic que la couleur jaune.
 (iv) Dans le Midi il fait plus chaud qu'en Angleterre.
  (v) Le Livarot est plus délicieux que le Camembert.
 (vi) Le théâtre est plus intéressant que le cinéma.
(vii) Mon imperméable est plus beau que votre anorak.
(viii) Catherine est plus petite que son frère.

### (d) Exercise 4

  (i) Asseyez-vous, s'il vous plaît. Vous voulez prendre un apéritif avant de manger?
 (ii) Oui, s'il vous plaît. Je vais prendre un martini.
(iii) Je crois que les enfants vont prendre des jus de fruit.
 (iv) On peut avoir le menu, s'il vous plaît? Certainement, monsieur.
  (v) Je voudrais le pâté et ma femme va prendre les escargots.
 (vi) Je n'aime pas beaucoup la viande. Je vais prendre une omelette.
(vii) À mon avis le canard est meilleur.
(viii) Ils ont faim, je crois, mais ils attendent patiemment.
 (ix) Qu'est-ce que vous voulez boire? Une carafe de vin rouge.
  (x) Quel repas délicieux! Et ce n'est pas encore fini!

**(e) Exercise 5**
(i)  Les enfants attendent patiemment.
(ii)  Robert, lui, aime la viande.
(iii)  Je reviens dans quelques minutes.
(iv)  Qu'est-ce que vous voulez comme apéritif?
(v)  Elle prend le canard mais lui préfère le coq.
(vi)  Nous sommes ravis de notre visite.

**Chapter 8**

**Section A**

**(a) Exercise 1**
Avec plaisir. Je ne suis pas pressé.
Oui, c'est ma première visite à Caen.
Je viens d'Angleterre.
Non, je suis dans un hôtel.
Non, je suis avec ma femme et mes deux enfants.
Je suis professeur. . . .
On se promène en ville. On visite les monuments. On fait des excursions.
Ma femme et moi, nous sommes ravis. Nous croyons que les gens sont aimables et nous aimons la ville.
Je vous en prie.

**(b) Exercise 2**
(i)  Je me réveille à sept heures.
(ii)  Je me lève à sept heures et demie.
(iii)  Je me lave à huit heures.
(iv)  Je déjeune à neuf heures du matin.
(v)  Je me promène en ville à dix heures du matin.
(vi)  Je me repose à huit heures du soir.
(vii)  Je me couche à dix heures du soir.

**(c) Exercise 3**
(i)  Quand est-ce que vous vous réveillez?
(ii)  Quand est-ce que vous vous levez?
(iii)  Quand est-ce que vous vous lavez?
(iv)  Quand est-ce que vous déjeunez?
(v)  Quand est-ce que vous vous promenez en ville?
(vi)  Quand est-ce que vous vous reposez?
(vii)  Quand est-ce que vous vous couchez?

**(d) Exercise 4**
(i)  Je vais à l'église. Je vais au jardin. Je vais au port. Je vais à Caen. Je vais au Syndicat d'Initiative.
(ii)  Je vais en France. Je vais en Normandie. Je vais en Bretagne. Je vais en Angleterre.
(iii)  Je viens de France. Je viens du château. Je viens de l'Hôtel de Ville. Je viens de Normandie. Je viens de l'école.

## Section B

### (e) Exercise 5

   (i)   Est-ce que vous pouvez répondre à quelques questions?
   (ii)  Vous venez d'où?
  (iii)  Vous parlez vraiment bien français.
  (iv)  Ce n'est pas votre première visite en France?
   (v)  Je viens en France chaque année, si possible.
  (vi)  En général on passe les vacances à Paris.
 (vii)  Il y a tellement de choses à faire.
(viii)  On aime se promener en ville. *Or,* Nous aimons nous promener en ville.
  (ix)  Votre femme est très inquiète.
   (x)  Il faut faire quelque chose.

### (f) Exercise 6

There are a number of possibilities here. The following are suggestions:
    Il a huit ans. Il est de taille moyenne et il porte un pullover noir et un pantalon bleu.
    Il a trente ans, et il porte un anorak jaune et un pantalon bleu.

## Chapter 9

## Section A

### (a) Exercise 1

    Je voudrais . . . une livre de beurre; du fromage; de la bière; un kilo de pommes de terre; une bouteille de limonade; quatre tranches de jambon; deux cents grammes de saucisson; du lait; du pain.

### (b) Exercise 2

    Je regrette madame, je n'ai pas de lait;
                      je n'ai pas de fromage;
                      je n'ai pas de bière.

### (c) Exercise 3

    Je voudrais une livre de beurre, un kilo de pommes de terre et du pain. Deux. Je voudrais aussi deux bouteilles de lait. Qu'est-ce que vous avez comme charcuterie?
    Je voudrais cinq tranches de jambon. Est-ce que vous avez du cidre? Non, je ne veux pas de bière. Je vais prendre une bouteille de limonade pour les enfants.
    Ça fait combien?

### (d) Exercise 4

   (i)  Je voudrais . . . du vin rouge; du vin blanc; du café; du chocolat; du thé; des fruits; des légumes; des oeufs; des croissants; de la farine; de la viande; des cigarettes; des allumettes; des aspirines.
       Je voudrais une boîte d'allumettes; une bouteille de vin; un paquet de

cigarettes; un kilo de farine; une livre de beurre; beaucoup de chocolat; peu de thé.

(ii) Je ne veux pas . . . de vin rouge; de vin blanc; de café; de chocolat . . . and so on.

## Section B

### (e) Exercise 5

(i) Je voudrais venir passer quelques jours sur la côte.
(ii) Est-ce qu'il est possible de louer une tente?
(iii) Il est difficile de répondre à vos questions.
(iv) Je voudrais réserver des casseroles, des couteaux et des fourchettes.
(v) Pour combien de temps?
(vi) Pour cinq jours à partir de demain . . . Je m'appelle . . .
(vii) Je voudrais du fromage, du beurre, du pain et du lait, s.v.p.
(viii) Combien de beurre est-ce que vous voulez?
(ix) Combien de baguettes et combien de fromage voulez-vous?
(x) Je suis désolé, je n'ai pas de lait.

### (f) Exercise 6

(i) Il est difficile de faire la cuisine.
(ii) Il est possible de louer une tente.
(iii) Il faut arriver à huit heures.
(iv) Je vais boire de la bière.
(v) Nous allons chercher les enfants.
(vi) Je veux écouter la radio.
(vii) Nous voulons aller à la côte.
(viii) Je peux acheter du jambon.
(ix) Nous pouvons venir au château.

This is just a selection of numerous sentences that can be formed on the same basis.

## Chapter 10

Translation of extracts from guide book given on p.88.

*The Avenue of the Champs Elysées*

From the Concorde to the Rond-Point

Go up towards the Étoile following the drives of chestnut trees lining the avenue. It's the part of the walk where there are most people. There are lots of children there, attracted by the little shops, the swings.

From the Rond-Point to the Étoile

Stroll up the avenue. One should walk on the right-hand side. It is the liveliest and the most typical. A street, a café and a cinema bear the name Colisée. One arrives at the Place de l'Étoile, at the base of the majestic arch.

*The Eiffel Tower*

This is the most universally known of the sights of Paris. Ascent: Every day from 10.45 until 6.00 pm (in July and August from 9.30 until 6.00 pm). For the visitor who climbs to the top, the view can extend as far as 67 kilometres.

*The Basilica of the Sacré Coeur*

The tall white silhouette now forms part of the Parisian landscape. The ascent to the dome (from 10.00 am to 1.00 pm and from 2.00 pm to 5.00 pm) offers a magnificent panorama.

*Paris, seen from its river*
There are regular services of pleasure boats every day from 1 April until 5 October. In winter there is one service per day at 3.15 pm. Embarcation point: Solferino bridge.

## Section A

### (a) Exercise 1

  (i) Je verrai l'Arc de Triomphe.
 (ii) Je visiterai la cathédrale Notre Dame.
(iii) Je ferai une excursion en bateau-mouche.
 (iv) Je déjeunerai dans un grand restaurant.
  (v) Je prendrai le métro.

### (b) Exercise 2

  (i) Oui, je le connais bien. J'espère le revoir.
 (ii) Non, ils ne le connaissent pas encore.
(iii) Oui, je le prendrai à sept heures vingt.
 (iv) Oui, je les aime beaucoup.
  (v) Oui, je la visiterai dans l'après-midi.

### (c) Exercise 3

   (i) C'est toujours un plaisir de vous revoir.
  (ii) Évidemment nous ne visiterons pas tous les musées.
 (iii) Vous verrez toutes sortes d'activités dans la cour devant le Centre Pompidou.
 (iv) Est-ce que vous aurez assez de temps pour faire une excursion en bateau-mouche?
  (v) Nous visiterons la Tour Eiffel. Nous voulons la voir de près.
 (vi) Le métro est plus vite que l'autobus, mais je préfère l'autobus parce qu'on voit la ville.
 (vii) Je déteste le métro. Il y a toujours tellement de monde.
(viii) Quand est-ce que vous reviendrez demain soir?
 (ix) Je viendrai vous chercher à la gare. Je vous verrai à huit heures.
  (x) Il va falloir partir de bonne heure.

### (d) Exercise 4

  (i) Les enfants ne le connaissent pas.
 (ii) Nous le prendrons.
(iii) Je les aime bien.
 (iv) Nous la ferons en bateau-mouche.
  (v) Je ne l'aime pas.

## Chapter 11

## Section A

### (a) Exercise 1

Quatre adultes, aller-retour à Paris, s'il vous plaît.
Il part à quelle heure, le train pour Paris?

Et de quelle voie?

À quelle heure est-ce qu'on arrive à Paris?

## (b) Exercise 2

   (i)  La Préfecture de Police se trouve en face de la Cathédrale.

  (ii)  La Cathédrale Notre-Dame se trouve en face de la Préfecture de Police.

 (iii)  Le Palais de Justice se trouve près du Marché aux Fleurs.

 (iv)  La rue de la Cité est située devant la Préfecture de Police.

  (v)  Le Marché aux Fleurs se trouve derrière la Préfecture de Police.

 (vi)  La Place du Parvis Notre-Dame est située devant la Cathédrale.

## (c) Exercise 3

Excusez-moi, monsieur, ces chaises sont libres?

Est-ce que je peux m'asseoir? Vous permettez?

Il y a tellement de monde en ville aujourd'hui.

Non, je passe un jour seulement à Paris avec ma famille.

Nous espérons visiter la Tour Eiffel, la cathédrale Notre-Dame et l'Arc de Triomphe.

## Section B

## (d) Exercise 4

   (i)  Je m'assieds ici, tout près; vous permettez?

  (ii)  On n'a pas le temps de s'ennuyer.

 (iii)  Nous allons bientôt partir. Vous avez l'heure?

 (iv)  Ils vont apprendre le français à l'école.

  (v)  On n'aura pas le temps de tout voir, bien entendu. *Or*

       Nous n'aurons pas le temps de tout voir.

## (e) Exercise 5

   (i)  ces

  (ii)  ce

 (iii)  cette

 (iv)  ce grand bâtiment-là

  (v)  cette

 (vi)  cet

## Chapter 12

## Section A

## (a) Exercise 1

Oui, nous avons passé une bonne journée. Nous avons tous beaucoup marché.

Non, nous avons mangé des sandwiches.

Moi, je n'ai rien acheté, mais ma femme a acheté une écharpe et les enfants ont acheté quelques souvenirs.

Nous y avons passé une heure environ.

**(b) Exercise 2**

    (i)   J'ai pris le bus.

   (ii)   Ma femme a eu le temps de se reposer.

  (iii)   Mon ami Michel a été souvent à Paris.

  (iv)   Nous avons pu voir la cathédrale.

   (v)   Vous avez fait une visite à Paris.

  (vi)   Mes enfants ont vu la Tour Eiffel.

 (vii)   Les Lebrun ont repris le train.

**(c) Exercise 3**

    (i)   Je n'ai pas pris le bus.

   (ii)   Ma femme n'a pas eu le temps de se reposer.

  (iii)   Mon ami Michel n'a pas été souvent à Paris.

  (iv)   Nous n'avons pas pu voir la cathédrale.

   (v)   Vous n'avez pas fait une visite à Paris.

  (vi)   Mes enfants n'ont pas pu voir la Tour Eiffel.

 (vii)   Les Lebrun n'ont pas pu reprendre le train.

**(d) Exercise 4**

    (i)   Nous avons eu de la chance avec le temps.

   (ii)   Nous n'avons pris qu'un petit sac pour notre piquenique.

  (iii)   Nous avons pu dîner dans le train.

  (iv)   Qu'est-ce que vous avez vu?

   (v)   Nous avons pris un bus pour aller à la Tour Eiffel.

  (vi)   On a pris un bateau-mouche pour se reposer. *Or*

          Nous avons pris un bateau-mouche pour nous reposer.

 (vii)   Qu'est-ce que vous avez fait après la Tour Eiffel?

(viii)   Je n'ai rien acheté, mais ma femme a trouvé quelques souvenirs.

  (ix)   Les enfants ont acheté des cartes postales.

   (x)   On a passé une journée formidable à Paris.

**(e) Exercise 5**

    (i)   Vous avez couché.

   (ii)   Ils ont dormi.

  (iii)   Vous avez goûté.

  (iv)   J'ai mangé ... j'ai vu.

   (v)   Vous avez visité.

  (vi)   Nous avons oublié.

## Chapter 13

### Section A

**(a) Exercise 1**

Je suis sorti de l'hôtel. Je me suis promené dans la rue.

Je suis allé acheter un journal. Je suis rentré. Je suis arrivé à l'hôtel vers neuf heures et demie.

(Women students should note that in giving an account such as this they will need to give past participles a *feminine* ending, for example:

Je suis sortie ... je me suis promenée ... je suis allée and so on.)

**(b) Exercise 2**

(i) Je suis sorti de l'hôtel. Je suis allé à la gare. J'ai pris le train. Je suis arrivé à Paris. J'ai visité les monuments. Je suis allé au théâtre. Je suis rentré à minuit.

(ii) Je suis sorti de l'hôtel. Je suis allé au bureau. J'ai travaillé toute la matinée. Je suis sorti déjeuner. Je suis retourné au bureau. Je suis rentré à six heures.

(iii) Je suis sorti de l'hôtel. Je me suis promené dans la rue. Je suis allé acheter un journal. Je suis retourné à l'hôtel. Je suis sorti pour la journée. J'ai fait une excursion. Je suis rentré à six heures.

## Section B

**(c) Exercise 3**

(i) Il est sorti il y a une heure pour acheter un journal.

(ii) Je l'ai vu sortir, mais il n'est pas rentré.

(iii) J'espère que vous avez raison. Je suis inquiet (inquiète) pour lui.

(iv) Nous aurons besoin de vous contacter. Quel est votre numéro de téléphone?

(v) Je suis en retard à cause d'un accident de la route.

(vi) Quelqu'un ne s'est pas arrêté au feu rouge.

(vii) Je viens d'arriver à Paris et j'espère que vous avez une chambre.

(viii) Nous sommes sortis déjeuner et nous avons vu un accident.

(ix) Est-ce que vous l'avez vu? Je l'ai vu il y a trois semaines.

(x) Qu'est-ce qui s'est passé? Est-ce que vous avez prévenu ma femme?

**(d) Exercise 4**

(i) Je l'ai vu en ville.

(ii) Nous les avons visités à Paris.

(iii) Il ne l'a pas entendu.

(iv) J'en ai besoin.

(v) Je l'ai prévenu et je l'ai appelé.

## Chapter 14

## Section A

**(a) Exercise 1**

(i) La cathédrale qui est à Bayeux.

(ii) La forêt qui est au sud de Bayeux.

(iii) Le timbre que vous avez acheté.

(iv) L'argent que vous avez perdu.

(v) L'ami qui habite dans le Midi.

(vi) Le sac que vous avez placé dans la voiture.

(vii) Les vaches qui sont dans le pré.

(viii) Le château qui est dans la forêt.

**(b) Exercise 2**

(i) Je lui ai déjà donné la bouteille.

(ii) Je lui ai déjà écrit la carte postale.

(iii) Je lui ai déjà présenté ce paquet.

(iv) Je leur ai déjà proposé une excursion.

(v) Je leur ai déjà téléphoné.

## (c) Exercise 3

Any number of items could be used in this exercise. Here are a few suggestions.

  (i) Il me faut du vin; Il me faut des pommes de terre; il me faut une livre de beurre; il me faut des cigarettes; il me faut du jambon, etc.

 (ii) Il vous faut des allumettes? Il vous faut des légumes? Il vous faut des aspirines? Il vous faut du fromage?

## (d) Exercise 4

  (i) Il faut absolument visiter Bayeux. Je n'ai jamais vu la tapisserie.

 (ii) Oui, d'accord. On prendra les enfants. Ça leur plaira.

(iii) J'y suis allé il y a bien des années. J'espère que le temps fera beau.

 (iv) Il y a un petit restaurant qu'un ami m'a recommandé.

  (v) On dit que le château vaut une visite.

 (vi) Nous sommes trop nombreux pour une auto. Où est-ce qu'on se retrouve?

(vii) Le paysage ici est tellement varié. On n'aura pas le temps de tout voir.

(viii) Je préfère le paysage qui se trouve de l'autre côté de la Seine.

 (ix) Je leur ai donné l'argent. Ils sont partis acheter un souvenir.

## Chapter 15

## Section A

## (a) Exercise 1

Quand j'etais jeune, j'habitais à la campagne. Mes parents n'étaient pas riches. J'ai commencé l'école à l'âge de cinq ans, mais j'habitais loin de l'école et je prenais le bus tous les jours. J'ai quitté l'école à quatorze ans et j'ai commencé à travailler dans un bureau. Il y avait des difficultés à cette époque-là. Je suis venu à la ville plus tard et j'ai changé de travail. La ville était petite à cette époque-là, mais elle est devenue plus grande.

## (c) Exercise 3

Here is a selection of the possible answers:

Autrefois les villages étaient plus calmes.

À cette époque-là la ville était petite.

Dans le temps mes parents habitaient à la campagne.

Quand j'étais jeune la campagne était plus paisible.

Tous les jours Pierre allait en ville.

Autrefois les langues intéressaient John.

À cette époque-là Pierre prenait l'autobus.

## Section B

### (d) Exercise 4

(i) Je me suis toujours intéressé aux langues.

(ii) Nous habitions à la campagne, mais il y a trois ans nous sommes venus à Caen.

(iii) À cette époque-là il y avait beaucoup de problèmes dans la ville.

(iv) Oui, ce n'était pas comme ça à la campagne. La vie était calme quand on était petit.

(v) Caen est devenu peu à peu un des centres régionaux les plus importants.

(vi) Je me souviens que tout était plus paisible et décontracté dans le Midi.

(vii) Il fait tellement chaud dans le Midi qu'il faut conserver son énergie.

(viii) Nous allions tous les jours à la plage, mais maintenant nous n'avons plus le temps.

(ix) Il faut admettre que les Anglais et les Normands ont beaucoup de traits en commun.

(x) Je travaillais dans mon bureau quand il est arrivé.

## Chapter 16

## Section A

### (a) Exercise 1

Je dois me lever à neuf heures. Je dois aller au bureau à dix heures.
Je dois déjeuner à midi et demi. À trois heures moins le quart je dois faire des courses. Je dois rentrer à quatre heures et je dois dîner à sept heures et demie.
À dix heures et demie je dois aller au lit.

### (b) Exercise 2

J'ai dû me lever à neuf heures. J'ai dû aller au bureau à dix heures.
J'ai dû déjeuner à midi et demi. À trois heures moins le quart j'ai dû faire des courses. J'ai dû rentrer à quatre heures et j'ai dû dîner à sept heures et demie.
À six heures et demie j'ai dû aller au lit.

### (c) Exercise 3

The model of the letter provided in the text should be followed with any changes as required.

## Section B

### (d) Exercise 4

Cher Jean,
    Maintenant que nos vacances touchent à leur fin nous devons vous écrire pour raconter ce que nous avons fait ici en Normandie. D'abord le temps

faisait mauvais et nous avons eu beaucoup d'averses. Heureusement il y avait beaucoup à faire et beaucoup d'endroits à visiter. Nous avons fait la connaissance de la ville de Caen, ce qui était un grand plaisir. Nous avons pu passer une journée à Paris, ce qui était très intéressant pour les enfants. Nous devrons retourner à Paris avec eux, parce qu'un jour n'est pas très long. Il y avait du soleil pendant cette excursion et depuis ce jour-là il a fait beau. On a pu profiter des belles plages de la région. Le temps a passé tellement vite qu'il est difficile de croire que nous devrons partir demain.

Bien amicalement,

### (e) Exercise 5

(i) Jeudi dernier j'ai dû quitter mon bureau de bonne heure.
Last Thursday I had to leave my office early.

(ii) Quand j'étais jeune mon père devait commencer son travail à sept heures.
When I was young my father had to start work at 7 o'clock.

(iii) Les enfants doivent rentrer à l'école aujourd'hui.
The children have to go back to school today.

(iv) Mardi prochain vous devrez venir me rendre visite.
Next Tuesday you will have to come and visit me.

## Chapter 17

## Section A

### (a) Exercise 1

Il a dit que ce n'était pas grave.
Il a dit que je n'avais aucune raison de m'inquiéter.
Il a dit que l'enfant était un peu enrhumé.
Il a dit qu'il avait un peu de fièvre.
Il a dit qu'il ne devait pas sortir.
Il a dit qu'il fallait lui donner deux comprimés par jour.
Il a dit qu'il fallait le laisser dormir, si possible.

### (b) Exercise 2

(i) Voilà deux bouteilles de vin. Celui-ci est sec, celui-là est doux.
(ii) Voilà deux sacs. Celui-ci est plein, celui-là est vide.
(iii) Voilà deux paniers. Celui-ci est lourd, celui-là est léger.
(iv) Voilà deux voitures. Celle-ci est rouge, celle-là est blanche.
(v) Voilà deux routes. Celle-ci est bonne, celle-là est mauvaise.

### (c) Exercise 3

(i) J'ai mal à la tête et mal à la gorge. Qu'est-ce que vous pouvez me donner?
(ii) Vous avez besoin de comprimés et de sirop. Prenez cette ordonnance chez le pharmacien.
(iii) Donnez-leur ces comprimés trois fois par jour et ne les laissez pas aller dans l'eau.

(iv) Vous vous êtes enrhumé, mais ce n'est pas grave. Vous n'avez pas de raison de vous inquiéter.

(v) Qu'est-ce qu'il aime comme vin? Celui-ci est sec.

(vi) Je crois qu'il va préférer celui-ci, probablement; ou celui-là est peut-être meilleur.

(vii) Voilà vos fromages. Gardez-les au frais jusqu'à votre départ.

(viii) Est-ce qu'il a dit qu'il fallait attendre ici? Vous en êtes sûr?

(ix) J'ai acheté des petits pains, mais nous n'en avons pas besoin maintenant.

(x) Au printemps nous devrons retourner en France.

## Chapter 18

### Section A

#### (a) Exercise 1

Si je gagnais, je ferais le tour du monde;
j'achèterais un château sur la Côte d'Azur;
je mangerais dans les meilleurs restaurants;
j'habiterais à la campagne;
j'aurais une grande voiture;
j'irais souvent au théâtre;
je viendrais tous les ans en France;
je passerais l'hiver dans le Midi.

#### (b) Exercise 2

Si je devais préparer ce poulet, je mettrais le cognac;
je ferais flamber; j'ajouterais le bouillon;
je laisserais cuire trente minutes; je terminerais
la sauce; je mélangerais bien.

### Section B

#### (a) Exercise 3

(i) Si nous avions plus de temps nous resterions plus longtemps mais il faut bien gagner sa vie.

(ii) Avant de partir vous devez visiter la vallée de la Seine.

(iii) Nous ferons tout notre possible pour vous rendre visite.

(iv) Qu'est-ce que cela veut dire? Je ne comprends pas.

(v) Vous savez où nous trouver. Nous espérons vous revoir bientôt.

(vi) Si je ne devais pas gagner ma vie, j'aimerais rester encore quelques jours.

(vii) Vous voulez bien vérifier l'huile et la pression des pneus, s'il vous plaît.

(viii) Si vous tombez en panne en route pour le Havre vous aurez du mal à trouver un garage.

(ix) Il vaut mieux que ça soit réparé immédiatement. Je ne crois pas que ça soit grave.

(x) Les bougies sont sales et huileuses. Vous savez ce que ça veut dire?

# Chapter 19

## Section A

### (a) Exercise 1

(i) Nous avions déjà pris du retard quand nous sommes arrivés au port.

(ii) Elle était déjà arrivée à la gare quand nous sommes allés la chercher.

(iii) Il avait déjà recommencé son travail quand sa femme est retournée au bureau.

(iv) L'hôtelier avait déjà renvoyé les articles quand je lui ai écrit.

(v) Mon ami avait déjà appris la langue quand il a visité le pays.

### (b) Exercise 2

Cher . . .

Ça fait déjà presque une semaine depuis que nous sommes rentrés. Le temps passe tellement vite. Nous avons beaucoup de bons souvenirs de la période que nous avons passée avec vous. Nous vous sommes très reconnaissants de votre accueil. Le voyage de retour n'a pas été une réussite. Nous avons dû attendre à un garage, puis nous sommes tombés en panne en route et ensuite nous avons pris du retard à cause de la circulation. Mais nous avons eu le temps de prendre un snack avant d'embarquer. Les vacances sont finies maintenant et je vais recommencer mon travail. Nous attendons avec plaisir de vous recevoir chez nous et nous vous envoyons toutes nos amitiés.

## Section B

### (c) Exercise 3

(i) Après avoir quitté l'hôtel, j'ai rencontré mon ami Pierre en route pour son bureau.

(ii) Nous étions déjà partis pour le Havre quand la voiture est tombée en panne.

(iii) Si vous écriviez la semaine prochaine je recevrais la lettre bientôt après.

(iv) J'espère que vous avez eu un bon voyage. Le nôtre n'a pas été une réussite.

(v) Il s'ennuie parce que son travail n'est pas intéressant, mais le mien est fascinant.

(vi) Se familiariser avec une autre culture c'est toujours un avantage quand on apprend une langue étrangère.

(vii) Quelquefois le contact humain manque quand on visite un pays comme touriste.

(viii) Nous sommes bien rentrés et nous avons des souvenirs heureux de notre visite.

(ix) C'est dommage que la voiture soit tombée en panne. On ira se promener en attendant.

(x) J'avais déjà lu le livre quand il me l'a acheté.

**Chapter 20**

20.1

**(a)**
- (i) Je vous présente mon mari.
- (ii) Je vous présente mes enfants, Catherine et Robert.
- (iii) Je vous présente mon ami Jean.
- (iv) Je vous présente mon père.
- (v) Je vous présente ma mère.

**(b)**
- (i) Est-ce que vous êtes Madame Smith?
- (ii) Est-ce que vous êtes Catherine?
- (iii) Est-ce que vous êtes libres ce soir?
- (iv) Est-ce que vous pouvez dîner chez nous?
- (v) Est-ce que vous restez en France?

**(c)** The answers to this exercise are already given in the exercise itself.

20.2

**(a)**
- (i) ils s'endorment
- (ii) ils se dépêchent
- (iii) Ils se cachent
- (iv) l'église se trouve
- (v) Je me lève
- (vi) se reposer . . . on se promène

**(b)**
- (i) Vous envoyez des cerises à votre père.
  Vous lui en envoyez.
- (ii) Mary achète de la crème dans la laiterie.
  Mary y en achète.
- (iii) John présente des cadeaux à ses enfants.
  John leur en présente.
- (iv) Nous avons acheté des timbres dans le tabac.
  Nous y en avons acheté.
- (v) La Normandie offre du fromage aux touristes.
  La Normandie leur en offre.
- (vi) Comme piquenique, l'hôtel fournit du pain et de la charcuterie à la famille.
  Comme piquenique l'hôtel leur en fournit.
- (vii) Elle explique des problèmes à sa fille.
  Elle lui en explique.

(viii) Ils achètent des crayons dans la papeterie.
Ils y en achètent.
(ix) Les enfants dépensent de l'argent dans les boutiques.
Les enfants y en dépensent.

**(c)**

(i) reviendrons
(ii) discuterons
(iii) sera
(iv) iront
(v) enverrai

**(d)**

(i) J'ai vu l'accident, bien entendu. J'allais vers le carrefour quand j'ai vu une auto brûler le feu et elle s'est emboutie dans une autre voiture.
(ii) Votre femme était très inquiète pour vous. Elle m'a demandé de lui téléphoner dans sa chambre.
(iii) Il est sorti de l'hôtel (or Il a quitté l'hôtel) il y a une demie-heure mais il n'est pas encore rentré. Quand je l'ai vu la dernière fois il achetait un journal au kiosk.
(iv) Elle regardait le paysage quand son fils est tombé.
(v) Ils étaient chez eux quand leur ami a téléphoné.

**(e)**

A selection of possible sentences. Others are also possible.
Les parents peuvent écouter la musique.
Les enfants doivent chanter une chanson populaire.
L'hôtelier veut frapper à la port.
La famille doit occuper les heures de loisir.
La femme de chambre peut expliquer la situation.
John veut acheter des fruits. And so on.

**(f)**

(i) Après être arrivé il s'est assis.
(ii) Avant de partir il m'a dit au revoir.
(iii) En travaillant il pense à ses vacances.
(iv) Elle avait déjà trouvé . . .
(v) Nous étions déjà rentrés . . .
(vi) Si vous veniez me chercher à la gare, il serait plus facile pour moi
(vii) Si je gagnais la Loterie Nationale, je partirais en vacances

# SUPPLEMENTARY
# VOCABULARIES

## 1  LA FAMILLE
**Masc.**

| | |
|---|---|
| le bébé | the baby |
| le cousin | cousin |
| le frère | brother |
| le grand-père | grandfather |
| un homme | man |
| le mariage | marriage |
| le neveu | nephew |
| un oncle | uncle |

## THE FAMILY
**Fem.**

| | |
|---|---|
| la cousine | cousin |
| la grand'mère | grandmother |
| la jeune-fille | girl |
| la ménagère | housewife |
| la nièce | niece |
| la soeur | sister |
| la tante | aunt |

## 2  LES VÊTEMENTS
**Masc.**

| | |
|---|---|
| le bouton | button |
| le chapeau | hat |
| les collants | tights |
| le costume | suit |
| le gant | glove |
| le jupon | petticoat |
| le mouchoir | handkerchief |
| le parapluie | umbrella |
| le sac à main | handbag |
| le short | shorts |
| le soulier | shoe |

## CLOTHES
**Fem.**

| | |
|---|---|
| la boucle d'oreille | ear-ring |
| la ceinture | belt |
| la chaussette | sock |
| la cravate | tie |
| la jupe | skirt |
| les lunettes | spectacles |
| les lunettes de soleil | sun-glasses |
| la montre | wristwatch |
| la poche | pocket |
| la robe | dress |

## 3  LES PARTIES DU CORPS
**Masc.**

| | |
|---|---|
| le bras | arm |
| le cou | neck |
| le doigt | finger |
| le dos | back |
| le front | forehead |
| le genou | knee |

## PARTS OF THE BODY
**Fem.**

| | |
|---|---|
| la barbe | beard |
| la cheville | ankle |
| la dent | tooth |
| la figure | face |
| la jambe | leg |
| la lèvre | lip |

| | | | | |
|---|---|---|---|---|
| le nez | nose | | la main | hand |
| un oeil (*plural*: | | | une oreille | ear |
| les yeux) | eye | | la poitrine | chest |
| le visage | face | | | |

## 4 LA NOURRITURE ET LA BOISSON

**FOOD AND DRINK**

**Masc.**

| | | | **Fem.** | |
|---|---|---|---|---|
| un agneau | lamb | | la confiture | jam |
| le bifteck | steak | | la crêpe | pancake |
| le boeuf | beef | | | |
| le foie | liver | | | |
| le gigot | leg of mutton | | | |
| le porc | pork | | | |
| le riz | rice | | | |
| le veau | veal | | | |
| le vinaigre | vinegar | | | |

## 5 LES FRUITS ET LES LÉGUMES

**FRUIT AND VEGETABLES**

**Masc.**

| | | | **Fem.** | |
|---|---|---|---|---|
| un abricot | apricot | | la banane | banana |
| un ananas | pineapple | | la framboise | raspberry |
| le chou | cabbage | | la pêche | peach |
| un haricot vert | French bean | | la poire | pear |
| les petits pois | green peas | | la prune | plum |

## 6 LES MAGASINS ET LES METIERS

**SHOPS AND PROFESSIONS**

**Masc.**

| | | | **Fem.** | |
|---|---|---|---|---|
| un agent d'affaires | estate agent | | la bijouterie | jewellers |
| | | | la boucherie | butchers |
| un agent de change | stockbroker | | la coiffeuse | hairdresser |
| | | | la confiserie | confectioners |
| un architecte | architect | | la gendarmerie | police station |
| un avocat | lawyer (barrister) | | une horlogerie | watchmaker |
| | | | une infirmière | nurse |
| un avoué | solicitor | | la librairie | bookshop |
| le banquier | banker | | la modiste | milliner |
| le charpentier | carpenter | | la pâtisserie | cake-shop |
| le chirurgien | surgeon | | la poissonnerie | fishmongers |
| le coiffeur | hairdresser | | la quincaillerie | ironmongers |
| le concierge | caretaker | | | |
| le dentiste | dentist | | | |
| un entrepreneur | builder; contractor | | | |
| le facteur | postman | | | |
| le gérant | manager | | | |
| un ingénieur | engineer | | | |
| le jardinier | gardener | | | |
| le juge | judge | | | |

**Masc.**

| le marchand | shopkeeper |
| le notaire | solicitor |
| un ouvrier | workman |
| le patron | employer; boss |
| le pêcheur | fisherman |
| le plombier | plumber |
| le pompier | fireman |
| le rédacteur | newspaper editor |
| le tailleur | tailor |
| le vétérinaire | vet |

## 6 L'AUTOMOBILISME ET LE TRANSPORT — MOTORING AND TRANSPORT

| **Masc.** | | **Fem.** | |
| un avion | aeroplane | une autoroute | motorway |
| le camion | lorry | la bicyclette | bicycle |
| le capot | bonnet | la crevaison | puncture |
| le coffre | boot | la moto | motorcycle |
| le cric | jack | la pile | battery |
| le démarreur | starter | la plaque | number-plate |
| un embrayage | clutch | la roue | wheel |
| le frein | brake | la roue de rechange | spare-wheel |
| le kilomètre | kilometre | la route nationale | 'A' Class road |
| le moteur | engine | | |
| le pare-choc | bumper | | |
| le phare | headlight | | |
| le radiateur | radiator | | |

## 7 LE CHEMIN DE FER — RAILWAY

| **Masc.** | | **Fem.** | |
| le chef de gare | station master | la consigne | left-luggage office |
| le chef de train | guard | la correspondance | changing trains |
| le compartiment | compartment | la locomotive | engine |
| le contrôleur | ticket-inspector | la salle d'attente | waiting-room |
| le filet | rack | la sortie | way-out |
| un indicateur | timetable | la valise | suitcase |
| le passage souterrain | subway | | |
| le porteur | porter | | |
| le rapide | express | | |
| le wagon | carriage | | |
| le wagon-lit | sleeping car | | |

## 8 LES PAYS — COUNTRIES

| **Masc.** | | **Fem.** | |
| le Pays de Galles (gallois) | Wales | l'Angleterre (anglais) | England |
| le Danemark (danois) | Denmark | l'Écosse (écossais) | Scotland |

| | | | |
|---|---|---|---|
| le Portugal (portugais) | Portugal | l'Irlande (irlandais) | Ireland |
| le Canada (canadien) | Canada | l'Allemagne (allemand) | Germany |
| le Japon (japonais) | Japan | la Belgique (belge) | Belgium |
| les Etats-Unis (américain) | USA | l'Espagne (espagnol) | Spain |
| | | la Grèce (grec) | Greece |
| | | la Hollande (hollandais) | Holland |
| | | l'Italie (italien) | Italy |
| | | l'Australie (australien) | Australia |
| | | l'Afrique (africain) | Africa |
| | | la Chine (chinois) | China |

# GRAMMAR
# REFERENCE SECTION

**CONTENTS**

# GRAMMAR
# REFERENCE SECTION

This summary of the main points of French grammar does not make any claim to be complete. The purpose of this section is to provide a reference section for the grammatical points that are dealt with in this book. Readers wishing to extend their knowledge beyond the outline given here, should consult one of the grammars given in the bibliography.

## 1   THE ARTICLE

### 1.1 THE DEFINITE ARTICLE

**(a) Forms**
Masc.    le; l'  ⎫
Fem.     la; l'  ⎬ equivalent to English 'the'
Plu.     les     ⎭

**(b)** Some cases where French uses the article and English does not:
   (i) Before nouns with a general sense, for example: j'aime les enfants – 'I like children'.
   (ii) Expressing price, for example: soixante francs la boîte – 'sixty francs a box'.
   (iii) With names of countries and provinces, for example: la France; la Normandie (but not after en, for example: en France).
   (iv) With names of days of the week, when talking about habitual actions, for example: le lundi, je vais au bureau – 'on Mondays, I go to the office'.

### 1.2 THE INDEFINITE ARTICLE

**(a) Forms**
Masc.    un   ⎫ 'a', 'an'
Fem.     une  ⎭
Plu.     des    'some'

**(b)** As a general rule the indefinite article is used much as in English, but note the following cases where French does not use the article.

(i) After quel, for example: quel dommage! — 'what a pity!'

(ii) With cent and mille, for example: cent kilomètres — a hundred kilometres.

## 1.3 THE PARTITIVE ARTICLE

The partitive article is used to express a portion or undetermined quantity and may not be omitted in French.

**(a) Forms**

Masc.   du; de l'
Fem.    de la; de l' } equivalent to English
Plu.     des       'some', 'any'.

**(b) Examples**

Je voudrais du pain, de la farine, des cigarettes et de l'ail (garlic).

**(c)** The form of the partitive article becomes de in the following cases:

(i) when following a negative verb, for example: je n'ai pas de pain.

(ii) in expressions of quantity, for example: beaucoup de fromage; une bouteille de vin.

(But note that there are certain exceptions to this last rule, notably: bien des enfants — 'many children'; la plupart du temps — 'most of the time'; encore du pain — 'more bread').

## 2 THE NOUN

## 2.1 GENDER

All words in French are either of the masculine or feminine gender. Getting the correct gender is largely a matter of experience, and words should always be learned with their gender.

**(a)** The following are masculine:

   (i) Names of males and male occupations, for example: le père; le médecin.
  (ii) Languages, for example: le français
 (iii) Days, months, seasons.
  (iv) Metric system, for example: le mètre, le litre.
   (v) Nouns ending in -er, for example: le panier.
  (vi) Nouns ending in -al, for example: le cheval.
 (vii) Nouns ending in -ent, for example: un accident (but, la dent — 'tooth').
(viii) Nouns ending in -eau, for example: le tableau (but note two exceptions, la peau (skin); l'eau (water).
  (ix) Nouns ending in -eur, for example: le moteur.
   (x) Nouns ending in -acle, for example: le spectacle.

**(b)** The following are feminine:

   (i) Names of females and female occupations, for example: la mère; la vendeuse.

(ii)  Names of countries ending in -e, for example: la France.

(iii)  Nouns ending in -ace, -oire, -ière, -tion, -sion, -cion, for example: la glace; une histoire; la bière; la prononciation.

(c) Some words can be of either gender, and their meaning changes accordingly. The only words in this book with the possibility of either gender are: la livre − 'pound'; le livre − 'book'; la tour − 'tower'; le tour − 'tour'.

**(d) Formation of the feminine of nouns**
There are several possibilities:

(i)  The most common change is to add -e to the masculine form, for example: le marchand (merchant; shopkeeper); la marchande.

(ii)  Masculine nouns ending in -x change -x to -se, for example: époux; épouse (husband, wife).

(iii)  Nouns ending in -er change -er to -ère, for example: le boulanger; la boulangère.

(iv)  Nouns ending in -eur change -eur to -euse, for example: vendeur; vendeuse.

(v)  A few nouns ending in -teur change -teur to -trice, for example: conducteur (driver); conductrice.

(vi)  In a few cases the masculine form is used to refer to both male and female members of a profession, for example: le médecin, le professeur.

## 2.2 PLURAL OF NOUNS

**(a)** The general rule is to add -s to the singular form.

**(b)** Nouns ending in -x do not change in the plural, for example: les toux.

**(c)** Nouns ending in -al change -al to -aux, for example: le cheval (horse) les chevaux. (But note le bal − les bals (dances).)

**(d)** Nouns ending in -au, -eau, -eu, -oeu all add -x in the plural, for example: les châteaux; les jeux.

**(e)** A few nouns ending in -ou, add -x, for example: les bijoux (jewels).

**(f)** Note the irregular plurals: un oeil − les yeux (eyes).
  le ciel − les cieux (skies; heavens).
  le travail − les travaux (road works).

**(g)** With family names, there is usually no indication of the plural, for example: les Lebrun − 'the Lebruns'.

**(h)** Some nouns are used only in the plural, for example: les environs − 'the surroundings'; les frais − 'fees', 'expenses'.

## 3  THE ADJECTIVE

### 3.1  Formation of the Feminine

**(a)** The general rule is to add -e to the masculine form, for example: petit − petite. When the adjective already ends in -e there is no change, for example, jeune.

**(b)** Adjectives ending in -er, -ier change their ending to -ère, -ière, for example: léger − légère.

**(c)** Adjectives ending in -as, -eil, -el, -en, -on, double the final consonant and add -e, for example: parisien − parisienne; bon − bonne; bas − basse.

**(d)** Adjectives ending in -et change to -ète, for example: inquiet − inquiète.
**(e)** Adjectives ending in -f change to -ve, for example: neuf − neuve (brand new).
**(f)** Adjectives ending in -x change to -se, for example: jaloux − jalouse (jealous).
**(g)** Adjectives ending in -c change to -che, for example: blanc − blanche

## 3.2 FORMATION OF THE PLURAL

**(a)** The general rule, as with nouns, is to add -s to the singular form.
**(b)** Adjectives ending in -s, and -x remain unchanged.
**(c)** Adjectives ending in -eau add -x, for example: nouveau − nouveaux.
**(d)** Most adjectives ending in -al change to -aux, for example: égal − égaux (equal). But note the exception, final − finals (final).

## 3.3 POSITION OF THE ADJECTIVE

**(a)** The general rule is that the adjective in French follows the noun it qualifies.
**(b)** Certain common adjectives always precede the nouns, notably: beau, bon, gentil, jeune, joli, long, mauvais, petit, vaste, vieux.
**(c)** Certain adjectives *always* follow the noun, namely:
  (i) Adjectives of nationality, for example: une femme française.
 (ii) Participles used as adjectives, for example: une église connue.
(iii) Adjectives of colour, and other physical qualities ('shape', 'temperature' and so on), for example: un pantalon gris; un jour chaud.

**(d)** Certain adjectives vary in meaning according to whether they precede or follow the noun. Note the following examples:
un cher ami (a dear friend); un repas cher (an expensive meal)
le dernier jour (the last day); la semaine dernière (last week)
un grand homme (a great man); un homme grand (a tall man)
la pauvre femme (the poor woman − that is, 'unfortunate'); la femme pauvre (the poor woman − that is, 'penniless')
la seule solution (the only solution); une personne seule (a person who is alone)

## 3.4 COMPARATIVE AND SUPERLATIVE OF ADJECTIVES

**(a) Regular forms**

joli    plus joli − 'prettier'                le plus joli − 'the prettiest'
joli    moins joli − 'less pretty'            le moins joli − 'the least pretty'
aussi joli que − 'as pretty as ...'
... n'est pas si joli que − ...'isn't as pretty as'.

**(b) Irregular forms**

bon    meilleur − 'better'                    le meilleur − 'the best'
                                              (or, la meilleure, les meilleurs and
                                              so on)
mauvais pire − 'worse'                        le pire − 'the worst'

## 3.5 POSSESSIVE ADJECTIVES

**(a) Forms**

|  | Masc. | Fem. | Plu. |
|---|---|---|---|
| my | mon | ma | mes |
| your (familiar) | ton | ta | tes |
| his | son | sa | ses |
| her | son | sa | ses |
| its | son | sa | ses |
| one's | son | sa | ses |
| our | notre | notre | nos |
| your | votre | votre | vos |
| their | leur | leur | leurs |

**(b)** The possessive adjective agrees with the object possessed, and *not with the possessor,* thus sa table may mean 'his table', 'her table' and so on.

**(c)** All nouns beginning with a vowel or mute h take the masculine form of the possessive adjective, for example: son école.

## 3.6 DEMONSTRATIVE ADJECTIVES ('this', 'that')

**(a) Forms**

| **Sing.** | **Masc.** | ce, cet |
|---|---|---|
|  | **Fem.** | cette |
| **Plu.** | **Masc.** | ces |
|  | **Fem.** | ces |

**(b)** Cet is used before masculine singular nouns beginning with a vowel or h mute, for example: cet homme.

**(c)** The French demonstrative adjective can mean either 'this' or 'that'. If it is necessary to stress the notion of 'that one over there', in order to draw a contrast, -là can be added, for example: cette église-là.

## 3.7 INTERROGATIVE ADJECTIVE

**(a) Forms**

|  | **Sing.** | **Plu.** |
|---|---|---|
| **Masc.** | quel | quels |
| **Fem.** | quelle | quelles |

**(b)** The interrogative adjective is used:
(i) In the sense of 'which...?'; 'what...?' when these words qualify a noun, for example: Quelle est votre profession?
(ii) In exclamations, for example: Quel plaisir!; Quel dommage!

## 3.8 INDEFINITE ADJECTIVES

These are a group of various adjectives representing unspecified amounts:

**(a)** Chaque, for example: chaque année – 'every year'.

**(b)** Quelque, quelques, for example: je suis ici depuis quelques jours – 'I have been here for a few days'.

**(c)** Plusieurs, for example: Elle a plusieurs enfants – 'She has several children'.

**(d)** tel, telle, tels, telles, for example:
un tel accident – 'such an accident';
une telle personne – 'such a person';
de tels accidents – 'such accidents'.

**(e)** Tout, toute, tous, toutes, for example:
tout mon argent – 'all my money';
toute la famille – 'all the family';
tous les gens – 'all the people'.

## 4  THE PRONOUN

## 4.1 PERSONAL PRONOUNS

**(a) Unstressed pronouns**

| SUBJECT | DIRECT OBJECT | INDIRECT OBJECT | REFLEXIVE |
|---------|---------------|-----------------|-----------|
| je | me | me | me |
| tu | te | te | te |
| il | le | lui | se |
| elle | la | lui | se |
| nous | nous | nous | nous |
| vous | vous | vous | vous |
| ils | les | leur | se |
| elles | les | leur | se |

*Note* also: y – 'there'
en – 'of it', 'of them'

Unstressed pronouns precede the verb, for example:
Je la vois – 'I see her';
Il lui offre un verre – 'He offers (to) him a glass'.

**(b) Order of unstressed pronouns before the verb**

When there is more than one pronoun preceding the verb, they always appear in the following order:

| me | | | | |
|----|----|----|----|----|
| te | le | | | |
| se | la | lui | y | en |
| nous | les | leur | | |
| vous | | | | |

For example:
Je vous le donne – 'I give it to you';
Il n'y en a pas – 'There isn't any (of it)';
Elle la lui offre – 'She offers it to him'.

Note that where a verb is followed by a dependent infinitive, the pronouns precede the infinitive, for example:
Je veux le voir – 'I want to see him'.

**(c) Order of pronouns after the imperative**

Where the verb is in the imperative mood, pronouns follow the verb in the following order:

| | | | |
|---|---|---|---|
| le | moi | | |
| la | toi | y | en |
| les | lui | | |
| | nous | | |
| | vous | | |
| | leur | | |

For example:

Donnez-le-moi — 'Give it (to) me'.

Donnez-m'en — 'Give me some (of it)'.

Note that in the written form the pronoun is linked to the verb by a hyphen, and the following pronouns are similarly linked.

When the imperative is used in the negative, pronouns precede the verb in the normal way, for example:

Ne le lui donnez pas — 'Don't give it (to) him'.

**(d) Use of en**

(i) As can be seen from several of the above examples, en is used in French where no equivalent is required in English, for example:

Donnez m'en — 'Give me some (of it)'.

The same is true when en is used with numerals, for example:

Combien en avez-vous? or, Vous en avez combien? — 'How many have you got (of them)?'

J'en ai trois — 'I've got three (of them)'.

(ii) En is also used as a pronoun in cases where a verb is followed by a dependent de, for example:

Je me souviens de mes vacances — je m'en souviens.

Est-ce que vous êtes sûr de la route? — Oui, j'en suis sûr ('Yes, I'm sure of it').

**(e) Stressed (Disjunctive) Pronouns**

(i) **Forms:**

| Sing. | Plu. |
|---|---|
| moi | nous |
| toi | vous |
| lui | eux |
| elle | elles |

(ii) Use after preposition, for example: avec eux; sans moi.

(iii) Use in double subject, for example: Son père et lui vont à l'église.

(iv) Used for emphasis, for example: Moi, je n'y vais pas.

(v) Used to give a one word answer, for example: Qui est là? — Moi!

## 4.2 RELATIVE PRONOUNS ('who', 'which')

**(a) Forms**

SUBJECT — qui

OBJECT — que, qu'

The relative pronoun can not be omitted in French, as it often is in English.

**(b) Uses**

(i) As subject of a relative clause, for example:

l'homme qui me connaît — 'the man who knows me'.

(ii) As object of a relative clause, for example:

l'homme que je connais — 'the man (whom) I know'.

(iii)  After a preposition, when referring to people, for example:
la femme, à qui je donne la lettre – 'the woman, to whom I give the letter'.

**(c)** Use of quoi, for example:
De quoi est-ce que vous parlez? – 'What are you talking about?'
**(b)** Use of où in relative clauses, for example:
le parc, où elle se promène – 'the park where she goes walking'.

## 4.3 COMPOUND RELATIVE PRONOUN

**(a) Forms**
ce qui; ce que

**(b) Uses**
(i)  To translate 'what' as used in the phrase, 'Do you know what I mean?'
– Est-ce que vous savez ce que je veux dire?
(ii)  To translate 'what' in phrases such as, What amuses me, is . . . – Ce qui
m'amuse, c'est . . .

## 4.4 DEMONSTRATIVE PRONOUN

**(a) Forms**

|        | Sing. | Plu.   |
|--------|-------|--------|
| **Masc.** | celui | ceux   |
| **Fem.**  | celle | celles |

**(b) Uses**
This pronoun never stands alone. It is followed by:
(i)  -ci, or -là, for example: Voilà deux voitures; est-ce que vous préférez
celle-ci ou celle-là? (That is, 'this one' or 'that one'.)
(ii)  The relative pronoun, for example: Voilà deux maisons; celle qui est à
gauche est la plus jolie.
(iii)  The preposition de, for example: mon auto et celle de mon ami – 'my
car and my friend's'.

## 4.5 POSSESSIVE PRONOUNS

**(a) Forms**

|          | Masc.     | Fem.       | Plu.       |              |
|----------|-----------|------------|------------|--------------|
| mine     | le mien   | la mienne  | les miens  | les miennes  |
| yours    | le tien   | la tienne  | les tiens  | les tiennes  |
| his      |           |            |            |              |
| hers     | le sien   | la sienne  | les siens  | les siennes  |
| its own  |           |            |            |              |
| one's own |          |            |            |              |
| ours     | le nôtre  | la nôtre   | les nôtres | les nôtres   |
| yours    | le vôtre  | la vôtre   | les vôtres | les vôtres   |
| theirs   | le leur   | la leur    | les leurs  | les leurs    |

**(b) Uses**
The possessive pronoun in French agrees with the thing possessed and not with
the possessor, for example: cette maison est la mienne; ce sac est le sien.

# 5  THE VERB

## 5.1  VERB FORMS

### (a) Regular Verbs

|               | donner        | choisir            | attendre         |
|---------------|---------------|--------------------|------------------|
| PRESENT TENSE | je donne      | je choisis         | j'attends        |
|               | tu donnes     | tu choisis         | tu attend        |
|               | il donne      | il choisit         | il attend        |
|               | elle donne    | elle choisit       | elle attend      |
|               | nous donnons  | nous choisissons   | nous attendons   |
|               | vous donnez   | vous choisissez    | vous attendez    |
|               | ils donnent   | ils choisissent    | ils attendent    |
|               | elles donnent | elles choisissent  | elles attendent  |
|               |               |                    |                  |
| IMPERFECT     | je donnais    | je choisissais     | j'attendais      |
|               | tu donnais    | tu choisissais     | tu attendais     |
|               | il donnait    | il choisissait     | il attendait     |
|               | elle donnait  | elle choisissait   | elle attendait   |
|               | nous donnions | nous choisissions  | nous attendions  |
|               | vous donniez  | vous choisissiez   | vous attendiez   |
|               | ils donnaient | ils choisissaient  | ils attendaient  |
|               | elles donnaient | elles choisissaient | elles attendaient |
|               |               |                    |                  |
| FUTURE        | je donnerai   | je choisirai       | j'attendrai      |
|               | tu donneras   | tu choisiras       | tu attendras     |
|               | il donnera    | il choisira        | il attendra      |
|               | elle donnera  | elle choisira      | elle attendra    |
|               | nous donnerons | nous choisirons   | nous attendrons  |
|               | vous donnerez | vous choisirez     | vous attendrez   |
|               | ils donneront | ils choisiront     | ils attendront   |
|               | elles donneront | elles choisiront | elles attendront |
|               |               |                    |                  |
| CONDITIONAL   | je donnerais  | je choisirais      | j'attendrais     |

and so on, adding the endings of the imperfect to the infinitive of the verb.

|                     | donné   | choisi      | attendu   |
|---------------------|---------|-------------|-----------|
| PAST PARTICIPLE     | donné   | choisi      | attendu   |
| PRESENT PARTICIPLE  | donnant | choisissant | attendant |

### (b) Spelling variations in regular verbs

There are a number of verbs which are regular except that they undergo certain small changes in pronunciation and spelling. The most frequent are:

(i) The stem of the infinitive of -er verbs ends in c, for example: commencer. To maintain the soft pronunciation of c, it must be written with a cedilla before o and a, for example, il commençait, nous commençons. (See pronunciation section p. 245)

(ii) The stem of the infinitive ends in g, for example: manger. To maintain the soft pronunciation of g, it must be written ge before o and a, for example, il mangeait, nous mangeons.

(iii) The infinitive ends in e + consonant + er, for example: mener – 'to lead'. The e of the infinitive changes to è in all forms of the present tense except nous, vous, for example: je mène, but, nous menons. The same change occurs throughout the future tense, for example: je mènerai, nous mènerons.

(iv) The infinitive ends in é + consonant + er. The é of the infinitive changes to è in all forms of the present tense except nous, vous, for example: préférer – je préfère, nous préférons; espérer – j'espère, nous espérons.

(v) The infinitive ends in -oyer, or -uyer. In these cases, the y of the infinitive changes to i in all forms of the present tense except nous, vous, for example: employer – 'to use'; j'emploie, nous employons. The same change occurs throughout the future tense, for example: j'emploierai, nous emploierons.

(vi) Most verbs ending in -eler and -eter double the l and t respectively in all forms of the present tense except nous, vous, for example: appeler – 'to call', j'appelle, nous appelons; jeter – 'to throw', je jette, nous jetons. The same change takes place throughout the future tense, for example: j'appellerai; je jetterai.

## (c) Être and avoir

These are the most important irregular verbs, so it is worth giving their forms in full. (Forms for il and elle are the same.)

|  | Être | Avoir |
|---|---|---|
| PRESENT TENSE | je suis | j'ai |
|  | tu es | tu as |
|  | il est | il a |
|  | nous sommes | nous avons |
|  | vous êtes | vous avez |
|  | ils sont | ils ont |
| IMPERFECT | j'étais | j'avais |
|  | tu étais | tu avais |
|  | il était | il avait |
|  | nous étions | nous avions |
|  | vous étiez | vous aviez |
|  | ils étaient | ils avaient |
| FUTURE | je serai | j'aurai |
|  | tu seras | tu auras |
|  | il sera | il aura |
|  | nous serons | nous aurons |
|  | vous serez | vous aurez |
|  | ils seront | ils auront |
| CONDITIONAL | je serais etc | j'aurais etc |
| PAST PARTICIPLE | été | eu |
| PRESENT PARTICIPLE | étant | ayant |

## (d) Principal parts of other common irregular verbs

| INFINITIVE | PRESENT TENSE | PRESENT PARTICIPLE | PAST PARTICIPLE |
|---|---|---|---|
| aller = 'to go' | je vais, tu vas il va, nous allons vous allez, ils vont | allant | allé |
| s'asseoir = 'to sit' | je m'assieds tu t'assieds il s'assied nous nous asseyons vous vous aseyez ils s'asseyent | s'asseyant | assis |
| boire = 'to drink' | je bois, tu bois il boit, nous buvons vous buvez, ils boivent | buvant | bu |
| conduire = 'to drive' | je conduis, tu conduis il conduit nous conduisons vous conduisez ils conduisent | conduisant | conduit |
| connaître = 'to know' | je connais, tu connais il connaît nous connaissons vous connaissez ils connaissent | connaissant | connu |
| courir = 'to run' | je cours, tu cours il court, nous courons vous courez, ils courent | courant | couru |
| croire = 'to believe' | je crois, tu crois il croit, nous croyons vous croyez, ils croient | croyant | cru |
| devoir = 'to owe', to have to' | je dois, tu dois il doit, nous devons vous devez, ils doivent | devant | dû |
| dire = 'to say' | je dis, tu dis il dit, nous disons vous dites, ils disent | disant | dit |
| dormir = 'to sleep' | je dors, tu dors il dort, nous dormons vous dormez, ils dorment | dormant | dormi |
| écrire = 'to write' | j'écris, tu écris il écrit, nous écrivons vous écrivez, ils écrivent | écrivant | écrit |
| faire = 'to make', 'to do' | je fais, tu fais il fait, nous faisons vous faites, ils font | faisant | fait |
| joindre (+ rejoindre) = 'to join' | je joins, tu joins il joint, nous joignons vous joignez, ils joignent | joignant | joint |

| | | | |
|---|---|---|---|
| lire<br>= 'to read' | je lis, tu lis<br>il lit, nous lisons<br>vous lisez, ils lisent | lisant | lu |
| mettre<br>= 'to put' | je mets, tu mets<br>il met, nous mettons<br>vous mettez, ils mettent | mettant | mis |
| offrir<br>= 'to offer' | j'offre, tu offres<br>il offre, nous offrons<br>vous offrez, ils offrent | offrant | offert |
| plaire<br>= 'to please' | je plais, tu plais<br>il plait, nous plaisons<br>vous plaisez, ils plaisent | plaisant | plû |
| pleuvoir<br>= 'to rain' | il pleut<br>(only used in the 3rd person singular) | pleuvant | plu |
| pouvoir<br>= 'to be able' | je peux, tu peux<br>il peut, nous pouvons<br>vous pouvez, ils peuvent | pouvant | pu |
| prendre<br>= 'to take' | je prends, tu prends<br>il prend, nous prenons<br>vous prenez, ils prennent | prenant | pris |
| recevoir<br>= 'to receive' | je reçois, tu reçois<br>il reçoit, nous recevons<br>vous recevez,<br>ils reçoivent | recevant | reçu |
| savoir<br>= 'to know' | je sais, tu sais<br>il sait, nous savons<br>vous savez, ils savent | sachant | su |
| sortir<br>= 'to go out' | je sors, tu sors<br>il sort, nous sortons<br>vous sortez, ils sortent | sortant | sorti |
| tenir<br>= 'to hold' | je tiens, tu tiens<br>il tient, nous tenons<br>vous tenez, ils tiennent | tenant | tenu |
| venir<br>= 'to come' | je viens (like tenir) | venant | venu |
| vivre<br>= 'to live' | je vis, tu vis<br>il vit, nous vivons<br>vous vivez, ils vivent | vivant | vécu |
| voir<br>= 'to see' | je vois, tu vois<br>il voit, nous voyons<br>vous voyez, ils voient | voyant | vu |
| vouloir<br>= 'to want' | je veux, tu veux<br>il veut, nous voulons<br>vous voulez, ils veulent | voulant | voulu |

## 5.2 USES

### (a) Present tense

(i) The French present tense can be rendered in three possible ways in English, for example: je vais can mean 'I go'. 'I am going' or 'I do go'.

(ii) The present tense is used with depuis in sentences such as Il est ici depuis une heure − 'He has been here for an hour'.

## (b) Imperfect tense

The imperfect tense can be formed by taking the stem of the present participle and adding the endings already given in *5.1* above, for example: present participle, allant, of which the stem is all-, and the imperfect is therefore, j'allais and so on. Only two verbs in the language do not fit into this pattern of forming the imperfect, namely, avoir (j'avais) and savoir (je savais). The imperfect tense is used in the following circumstances:

(i) To describe a continuous action in the past, for example: Lundi dernier il pleuvait sans cesse − '... it went on and on raining'.

(ii) To describe a habitual action in the past, for example: Quand j'étais jeune, j'allais tous les jours à l'école − '... I used to go ...'.

(iii) To express description in the past, for example: C'était une grande maison, mais le jardin était petit.

(iv) After si (if) used with a conditional, for example: S'il venait me voir, je resterais à la maison − 'If he came ... I would stay ...'.

## (c) Future tense

The future tense is formed by taking the infinitive of the verb and adding the future endings already shown in *5.1* above:

There are a few irregular futures, notably:

| | | |
|---|---|---|
| être − je serai | faire − je ferai | tenir − je tiendrai |
| avoir − j'aurai | pouvoir − je pourrai | venir − je viendrai |
| aller − j'irai | recevoir − je recevrai | voir − je verrai |
| courir − je courrai | savoir − je saurai | vouloir − je voudrai |

As will be seen from many examples in the dialogues, there is a tendency in contemporary French to use the construction aller + infinitive instead of the future.

## (d) Conditional

The conditional is formed from the infinitive with the same endings as the imperfect. The irregular forms are the same as those given for the future. The conditional has two main uses:

(i) In conditional si clauses, for example:
Si j'avais assez d'argent, j'irais à Paris.

(ii) To express a polite form of request or statement, for example:
Je voudrais du pain, s'il vous plaît − 'I would like ...'.
Est-ce que je pourrais payer par chèque? − 'Could I possibly pay ...'.

## (e) Present Participle

The present participle has two main uses:

(i) Certain present participles are commonly found as adjectives, for example: charmant − 'charming'; fatigant − 'tiring'.

(ii) With a verbal function similar to the English present participle, for example: en passant − 'in passing'. French also uses the present participle where English might prefer a clause, for example:
En sortant du bureau, j'ai vu mon ami − 'As I was leaving the office ...' and so on.

(iii) Note that the only preposition which can precede the present participle is en. With other prepositions, French usage is different from English, for example:

avant de partir – 'before leaving';
après avoir vu – 'after seeing'.

### (f) Past Participle

The past participle is used to form the perfect and pluperfect tenses. Each of these tenses is formed by combining an auxiliary verb (être or avoir) with the past participle. Note the following points:

(i) *Auxiliary verbs*. The majority of verbs in French use avoir as the auxiliary verb, for example: j'ai mangé. A number of verbs use être as auxiliary, notably, all reflexive verbs, for example: je me suis levé, and verbs of motion, that is, aller, arriver, descendre, monter, partir, rentrer, retourner, revenir, sortir, tomber, venir. Note also devenir, 'to become'. When a verb takes être as its auxiliary, the past participle agrees with the subject of the verb, as follows: le père est revenu; la mère est revenue; les garçons sont revenus; les fillettes sont revenues. There is no agreement with the subject required when the auxiliary verb is avoir. Verbs with the auxiliary avoir only agree if a feminine or plural direct object precedes the verb, for example: je les ai vus.

(ii) *Perfect Tense*. This is formed by the forms of the present tense of the auxiliary verb plus the past participle. The perfect tense in French is used to convey both the sense of English past definite and English perfect, thus je suis venu might be translated 'I came' or 'I have come' according to context. Note these examples:

Quand est-ce que vous êtes arrivé en France? – 'When did you arrive . . .?'
Je suis arrivé la semaine dernière – 'I arrived last week'.
J'ai déjà écrit deux fois – 'I have already written twice'.

(iii) *Pluperfect Tense*. This is exactly equivalent to the English pluperfect, that is, it conveys the meaning of something that happened in the more remote past, for example:

J'étais déjà parti quand elle est arrivée – 'I had already left when she arrived'.
J'avais écrit la lettre avant de partir – 'I had written the letter before leaving'.

The pluperfect is formed by combining the imperfect of the auxiliary verb with the past participle. The rules for the use of être and avoir are the same as explained in (ii) above.

(iv) *Position of pronouns*. Note that in the perfect and pluperfect tenses the pronouns always precede the auxiliary verb, for example: je le lui ai donné; il leur a parlé; je lui avais donné le livre.

## 5.3 REFLEXIVE VERBS

### (a) Forms

The forms of reflexive verbs in the various tenses are identical with those already described for all other verbs, with the additional element of the reflexive pronoun, for example: je me lève; est-ce que vous vous souvenez? The forms of the reflexive pronouns are given in *4.1 (a)*.
Note the following points of usage:

(i) The imperative of reflexive verbs includes the reflexive pronoun, for example: levez-vous.

(ii) In the perfect and pluperfect tenses the auxiliary verb être is used, with agreement of the past participle as explained in *5.2 (f)(i)*.

**(b) Uses**

Note that although many reflexive verbs are equivalent to English reflexives, there are a number of French reflexive verbs which are expressed by a simple verb in English. The most common are:

| | | | |
|---|---|---|---|
| s'arrêter | to stop | se promener | to go for a walk |
| s'endormir | to fall asleep | se réveiller | to wake up |
| se lever | to get up | se souvenir de | to remember |
| se plaindre | to complain | se servir de | to use |

## 5.4 THE PASSIVE VOICE

**(a) Forms**

The passive voice in French is formed, as in English, by combining the tense of the verb 'to be' (être) with the past participle, for example:

ACTIVE    Le garçon ferme la porte

PASSIVE   La porte est fermée par le garçon

**(b) Uses**

This course has made little use of the passive voice, since it is not as much used in French as in English, and there are a number of ways in which its use can be avoided. that is:

   (i) by using the active form of expression, as in the example above.

   (ii) by using the pronoun on, for example:

Ici on parle français – 'French is spoken here'.

   (iii) by using a reflexive verb, for example:

Les oeufs se vendent au marché – 'Eggs are sold in the market'.

## 5.5 THE SUBJUNCTIVE MOOD

**(a) Forms**

The present subjunctive is formed by taking the stem of the 3rd person plural and adding the endings given below:

donner: 3rd person plural – donnent; stem + endings = donn +:

je donn*e*, tu donn*es*, il donn*e*, nous donn*ions*, vous donn*iez*, ils donn*ent*.

There are a number of irregular subjunctives, of which the most common are: avoir (j'aie); aller (j'aille, nous allions); être (je sois, nous soyons); faire (je fasse); pouvoir (je puisse); savoir (je sache); venir (je vienne, nous venions).

**(b)** The subjunctive is not widely used in modern French, and it can often be avoided, or else the forms of the verb are identical with the ordinary present tense. The only forms of use introduced in this book are the most common, thus:

   (i) after il faut que ..., for example: il faut que je m'en aille; il faut qu'il fasse son travail.

   (ii) after je veux que ...; je préfère que, for example: je veux qu'il fasse un effort.

   (iii) after bien que – 'although', for example: bien qu'il soit riche.

## 5.6 IMPERSONAL VERBS

These are verbs which are only found in the form of the 3rd person singular, in particular:

(i)  Il fait, to express aspects of the weather, for example: il fait beau; il fait froid

(ii)  other verbs describing weather conditions, for example: il pleut; il neige

(iii)  il est + certain adjectives, for example: il est nécessaire de partir; il est possible de voir
(it should be noted that there is a tendency in modern spoken French to use c'est instead of il est in such expressions).

(iv)  il y a – 'there is', 'there are'

(v)  il est in stating the time, for example: il est trois heures

(vi)  il faut – to express necessity, for example: il faut partir – 'we must leave', or 'I must leave'. Since il faut is impersonal, the expression can refer to any subject which is appropriate in context.

## 5.7 THE INFINITIVE

The infinitive, when it follows another verb, may stand alone without a preposition, or it may be preceded by à or de.

### (a) The infinitive used alone

(i)  After verbs of motion, for example: aller; venir. Je suis venu voir la maison; je vais fermer la porte.

(ii)  After certain verbs of perception, for example: écouter, regarder; voir. Je le vois venir – 'I see him coming'.

(iii)  After the following verbs used as auxiliaries: devoir (vous devez aller); faire; laisser; pouvoir; savoir; vouloir.

(iv)  After verbs expressing hope or belief, for example: croire; espérer. J'espère vous voir avant les vacances.

**(b)** The infinitive is preceded by à when following these verbs: apprendre à; commencer à; s'intéresser à; inviter à; se mettre à ('to begin'); penser à; se préparer à.
For example: Il apprend à nager – 'He's learning to swim'. Je vous invite à dîner chez nous.

**(c)** The infinitive is preceded by de when following these verbs:
continuer de; décider de; essayer de; finir de; oublier de. For example: Il a continué de travailler; j'ai oublié de vous le dire.

**(d)** The infinitive stands after the prepositions pour and sans, for example: pour aller à la gare; sans dire un mot.

**(e)** Note the following constructions:
Demander à quelqu'un de faire quelque chose, for example: Je lui ai demandé de venir – 'I asked him to come'.
Dire à quelqu'un de faire quelque chose, for example: Dites-lui de partir! – 'Tell him to leave'.

**(f)** Note the use of venir de + infinitive, for example: Il vient de partir – 'He has just left'.

## 5.8 MODAL AUXILIARY VERBS

Besides the common auxiliary verbs être and avoir used to form the perfect and pluperfect tenses, there are a number of other verbs commonly used as auxiliaries in conjunction with infinitives, notably:

**(a)** Aller, to express future intention, for example: je vais visiter la Normandie.

**(b)** Devoir, to express compulsion, for example: je dois bientôt partir. Note the English equivalents of the tenses of devoir:

| | |
|---|---|
| je dois | I must, I have to |
| je devrai | I shall have to |
| je devrais | I ought to, I should |
| je devais | I had to ('habitual', that is, 'I used to have to ...') |
| j'ai dû | I had to, I have had to, I must have |
| j'avais dû | I had had to |
| j'aurais dû | I ought to have |

**(c)** Faire, 'to make', 'to have something done', for example:
Faites-le parler! – 'Make him speak'
Il se fait couper les cheveux – 'He's having his hair cut'.

**(d)** Laisser – 'to let', 'to allow', for example: laissez-le entrer!

**(e)** Pouvoir – 'to be able', for example:
Est-ce que je peux sortir? – 'Can I go out?';
Je pourrai vous voir demain – 'I shall be able to see you tomorrow'.

**(f)** Savoir – 'to know about something', for example:
Je sais nager – 'I know how to swim'.

**(g)** Vouloir – 'to express wishes', for example: je veux partir demain. Note the use of other tenses, for example:
J'ai toujours voulu visiter la Normandie. Je voudrais du pain, s'il vous plaît – 'I should like ...'.

## 5.9 THE VERB AND ITS OBJECT

**(a)** Verbs requiring a direct object in French but used with a preposition in English:

| | | | |
|---|---|---|---|
| approuver | to approve of | écouter | to listen to |
| attendre | to wait for | espérer | to hope for |
| chercher | to look for | regarder | to look at |
| demander | to ask for | | |

**(b)** Verbs requring a direct object in English, but requiring à in French:

| | | | |
|---|---|---|---|
| convenir à | to suit | promettre à | to promise |

| permettre à | to permit | répondre à | to answer |
|---|---|---|---|
| plaire à | to please | | |

**(c)** Verbs requiring a direct object in English, but requiring de in French:

| s'approcher de | to approach | se servir de | to use |
|---|---|---|---|
| avoir besoin de | to need | se souvenir de | to remember |
| partir de | to leave | (for example: il part du port 'he leaves the port') | |

**(d)** Verbs requiring de in French but a different preposition in English.

| se moquer de | to laugh at |
|---|---|
| profiter de | to profit from |
| remercier de | to thank for |

**(e)** Some verbs require both a direct and an indirect object.

Demander — il demande un bonbon à sa mère — 'he asks his mother for a sweet';

Présenter — je vous présente ma femme — 'I introduce my wife to you'.

## 5.10 NEGATIVES

**(a)** When used with a verb, the following negative forms all have ne before the verb and the second part of the negative after the verb, for example:

ne ... pas — je ne le vois pas — 'I don't see him'.

ne ... plus — elle ne voit plus son ami — 'she doesn't see her friend any more'.

ne ... rien — je n'ai rien à déclarer — 'I have nothing to declare'.

ne ... personne — je ne connais personne à Caen — 'I don't know anyone in Caen'.

ne ... jamais — je ne suis jamais allé en France — 'I've never been to France'.

ne ... ni ... ni — chez l'épicier il n'y a ni pommes ni poires — 'at the grocer's there are neither apples nor pears'.

ne ... aucun — vous n'avez aucune raison de vous inquiéter — 'you have absolutely no reason to worry.'

From the above examples you will note:

(i) that in the perfect tense, the parts of the negative come before and after the auxiliary verb, for example: je ne suis jamais allé ....

(ii) that where there are pronouns preceding the verb, the negative ne comes before the pronouns, for example: je ne le vois pas.

(iii) It is also worth noting that the ne is very often omitted in everyday spoken French, though never in writing; for example, you will hear je sais pas — 'I don't know'.

**(b)** The negative forms may also stand alone, for example: rien — 'nothing'; jamais — 'never'.

## 5.11 INTERROGATIVES

**(a) Ways of forming the interrogative** (that is, putting questions)

(i) The direct form of statement is used, and the question indicated by the

rising intonation of the voice, for example:
  Vous partez aujourd'hui? – 'Are you leaving today?'
  (ii) The direct form of the statement is maintained but preceded by est-ce
que ..., Est-ce que vous partez aujourd'hui?
  (iii) The verb and its subject are inverted, that is, the order is reversed, for
example: Partez-vous aujourd'hui?
Inversion of the verb is not now very widespread in everyday spoken French.
  (iv) Note that in all the forms of questions given above, French can combine
the noun and the pronoun, in a way which would never occur in English, for
example:
  Il est déjà parti, le garçon? – 'Has the boy already left?'
  Est-ce qu'il est déjà parti, le garçon?
  Le garçon, est-il déjà parti?

**(b) Common interrogatives**
combien?    how much? how many?
quand?      when?
comment?    how?
où?         where?
pourquoi    why?
All these words can be followed by est-ce que or by inversion of the verb and
subject, for example:
  Pourquoi est-ce que vous partez?, or, Pourquoi partez-vous?
  Où est-ce que vous allez?, or, Où allez-vous?

**(c) Negative interrogative**
When putting questions in the negative, the usual pattern of forming the
negative is followed, for example:
  Est-ce que vous n'allez pas en France?
If the inverted form of the verb is used, the second part of the negative comes
after the subject pronoun, for example:
  N'allez-vous pas en France?
Note that when answering a negative question with a 'yes', French uses si
instead of oui, for example:
  Vous n'allez pas en France cette année? – mais si, j'y vais – 'Yes, on the
contrary, I am going there'.


# 6 ADVERBS

An adverb modifies a verb, an adjective or another adverb.

**(a) Forms**
  (i) The most common way of forming adverbs is to add the ending -ment to
the feminine form of the adjective, for example: heureusement – 'happily'.
  (ii) Adjectives ending in -ant and -ent, form adverbs in -amment and
-emment respectively, for example: constant – constamment, évident –
évidemment.
  (iii) Certain adverbs add an acute accent to the feminine e of the adjective,
for example: énormément; profondément.

(iv) There are a number of irregular adverbial formations, for example

bon — bien
gentil — gentiment
mauvais — mal
meilleur — mieux
petit — peu

**(b) Comparison of adverbs**

This is carried out in the same way as with adjectives, for example: plus heureusement.

Note the irregular form mieux — 'better', for example:

Il chante mieux que moi — 'He sings better than I'.

**(c)** In a few cases, adjectives are used as adverbs, for example:

| | | | |
|---|---|---|---|
| bref | in short | même | even |
| exprès | on purpose | soudain | suddenly |
| fort | loud(ly) | vite | quickly |
| juste | exactly | | |

**(d) Position of the adverb**

This can vary, but the main rule is that the adverb can never be placed between the subject and the verb as happens in English, for example:

Je le vois souvent — 'I often see him'.

# 7    THE PREPOSITION

## 7.1 COMMON PREPOSITIONS

| | | | |
|---|---|---|---|
| à | at; to | jusque | till; until |
| après | after | malgré | in spite of |
| avant | before (time) | par | by |
| avec | with | parmi | among |
| chez | at the house of | pendant | during |
| contre | against | pour | for |
| dans | in | sans | without |
| de | of; from | sauf | except |
| depuis | since | selon | according to |
| derrière | behind | sous | under |
| devant | in front of | sur | on |
| en | in | vers | towards |
| entre | between | | |

## 7.2 IDIOMS

It has been clear in previous explanations that prepositions can often not be translated by a single word, and that they are used differently in a wide variety of idioms. Below is a selection of such idioms, where translations of English prepositions could give problems.

| about | de quoi parlent-ils? | What are they talking about? |
|---|---|---|
| | vers quatre heures | about four o'clock |
| | il a environ 30 ans | he's about 30 |
| above | avant tout | above all |
| at | regardez l'heure | look at the time |
| | chez moi | at my house |
| | au travail | at work |
| | enfin | at last |
| | de toute façon | at all events |
| | surpris de | surprised at |
| by | près de moi | by me, by my side |
| | par hasard | by chance |
| | à propos | by the way |
| for | par exemple | for example |
| in = à | s'interésser à | to take an interest in |
| | à temps | in time |
| | au printemps | in spring |
| | à l'avenir | in future |
| | à la campagne | in the country |
| | au mois de mai | in May |
| | au lit | in bed |
| | au soleil | in the sun |
| | à Caen | in Caen |
| in = dans | dans quelques minutes | in a few minutes |
| in = en | en France | in France |
| in = de | à six heures du matin | at six o'clock in the morning |
| in not translated | le matin | in the morning |
| | l'après-midi | in the afternoon |
| on = à | à bicyclette | on a bicycle |
| | à pied | on foot |
| | au contraire | on the contrary |
| on = en | en voyage | on a journey |
| | en vente | on sale |
| | en grève | on strike |
| | en route | on the way |
| | en vacances | on holiday |
| on not translated | le onze mai | on the eleventh of May |
| to | écouter la radio | to listen to the radio |
| | trois heures moins dix | ten minutes to three |
| with | être content de | to be pleased with |
| | fâché contre | annoyed with |

# 8  CONJUNCTIONS

## 8.1 CONJUNCTIONS OF CO-ORDINATION

The following conjunctions have a linking or co-ordinating function in the sentence:

| | | | |
|---|---|---|---|
| mais | but | alors | then, so |
| ou | or | ou bien | or else |
| et | and | puis | then |
| donc | therefore | aussi | also |
| | | ensuite | next |

## 8.2 CONJUNCTIONS OF SUBORDINATION

The following conjunctions introduce a subordinate clause:

| | |
|---|---|
| comme | as, like |
| parce que | because |
| quand | when |
| pendant que | while |

pendant que    while   (Note the difference between pendant as a preposition, for example: pendant votre séjour; and pendant que as a conjunction, for example: pendant que vous êtes à Caen).

# 9  MISCELLANEOUS

## 9.1 NUMERALS

### (a) Cardinal numbers

| | | | | | |
|---|---|---|---|---|---|
| 1 | un, une | 11 | onze | 21 | vingt-et-un (une) |
| 2 | deux | 12 | douze | 22 | vingt-deux |
| 3 | trois | 13 | treize | 23 | vingt-trois |
| 4 | quatre | 14 | quatorze | 30 | trente |
| 5 | cinq | 15 | quinze | 31 | trente-et-un (une) |
| 6 | six | 16 | seize | 32 | trente-deux |
| 7 | sept | 17 | dix-sept | 40 | quarante |
| 8 | huit | 18 | dix-huit | 50 | cinquante |
| 9 | neuf | 19 | dix-neuf | 60 | soixante |
| 10 | dix | 20 | vingt | 70 | soixante-dix |

| | | | |
|---|---|---|---|
| 71 | soixante-et-onze | 82 | quatre-vingt-deux |
| 72 | soixante-douze | 90 | quatre-vingt-dix |
| 73 | soixante-treize | 91 | quatre-vingt-onze |
| 74 | soixante-quatorze | 92 | quatre-vingt-douze |
| 75 | soixante-quinze | 100 | cent |
| 76 | soixante-seize | 101 | cent un (une) |
| 77 | soixante-dix-sept | 200 | deux cents |
| 78 | soixante-dix-huit | 201 | deux cent un (une) |
| 79 | soixante-dix-neuf | 1000 | mille |
| 80 | quatre-vingts | 2000 | deux mille |
| 81 | quatre-vingt-un (une) | 1,000,000 | un million |

### (b) Ordinal numbers

| | | | |
|---|---|---|---|
| first | premier(-ère) | fifth | cinquième |
| second | deuxième | sixth | sixième |
| third | troisième | seventh | septième |
| fourth | quatrième | eighth | huitième |

| ninth | neuvième | twelfth | douzième |
|---|---|---|---|
| tenth | dixième | thirteenth | treizième |
| eleventh | onzième | | |

*Note* that onze, douze, treize, lose their final -e when adding -ième. All the ordinal numbers then follow this pattern, but note that in compound numbers such as twenty-first, premier is not used, for example: vingt-et-unième.

## 9.2 DATES AND TIMES

### (a) Days of the week

| lundi | Monday | vendredi | Friday |
|---|---|---|---|
| mardi | Tuesday | samedi | Saturday |
| mercredi | Wednesday | dimanche | Sunday |
| jeudi | Thursday | | |

All days of the week are masculine. They are written in French with a small letter, unless they begin a sentence.

### (b) Months of the year

| janvier | January | juillet | July |
|---|---|---|---|
| février | February | août | August |
| mars | March | septembre | September |
| avril | April | octobre | October |
| mai | May | novembre | November |
| juin | June | décembre | December |

All the names of months are written with a small letter in French. When saying 'in January', 'in May' and so on, you may either say en janvier, en mai, or au mois de janvier, au mois de mai.

### (c) Dates

(i) The first day of the month is referred to by the ordinal, that is, le premier juin − 'the first of June'. Other dates make use of the cardinal numbers in French, for example: le deux janvier; le cinq avril, and so on.

(ii) The year may be expressed in hundreds, for example, 1982 is dix-neuf cent quatre-vingt-deux; alternatively the word mil may be used, for example: mil neuf cent quatre-vingt-deux. (*Note* that mille is never used in dates).

### (d) Seasons

| le printemps | spring | au printemps | in spring |
|---|---|---|---|
| l'été | summer | en été | in summer |
| l'automne | autumn | en automne | in autumn |
| l'hiver | winter | en hiver | in winter |

### (e) Times

Quelle heure est-il? − 'What time is it?'

| (i) | Hour: | il est une heure | it is 1 o'clock |
|---|---|---|---|
| | | il est deux heures | it is 2 o'clock |
| | | il est midi | it is midday |
| | | il est minuit | it is midnight |
| (ii) | ½ Hour: | une heure et demie | half past one |
| | | midi et demi | half past midday |
| (iii) | ¼ Hour: | une heure et quart | 1.15 |

|  |  | deux heures et quart | 2.15 |
|---|---|---|---|
|  |  | midi et quart | 12.15 pm |
| (iv) | ¾ Hour: | une heure moins le quart | 12.45 |
|  |  | deux heures moins le quart | 1.45 |
|  |  | midi moins le quart | 11.45 am |
| (v) | Minutes: | une heure vingt | 1.20 |
|  |  | trois heures vingt-cinq | 3.25 |
|  |  | quatre heures moins cinq | 3.55 |
|  |  | cinq heures moins vingt | 4.40 |

(vi) Am/pm: the 24 hour clock is used extensively to avoid ambiguity, particularly with timetables and opening times. Otherwise 'am' is expressed by du matin, and 'pm' by de l'après-midi or du soir. Thus, 4.30 pm might be expressed as seize heures trente, or as, quatre heures et demie de l'après-midi.

## 9.3 ALPHABET

When spelling names and so on, it is necessary to know how the letters of the alphabet are pronounced in French.

The French names for the letters of the alphabet are as follows:
(See pronunciation section for information on the pronunciation of these sounds).

| a | a | n | en |
|---|---|---|---|
| b | bé | o | ô |
| c | cé | p | pé |
| d | dé | q | ku |
| e | é | r | er |
| f | ef | s | ess |
| g | gé | t | té |
| h | âche | u | u |
| i | i | v | vé |
| j | ji | w | double vé |
| k | ka | x | iks |
| l | el | y | i grec |
| m | em | z | zed |

## 9.4 COMMON ABBREVIATIONS

| cie | compagnie | company |
|---|---|---|
| dl | décilitres | decilitre |
| F | francs | francs |
| g | grammes | grammes |
| h | heure | o'clock |
| l | litres | litres |
| M | monsieur | Mr |
| Mme | madame | Mrs |
| Mlle | mademoiselle | Miss |
| MM | messieurs | gentlemen |
| No | numéro | number |
| ORTF | Office de Radio et Télévision Française | French Radio and TV |

| | | |
|---|---|---|
| PTT | Postes, Télégraphes, Téléphones | equivalent of GPO |
| RATP | Réseau Autonome des Transports Parisiens | Paris public transport |
| RSVP | répondez s'il vous plaît | please send a reply |
| qn | quelqu'un | someone |
| qch | quelque chose | something |
| SNCF | Société Nationale des Chemins de Fer Français | French Railways |
| TSVP | tournez s'il vous plaît | PTO (please turn over) |

# GUIDE TO PRONUNCIATION

It should be stressed that the following summary of rules for French pronunciation can only be a rough guide. The student should use this guide in conjunction with the cassette accompanying the course. The way to get a good French accent is to listen to the sounds and copy them, especially when they occur in sentences and phrases. This is because the rhythm and intonation of French phrases are quite different from the English. So you have to approach the pronunciation at two levels; firstly the way in which the separate vowels and consonants are pronounced; secondly the pattern of intonation in the whole phrase or sentence.

## SPELLING

The spelling of French, like the spelling of English, has not changed significantly over the centuries, while pronunciation has altered in many ways. The written form of the language therefore looks very different from the spoken form, and each sound can be spelt in a number of ways. In the table below, each sound is given its approximate value compared with English, and a summary of the ways in which you might expect to find it written. It should be stressed that the English comparison can only be approximate, and only listening to the tape or to other examples of spoken French will give you the exact sound.

## VOWELS

The main characteristic of French vowels is that each sound is pure, and does not 'slide' as happens in standard English. Compare the vowel sound in the words 'boat' and 'grass' as pronounced in BBC English and in North Country accents. The latter are pure in the sense that the vowel has a single sound. You would hear the same differences between the French word 'beau' and the English 'bow'. French vowels are all pronounced with more energy than English vowels, and more exactness – English vowels sound rather lazy in comparison. It is also the case that French vowels almost always keep their full value wherever they occur in the word. In the English word 'magnificent', for example, the stress falls heavily on the 'if' syllable, whereas the other vowels are much less prominent. The French equivalent magnifique gives each vowel its full value. (See more about this in the paragraph on stress). Because of these differences, the suggestions in the table below for English sounds which are equivalent to French sounds are bound to be only rough approximations. Listen to the tape to get them right.

| Approximate sound | Written forms in French | Examples |
|---|---|---|
| like 'a' in made | 1 é, ée, és, ées | été; poupées; écrire |
| | 2 ez | allez; chez |
| | 3 er (final) | aller; plancher (an exception is cher pronounced like 'share'). |
| | 4 ed, ied, ieds | pied; assieds-toi |
| | 5 ef | clef |
| | 6 et, es in monosyllables | les; mes; des; et |
| like 'e' in 'bed' | 1 è, ê | père; tête |
| | 2 ai, ei | palais; reine |
| like 'e' in 'perhaps' (but very much shorter) | e in unstressed position and in monosyllables with no other letter following. (Note that this vowel is the only exception to the statement made earlier that French vowels are given their full value. Often, when it occurs between two consonants, it disappears completely in pronunciation. The pronunciation of the examples above is therefore boul'vard; av'nue; méd'cin.) | le; te; de; que; boulevard; avenue; médecin |
| like 'a' in 'rack' | 1 a | cheval; ami |
| | 2 emm | femme |
| like 'a' in 'father' | 2 â | château; âge |
| | 2 as | pas; gras |
| | 3 ase | phrase |
| | 4 able | aimable |
| like 'o' in 'hope' | 1 o when final (consonant not pronounced) | dos; trop |
| | 2 au, eau, aux | autre; auto; beau |
| | 3 ô | côté |
| | 4 o followed by se, sse, tion | chose; grosse; émotion |
| like 'o' in 'lot' | followed by pronounced consonant | robe; comme; bonne |
| like 'u' in 'true' | ou | vous; chou; toujours |
| like 'ee' in 'keen' | i, î | fini; dîner |

There are some vowels for which not even an approximate pronunciation can be given because they do not exist in English. They are as follows:

u – Put your lips into position to pronounce 'oo' in English 'pool'. Now, keep your lips in that position and try to pronounce the sound of 'ee' in

English 'peel'. You will produce a sound which must not be allowed to slip into the English 'oo' sound, or the sound of the French ou listed above. Practise with sur, vue, plus.

eu — When followed by 'r' this sound is a little like 'ur' in English 'murder' (as in soeur, peur). When not followed by 'r' it is a very similar sound, but much shorter (as in feu, peu, deux).

## NASAL VOWELS

One of the most marked characteristics of French is the nasal vowel. Whereas with all English vowels, the sound is produced by a passage of air through the mouth, in nasal vowels some of the air comes through the nose as well. Compare the word 'say' as pronounced in standard English and as pronounced by an American. American English is more nasalised than standard English. Once again, the only good advice is to listen to the tape or to other examples of spoken French. In written French the nasal sound is always indicated by an 'm' or 'n' after the vowel. This 'm' or 'n' is not pronounced. It stands there only as a sign that the preceding vowel is nasal.

| Written form | Examples |
| --- | --- |
| in, im, ain, aim, ein | fin; main; faim |
| un, um | un; parfum; lundi |
| on, om | bon; mont |
| an, am, en, em | quand; camp (note that these two words are pronounced the same); |
| | lent; client |

Notice that the nasal quality is lost when the 'n' is doubled (for example, bonne is pronounced with the 'o' as in 'lot'), or when the 'n' is followed by a vowel (for example, in fini both vowels are pronounced like English 'ee').

## SEMI VOWELS

| Approximate sound | Written forms in French | Examples |
| --- | --- | --- |
| like 'y' in 'yes' | 1 i or y before a vowel | piano; pierre; yeux |
| | 2 -ill- in the body of a word | briller; travailler bouillon |
| | 3 il or ille at the end of a word | fille; feuille |
| | (There are a small number of exceptions when the final 'l' is pronounced, for example, mille; ville; tranquille.) | |
| like 'w' in 'wait' | 1 ou before a vowel | oui; alouette |
| | 2 oi, oy (pronounced 'wa') | oiseau; loi; voilà; trois |
| | 3 oin is the same sound as oi but nasalised | coin |

# CONSONANTS

The main characteristic to note is that the French consonants are not pronounced with such an escape of breath as the English ones. The 'p' in English 'pair' is pronounced with a puff of breath which does not occur in the French equivalent paire. The French consonants are thus more tense and precise in their pronunciation. As far as the written language is concerned you will already have noticed from the examples given when discussing vowels, that the final consonants in French words are hardly ever pronounced, for example you have already met the words dos, trop, palais, pied, and so on. In the pronunciation of these words you can ignore the final consonant. But the consonant is sounded if the word ends with a consonant plus e. Note the difference between vert (pronounced as though the t wasn't there) and verte (now the t is sounded).

In the list below, no further explanation is given for the consonants which are most similar to English (b, d, f, m, n, p, t, v), but even so you should remember that the sounds are not exactly as in English, and you should listen and copy.

| Approximate sound | Written forms in French | Examples |
|---|---|---|
| like 'c' in 'cat' | 1 c (before a, o, u) | Cannes; cognac; curé |
| | 2 k | képi |
| | 3 qu | queue |
| like 'g' in 'gate' | g (before a, o, u) | gare |
| like 's' in 'pleasure' | g, j (before e, i) | plage; gentil, jour |
| like 's' in 'save' | 1 s (initial and after nasal n) | santé; service; danser |
| | 2 c (before e, i) | ciel; ici |
| | 3 ç | française |
| | 4 ss | poisson |
| | 5 sc | scène |
| | 6 ti (in words ending tion) | émotion |
| like 'z' in 'zoo' | 1 z | gazon |
| | 2 s when between two vowels | chaise; chose |
| like 'sh' in 'shine' | ch | chéri |
| like 'ni' in 'onion' | gn | gagner; magnifique |

Among the other letters you will meet, note that, h is silent.

th is pronounced like 't' (for example thé)

x is pronounced 'gs' before a vowel (for example, examen)
'ks' before a consonant (for example, excuser)

w only occurs in words of foreign origin and is pronounced like 'v' (for example, wagon)

l and r offer particular difficulties.

l. This is a very different sound from the English, as you can see if you compare the English 'bell' and the French belle. In English the 'l' sound is pronounced with the tongue turned up and touching the ridge of the hard palate. In French the tongue is placed further forward so that it is touching the point at which the incisors meet the gums. Note also that l is one of the consonants that is nearly always pronounced when it is final − cheval. (Note however that the final l is not pronounced in the word gentil.) For the pronunciation of ill see the section on vowels.

r   This is perhaps the most characteristic sound of French, and the most difficult for foreigners to imitate. It is pronounced well back in the throat by bringing the soft palate down to meet the back of the tongue. The best way to explain it is to say that it is rather like the action of tongue and palate when gargling! Examples: jardin; grand; cri.

## LIAISON

As was stated above, final consonants are generally silent in French. But when the following word begins with a vowel or with a silent h the final consonant is usually pronounced together with the initial vowel which follows, for example, les_enfants; très_important; un petit_homme and so on. This process is called liaison. Note that there is no break of any kind between the words linked in this way. Each of the groups of words above sounds like a single word.

Although liaison is essential in the examples given, there are many cases where liaison might be expected but does not always occur in modern spoken French. For example you may hear je veux_aller or je veux/aller. This is again a question of listening to the tape and copying the examples given.

## STRESS AND INTONATION

It was pointed out earlier that English places a heavy stress on one syllable in a word (for example, 'magni*fi*cent'). French is characterised by a very even stress applied to each syllable, so that each vowel retains its full value wherever it occurs in the word. This is also true when words are grouped together, and it is also the case that the note of the voice is much more regular in French. In French ears, English has a sing-song accent, with lots of ups and downs of the voice. French retains an even accent and remains on a constant note until the voice drops at the end of the phrase. In Chapter 1, for example, you will find the statement: Vous_avez une chambre pour ma famille − 'You have a room for my family'. The voice does not vary its note until it drops on the syllable -mille.

# BIBLIOGRAPHY AND SOURCES OF INFORMATION

## 1  WORKS OF REFERENCE

### 1.1  GRAMMARS

(a) J. E. Mansion, *A Grammar of Present Day French* (Harrap and Co.)
(b) H. Ferrar, *A French Reference Grammar* (OUP.)

### 1.2  DICTIONARIES

(a) *Harrap's Concise French and English Dictionary* (Harrap and Co.)
(b) *Collins-Robert French and English Dictionary* (Collins and Co.)
(c) *Oxford Concise French and English Dictionary* (OUP.)

## 2  OPPORTUNITIES FOR HEARING FRENCH

Radio broadcasts from France may help to get the feel of the intonation and pronunciation of the language, but they will certainly be too difficult for learners at the early stages of French. The best source of opportunities for hearing French is the BBC, with programmes intended for adult listeners and for schools. ITV also broadcasts TV French programmes for schools.

### (a)  Adult Education Series (BBC)
  (i) *Ensemble*;
  (ii) *Sur le Vif*;
  (iii) *Allez France*.
This sequence of programme series for learners of French can provide many opportunities for listening. *Ensemble* is a series combining both TV and radio programmes, whereas *Sur le Vif* and *Allez France* are both radio alone. In addition to the programmes, BBC Publications market records and cassettes to accompany each course.
  (iv) *Get by in French*. This is a basic course in 'survival' French for travellers, and is also available on cassette.

**(b) Schools Broadcasts**

Although the timing of Schools Broadcasts will not be convenient for many adult students, it is worth noting that there are a number of series which could provide useful opportunities for supplementing one's chances of hearing spoken French.

   (i) BBC Schools TV series, *Dès le Début* and *Rendezvous France.*

   (ii) Schools Radio Series, *Salut les Jeunes*; *La Parole aux Jeunes*; *La France Aujourd'hui.*

   (iii) ITV Schools TV series, *Action Télé*; *Bric à Brac*; *Comment dit-on . . . ? La France telle qu'elle est*; *Au Travail.*


# 3  OTHER SOURCES OF INFORMATION ABOUT FRANCE OR THE FRENCH LANGUAGE

(a) Institut Français, Queensberry Place, South Kensington, London SW7.

(b) French Government Tourist Office, Piccadilly, London.

(c) French Railways, Picadilly, London.

(d) CILT (Centre for Information on Language Teaching and Research), 20, Carlton House Terrace, London SW1Y 5AP. The Centre offers an information service on all aspects of language learning, course materials and so on. There is also an extensive library where most current course materials, both book and audio materials, may be consulted.

# GLOSSARY OF WORDS INTRODUCED IN THIS BOOK

(The number in brackets refers to the chapter where the word is first introduced. SV refers to the Supplementary Vocabularies. Gender is indicated by *(m)* or *(f)* following a noun. (Parts of verbs, numerals and pronouns are not included.)

## A

| | |
|---|---|
| à | at **(1)** |
| d'abord | at first **(12)** |
| abricot *(m)* | apricot (SV) |
| absent | absent **(8)** |
| absolument | absolutely **(14)** |
| accident *(m)* | accident **(13)** |
| accompagner | to accompany **(14)** |
| d'accord | OK, agreed **(14)** |
| accueil *(m)* | welcome **(18)** |
| accueillir | to welcome **(19)** |
| acheter | to buy **(5)** |
| activité *(f)* | activity **(10)** |
| addition *(f)* | bill **(2)** |
| admettre | to admit **(15)** |
| adresse *(f)* | address **(13)** |
| adulte *(m)* | adult **(3)** |
| afin de | in order to **(16)** |
| africain | African (SV) |
| Afrique | Africa (SV) |
| âge *(m)* | age **(7)** |
| âgé | aged **(10)** |
| agent *(m)* | policeman **(1)** |
| agneau *(m)* | lamb (SV) |
| agréable | pleasant **(12)** |
| agréer | to accept **(16)** |
| aider | to help **(16)** |
| aimable | kind **(3)** |
| aimer | to like **(6)** |
| air *(m)* | appearance **(7)** |
| ajouter | to add **(18)** |
| allée *(f)* | drive **(10)** |
| Allemagne | Germany (SV) |
| allemand | German (SV) |
| aller | to go **(1;3)** |
| aller-retour | return (ticket) **(11)** |
| allô | hello (on 'phone) **(4)** |
| alors | well; then **(1)** |
| allumettes *(m,pl)* | matches **(9)** |
| s'améliorer | to improve **(19)** |
| ami *(m)* | friend **(7)** |
| amical | friendly **(19)** |
| amicalement | in a friendly way **(16)** |
| amitié *(f)* | friendship **(10)** |
| s'amuser | to amuse oneself, to enjoy **(5)** |
| an *(m)* | year **(8)** |
| ancien | ancient; former **(11)** |
| anglais | English **(2)** |
| Angleterre | England **(5)** |
| angle *(m)* | angle **(12)** |
| animé | animated, lively **(10)** |
| année | year **(7)** |
| anorak *(m)* | anorak **(5)** |
| à part | except for **(7)** |

| à partir de | with effect from (18) |
| apéritif *(m)* | aperitif (7) |
| à peu près | approximately (8) |
| s'appeler | to be called (1) |
| appétit *(m)* | appetite (4) |
| apporter | to bring (2) |
| apprendre | to learn (11) |
| après | after (4) |
| après-midi *(m)* | afternoon (4) |
| arbre *(m)* | tree (11) |
| arc *(m)* | arch (9) |
| argent *(m)* | money, silver (2) |
| arrêt *(m)* | stop (3) |
| s'arrêter | to stop (13) |
| arrhes *(f,pl)* | deposit (16) |
| arriver | { to arrive (7) / to happen (13) |
| article *(m)* | article (19) |
| ascension *(f)* | ascent (10) |
| aspirine *(f)* | aspirin (8) |
| s'asseoir | to sit down (7) |
| assez | enough (3) |
| assiette *(f)* | plate (7) |
| assurer | to assure, ensure (18) |
| attirer | to attract (10) |
| attraper | to catch (17) |
| aujourd'hui | today (4) |
| aussi | also (2) |
| Australie *(f)* | Australia (SV) |
| australien | Australian (SV) |
| auto *(f)* | car (10) |
| autobus *(m)* | bus (3) |
| automne *(m)* | autumn (16) |
| autoroute *(f)* | motorway (SV) |
| autour de | around (14) |
| autre | other (12) |
| autrefois | in the old days (15) |
| autrement | otherwise (14) |
| Autriche *(f)* | Austria (SV) |
| autrichien | Austrian (SV) |
| avant | before (7) |
| avantage | advantage (19) |
| avec | with (1) |
| aventureux | adventurous (15) |
| avenue *(f)* | avenue (4) |
| averse *(f)* | shower (16) |
| avion *(m)* | aeroplane (SV) |
| avis *(m)* | opinion (7) |
| avoir | to have (1) |

| avoir besoin | to need (13) |
| avoir faim | to be hungry (7) |
| avoir lieu | to take place (16) |
| avoir raison | to be right (7) |

**B**

| bagages *(m, pl)* | luggage (12) |
| baguette *(f)* | French loaf (9) |
| se baigner | to bathe (14) |
| bain *(m)* | bath (18) |
| balançoire *(f)* | swing (9) |
| balle *(f)* | ball (19) |
| banane *(f)* | banana (SV) |
| banque *(f)* | bank (2) |
| banquier *(m)* | banker (SV) |
| barbe *(f)* | beard (SV) |
| basilique *(f)* | basilica (4) |
| bassin *(m)* | dock (3) |
| bâtiment *(m)* | building (11) |
| bavarois | bavarian (18) |
| beau (belle) | beautiful, fine (6) |
| beaucoup | a lot, much (2) |
| bébé *(m)* | baby (SV) |
| belge | Belgian (SV) |
| Belgique | Belgium (SV) |
| besoin *(m)* | need (13) |
| beurre *(m)* | butter (9) |
| bicyclette *(f)* | bicycle (SV) |
| bien | well, good (1) |
| bien des | a lot of (14) |
| bientôt | soon (1) |
| bière *(f)* | beer (9) |
| biftek *(m)* | steak (SV) |
| bijouterie *(f)* | jeweller's (SV) |
| blanc | white (7) |
| bleu | blue (5) |
| boeuf *(m)* | beef (SV) |
| bois *(m)* | wood (14) |
| boisson *(f)* | drink (7) |
| boîte *(f)* | box, tin (9) |
| bombardement *(m)* | bombing (15) |
| bord *(m)* | edge, bank (6) |
| bordant | bordering (10) |
| bouche *(f)* | mouth (17) |
| boucherie *(f)* | butcher's (SV) |
| boucle d'oreille *(f)* | ear-ring (SV) |
| bougie *(f)* | candle, sparking-plug (18) |
| bouillir | to boil (18) |

bouillon *(m)* — stock **(18)**
boulangerie *(f)* — bakery **(17)**
boulevard *(m)* — boulevard **(10)**
bouquiniste *(m)* — bookseller **(10)**
bouteille *(f)* — bottle **(9)**
boutique *(f)* — shop **(10)**
boire — to drink **(9)**
bouton *(m)* — button (SV)
bras *(m)* — arm (SV)
brûler — to burn **(13)**
buanderie *(f)* — laundry **(9)**
bus *(m)* — bus **(12)**

**C**

ça — this, that **(1)**
(se) cacher — to hide (oneself) **(2)**
cadeau *(m)* — present **(2)**
caennais — native to Caen **(15)**
café *(m)* — café, coffee **(2)**
caisse *(f)* — cash-desk **(2)**
calme — calm **(15)**
se calmer — to quieten down **(8)**
camion *(m)* — lorry (SV)
campagne *(f)* — country **(15)**
camping *(m)* — camping (site) **(8)**
Canada *(m)* — Canada (SV)
canadien — Canadian (SV)
canard *(m)* — duck **(7)**
capable — capable **(19)**
capot *(m)* — bonnet (car) (SV)
caractéristique — characteristic **(15)**
carafe *(f)* — carafe, jug **(7)**
carrefour *(m)* — crossroads **(13)**
carte *(f)* — map, card **(12)**
casserole *(f)* — saucepan **(9)**
cathédrale *(f)* — cathedral **(11)**
à cause de — because of **(13)**
cela — this, that **(4)**
célèbre — famous **(11)**
centre *(m)* — centre **(10)**
ceinture *(f)* — belt (SV)
cerfeuil *(m)* — chervil **(18)**
cerise *(f)* — cherry **(20)**
certain — certain **(8)**
certainement — certainly **(2)**
chacun — each one **(17)**
chaise *(f)* — chair **(11)**
chambre *(f)* — bedroom **(1)**
chance *(f)* — luck **(6)**
changer — to change **(2)**

chanson *(f)* — song **(20)**
chanter — to sing **(20)**
chaos *(m)* — chaos **(15)**
chapeau *(m)* — hat (SV)
chaque — each **(2)**
charcuterie *(f)* — cold meats **(7)**
chargé — loaded **(11)**
charpentier *(m)* — carpenter (SV)
charte *(f)* — charter **(19)**
chasseur *(m)* — hunter **(18)**
château *(m)* — castle **(3)**
chaussette *(f)* — sock (SV)
chaud — hot **(6)**
chef de gare *(m)* — station-master (SV)
chef de train *(m)* — guard (SV)
chemisier *(m)* — shirt-blouse **(2)**
chèque *(m)* — cheque **(2)**
cher — dear, expensive **(9;14)**
chercher — to look for **(6)**
chéri — dear, darling **(7)**
cheveux *(m,pl)* — hair **(8)**
cheville *(f)* — ankle (SV)
chez — at house of **(1)**
chic — smart **(6)**
chirurgien — surgeon (SV)
choc *(m)* — shock, crash **(13)**
chocolat *(m)* — chocolate **(2)**
choisir — to choose **(8)**
choix *(m)* — choice **(17)**
chose *(f)* — thing **(7)**
chou *(m)* — cabbage (SV)
cidre *(m)* — cider **(9)**
cigarette *(f)* — cigarette **(9)**
ciel *(m)* — sky **(9)**
cinéma *(m)* — cinema **(10)**
circulation *(f)* — traffic **(19)**
cité *(f)* — city **(11)**
citron *(m)* — lemon **(11)**
classe *(f)* — class **(19)**
clef *(f)* — key **(1)**
climat *(m)* — climate **(5)**
coeur *(m)* — heart **(10)**
coffre *(m)* — boot (car) (SV)
cognac *(m)* — brandy **(12)**
coiffeur *(m)* — hairdresser (SV)
coiffeuse *(f)* — hairdresser (SV)
collants *(m,pl)* — tights (SV)
collègue *(m)* — colleague **(8)**
combien — how much? how many? **(5)**

| | | | |
|---|---|---|---|
| comme | like, as (5) | coup *(m)* | blow (10) |
| commencer | to begin (4) | courir | to run (14) |
| comment | how? (1) | court | short (8) |
| commissariat *(m)* | police station (16) | cousin(e) | cousin (SV) |
| | | couteau *(m)* | knife (9) |
| commun | common (19) | coûter | to cost (14) |
| commune *(f)* | parish, commune (19) | couvrir | to cover (18) |
| | | crayon *(m)* | pencil (20) |
| compagnie *(f)* | company (15) | cravate *(f)* | tie (SV) |
| compartement *(m)* | compartment (SV) | créer | to create (19) |
| | | crème *(f)* | cream (2) |
| complet | full up (4) | crêpe *(f)* | pancake (SV) |
| comprendre | to understand (8) | crevaison *(f)* | puncture (SV) |
| comprimé *(f)* | tablet (17) | cric *(m)* | jack (SV) |
| compris | included (2) | critiquer | to criticise (19) |
| concernant | concerning (16) | croire | to believe (6) |
| concierge *(m)* | caretaker (SV) | croissant *(m)* | croissant (9) |
| confiserie *(f)* | confectioner's (SV) | cuillère *(f)* | spoon (9) |
| | | cuillerée *(f)* | spoonful (18) |
| confiture *(f)* | jam (SV) | cuisine *(f)* | kitchen (9) |
| confortable | comfortable (11) | cuit | cooked (7) |
| connaître | to know (5) | cultivateur | farmer (6) |
| connaissance *(f)* | acquaintance (2) | culture | culture, farming (14;19) |
| connu | well-known (3) | | |
| conserver | to preserve (15) | | |
| consigne *(f)* | left-luggage (SV) | **D** | |
| construction *(f)* | construction (14) | dame *(f)* | lady (4) |
| construit | built (14) | Danemark *(m)* | Denmark (SV) |
| consultation *(f)* | consultation (17) | dans | in (2) |
| contact *(m)* | contact (19) | date *(f)* | date (16) |
| contacter | to contact (17) | davantage | more (17) |
| contestataire | argumentative (15) | de | of, from (3) |
| | | débarquement *(m)* | landing (4) |
| contraire *(m)* | opposite (12) | début *(m)* | beginning (11) |
| contrôleur *(m)* | ticket-collector (SV) | décider | to decide (14) |
| | | déclaration *(f)* | declaration (16) |
| copie *(f)* | copy (16) | décontracté | relaxed (15) |
| coq *(m)* | cock (7) | déjà | already (2) |
| cordial | cordial (19) | déjeuner *(m)* | lunch (2) |
| correct | correct (16) | déjeuner | to have lunch, breakfast (2) |
| correspondance *(f)* | changing trains (SV) | | |
| | | délicieux | delicious (7) |
| costume *(m)* | suit (SV) | demain | tomorrow (9) |
| côte *(f)* | coast (9) | demander | to ask (8) |
| côté *(m)* | side (10) | démarreur *(m)* | starter (SV) |
| à côté de | beside (11) | demi | half (2) |
| cou *(m)* | neck (SV) | demi-tarif | half-price (11) |
| coucher | to put to bed (12) | dent *(f)* | tooth (SV) |
| | | dentiste *(m)* | dentist (SV) |
| se coucher | to go to bed (8) | départ *(m)* | departure (16) |
| couleur *(f)* | colour (6) | département | department (14) |

| | | | |
|---|---|---|---|
| dépendre de | to depend on (6) | écolier (m) | schoolchild (15) |
| dépenser | to spend (20) | économie (f) | economy (14) |
| depuis | since (8) | écossais | Scottish (SV) |
| déranger | to disturb (5) | Écosse (f) | Scotland (SV) |
| descendre | to go down (13) | écouter | to listen to (9) |
| description (f) | description (8) | écrire | to write (14) |
| désirer | to want (2) | effort (m) | effort (14) |
| désolé | sorry (2) | église (f) | church (3) |
| dessert (m) | dessert (7) | élément (m) | element (19) |
| détail (m) | detail (16) | s'élever | to rise (14) |
| se détendre | to relax (14) | embarquer | to go on board (19) |
| devant | in front of (3) | | |
| devenir | to become (15) | embarras (m) | too many (18) |
| devoir | to owe, to have to (17) | emboutir | to bump into (13) |
| dévoué | devoted (16) | embrayage (m) | clutch (SV) |
| différence (f) | difference (19) | emporter | to take away (17) |
| différent | different (14) | employé (m) | employee (2) |
| difficile | difficult (14) | en | in (1) |
| difficulté (f) | difficulty (15) | enchanté | delighted (1) |
| dîner | to dine (1) | encombré | cluttered up (19) |
| directement | directly (14) | encore | yet, again (4;5) |
| direction (f) | direction (4) | endroit (m) | place (8) |
| discussion (f) | discussion (15) | énergie (f) | energy (15) |
| discuter | to discuss (20) | enfant (m) | child (1) |
| disposition (f) | disposal (7) | enfin | at last (9) |
| distingué | distinguished (16) | ennuyer | to bore (19) |
| docteur (m) | doctor (17) | s'ennuyer | to get bored (11) |
| document (m) | document (16) | énorme | enormous (6) |
| doigt (m) | finger (SV) | enrichissement | enrichment (19) |
| dôme (m) | dome (10) | ensoleillé | sunny (14) |
| domicile (m) | home address (16) | ensuite | next (7) |
| | | entente (f) | understanding (19) |
| dommage (m) | pity (4) | | |
| donc | therefore (8) | entr'acte (m) | interval (4) |
| donner | to give (10) | entre | between (7) |
| dormir | to sleep (12) | entrée (f) | entrance (3) |
| dos (m) | back (SV) | entrepreneur (m) | contractor (SV) |
| douane (f) | customs (17) | entreprise (f) | business, firm (15) |
| douche (f) | shower (9) | | |
| doux | sweet (17) | entrer | to enter (1) |
| droit | straight (3) | environ | approximately (3) |
| droite | right (3) | envoyer | to send (14) |
| durer | to last (17) | épicerie (f) | grocer's (9) |
| | | époque (f) | period (15) |
| **E** | | épuisé | exhausted (12) |
| eau (f) | water (17) | équivalent (m) | equivalent (15) |
| échalote (f) | shallot (18) | erreur (f) | mistake (18) |
| échange (m) | exchange (15) | escalier (m) | staircase (8) |
| écharpe (f) | scarf (12) | escalope (f) | cutlet (7) |
| école (f) | school (8) | escargot (m) | snail (7) |

| | |
|---|---|
| espace *(m)* | space **(11)** |
| espérer | to hope **(10)** |
| essayer | to try **(6)** |
| essence *(f)* | petrol **(18)** |
| Espagne *(f)* | Spain (sv) |
| espagnol | Spanish (sv) |
| estragon *(m)* | tarragon **(18)** |
| et | and **(1)** |
| États-Unis *(m,pl)* | USA (sv) |
| été *(m)* | summer **(6)** |
| étoile *(f)* | star **(9)** |
| étonner | to astonish **(13)** |
| étranger *(m)* | foreigner, stranger **(3)** |
| être | to be **(1)** |
| étude *(f)* | study **(15)** |
| étudiant *(m)* | student **(11)** |
| évacuer | evacuate **(15)** |
| évidemment | evidently **(10)** |
| évident | evident **(16)** |
| exact | exact **(6)** |
| excellent | excellent **(7)** |
| excursion *(f)* | excursion **(8)** |
| excuser | to excuse **(4)** |
| exemple *(m)* | example |
| expliquer | to explain **(20)** |
| expression *(f)* | expression **(16)** |
| extrait *(m)* | extract **(14)** |

### F

| | |
|---|---|
| en face de | opposite **(11)** |
| facile | easy **(16)** |
| facilité *(f)* | facility **(9)** |
| façon *(f)* | way **(10)** |
| facteur *(m)* | postman (sv) |
| faim *(f)* | hunger **(7)** |
| faire | to make, do **(1)** |
| faire des courses | to go shopping **(5)** |
| falaise *(f)* | cliff **(9)** |
| se familiariser | to get to know **(19)** |
| famille *(f)* | family **(1)** |
| fascinant | fascinating **(10)** |
| farine *(f)* | flour **(9)** |
| fatigant | tiring **(12)** |
| fatigué | tired **(10)** |
| il faut | it is necessary **(3)** |
| faute *(f)* | fault **(5)** |
| faveur *(f)* | favour **(19)** |
| femme *(f)* | wife, woman **(1)** |

| | |
|---|---|
| feu *(m)* | fire **(13)** |
| feuille *(f)* | leaf **(18)** |
| fier | proud **(15)** |
| fièvre *(f)* | fever **(17)** |
| figure *(f)* | face (sv) |
| filet *(m)* | rack, net (sv) |
| fille *(f)* | daughter **(8)** |
| fillette *(f)* | little girl **(6)** |
| fils *(m)* | son **(8)** |
| fin | fine **(12)** |
| fin *(f)* | end **(18)** |
| fini | finished **(6)** |
| finir | to finish **(15)** |
| flamber | to set alight **(18)** |
| flânant | strolling **(10)** |
| flèche *(f)* | spire, arrow **(3)** |
| flegmatique | phlegmatic **(15)** |
| fleuve *(m)* | river **(10)** |
| foie *(m)* | liver (sv) |
| fois *(f)* | time **(3)** |
| forêt *(f)* | forest **(14)** |
| formidable | terrific **(12)** |
| fort | strong **(7)** |
| fourchette *(f)* | fork **(9)** |
| fournir | to supply **(10)** |
| foyer *(m)* | home **(19)** |
| frais *(m,pl)* | expenses **(17)** |
| fraise *(f)* | strawberry (sv) |
| framboise *(f)* | raspberry (sv) |
| franc *(m)* | franc **(2)** |
| français | French **(7)** |
| France *(f)* | France **(1)** |
| frapper | to knock **(20)** |
| frein *(m)* | brake (sv) |
| fréquent | frequent **(10)** |
| fréquenté | busy **(10)** |
| frère *(m)* | brother (sv) |
| froid | cold **(18)** |
| fromage *(m)* | cheese **(7)** |
| front *(m)* | forehead (sv) |
| fruit *(m)* | fruit **(7)** |
| fuite *(f)* | leak **(18)** |

### G

| | |
|---|---|
| gagner | to earn, win **(18)** |
| galerie *(f)* | gallery **(10)** |
| gallois | Welsh (sv) |
| gant *(m)* | glove (sv) |
| garage *(m)* | garage **(18)** |
| garagiste *(m)* | garage owner **(18)** |

| | | | |
|---|---|---|---|
| garçon *(m)* | boy, waiter **(6)** | historique | historical **(14)** |
| garder | to keep **(17)** | hiver *(m)* | winter **(17)** |
| gare *(f)* | station **(10)** | hollandais | Dutch (sv) |
| garer | to park **(9)** | Hollande *(f)* | Holland (sv) |
| gauche | left **(3)** | homme *(m)* | man **(20)** |
| gelatine *(f)* | gelatine **(18)** | honneur *(f)* | honour **(16)** |
| gendarmerie *(f)* | police station (sv) | horlogerie *(f)* | watchmaker's (sv) |
| général | general **(8)** | hors d'oeuvre *(m,pl)* | hors d'oeuvre **(7)** |
| généralement | generally **(8)** | | |
| genou *(m)* | knee (sv) | hôtelier *(m)* | hotelier **(1)** |
| gens *(m,pl)* | people **(8)** | huile *(f)* | oil **(18)** |
| gentil | kind, nice **(1)** | huileux | oily **(18)** |
| gérant *(m)* | manager (sv) | humain | human **(19)** |
| gigot *(m)* | leg of mutton (sv) | | |
| | | | **I** |
| glace *(f)* | ice **(2)** | ici | here **(3)** |
| gorge *(f)* | throat **(17)** | idée *(f)* | idea **(3)** |
| goût *(m)* | taste **(17)** | île *(f)* | island **(11)** |
| goûter | to taste **(7)** | il y a | there is **(2)** |
| grand | big, tall **(3)** | il y a | ago **(13)** |
| grand'chose | a lot **(12)** | immédiatement | immediately **(12)** |
| grandiose | majestic **(10)** | impression *(f)* | impression **(8)** |
| grand-père | grandfather (sv) | important | important **(2)** |
| grand'mère | grandmother (sv) | inconnu | unknown **(8)** |
| gras | fat **(12)** | incorporer | to incorporate **(18)** |
| grave | serious **(2)** | | |
| grec | Greek (sv) | incroyable | unbelievable **(13)** |
| Grèce *(f)* | Greece (sv) | industriel | industrial **(14)** |
| grève *(f)* | strike **(2)** | infirmière *(f)* | nurse (sv) |
| grippe *(f)* | 'flu **(17)** | influence *(f)* | influence **(15)** |
| gris | grey **(8)** | ingénieur *(m)* | engineer (sv) |
| guerre *(f)* | war **(15)** | inquiet | worried **(8)** |
| guichet *(m)* | ticket-window **(11)** | intention *(f)* | intention **(8)** |
| | | intéressant | interesting **(3)** |
| guide *(m)* | guide **(3)** | s'intéresser à | to be interested in **(15)** |
| | | invasion *(f)* | invasion **(15)** |
| | **H** | invitation *(f)* | invitation **(18)** |
| s'habiller | to get dressed **(14)** | inviter | to invite **(5)** |
| | | irlandais | Irish (sv) |
| habitant *(m)* | inhabitant **(15)** | Irlande *(f)* | Ireland (sv) |
| habiter | to live **(15)** | Italie *(f)* | Italy (sv) |
| hâcher | to chop up **(18)** | italien | Italian (sv) |
| haricot vert *(m)* | French bean (sv) | | |
| haut | high **(10)** | | |
| hein? | isn't it? etc **(12)** | | **J** |
| hésiter | to hesitate **(7)** | jamais | never **(6)** |
| heure *(f)* | hour **(1)** | jambe *(f)* | leg (sv) |
| heureusement | happily **(6)** | jambon *(m)* | ham **(9)** |
| heureux | happy **(15)** | Japon *(m)* | Japan (sv) |
| histoire *(f)* | story, history **(15)** | japonais | Japanese (sv) |

| | | | |
|---|---|---|---|
| jardin *(m)* | garden **(3)** | livre *(m)* | book **(12)** |
| jardinier *(m)* | gardener (SV) | locomotive *(f)* | engine (SV) |
| jaune | yellow **(6)** | loger | to put up **(8)** |
| jeu *(m)* | game **(9)** | logique | logical **(7)** |
| jeune | young **(15)** | loin | far **(3)** |
| jeune-fille *(f)* | girl (SV) | loisir *(m)* | leisure **(20)** |
| joli | pretty **(6)** | long | long **(10)** |
| jongleur *(m)* | juggler **(10)** | longtemps | a long time **(11)** |
| jouer | to play **(14)** | longueur *(f)* | length **(19)** |
| jouet *(m)* | plaything **(19)** | louer | to hire, to let **(9)** |
| jour *(m)* | day **(1)** | lourd | heavy **(17)** |
| journal *(m)* | newspaper **(13)** | lumière *(f)* | light **(4)** |
| juge *(m)* | judge (SV) | lundi *(m)* | Monday **(16)** |
| jupe *(f)* | skirt (SV) | lunettes *(f,pl)* | (sun) glasses (SV) |
| jupon *(m)* | petticoat (SV) | (de soleil) | |
| jumelage *(m)* | twinning **(19)** | | |
| jumelé | twinned **(14)** | | |

| | | | |
|---|---|---|---|
| jus *(m)* | juice **(7)** | | **M** |
| juste | just **(17)** | magasin *(m)* | shop **(12)** |
| jusque | as far as; until **(4)** | magnifique | magnificent **(10)** |
| | | maintenant | now **(2)** |
| | | mais | but **(2)** |
| | **K** | maison *(f)* | house **(19)** |
| kilo *(m)* | kilo(gram) **(9)** | majestueusement | majestically **(14)** |
| kilomètre *(m)* | kilometre (SV) | malheureusement | unfortunately **(20)** |
| kiosk *(m)* | newspaper stand, kiosk **(20)** | manger | to eat **(3)** |
| | | manquer | to miss, to be lacking **(19)** |
| | **L** | marchand *(m)* | shopkeeper (SV) |
| là | there **(1)** | marché *(m)* | market **(8)** |
| là-bas | over there **(6)** | marcher | to walk **(10)** |
| laid | ugly **(16)** | mardi *(m)* | Tuesday **(16)** |
| laisser | to let, leave **(17;18)** | mari *(m)* | husband **(13)** |
| lait *(m)* | milk **(9)** | mariage *(m)* | marriage (SV) |
| laiterie *(f)* | dairy **(20)** | marinier | marine **(7)** |
| langue *(f)* | tongue, language **(15)** | maritime | maritime **(1)** |
| se laver | to wash **(8)** | marquis *(m)* | marquis **(14)** |
| légume *(m)* | vegetable **(9)** | marronnier *(m)* | chestnut tree **(10)** |
| lent | slow **(15)** | matériel *(m)* | equipment **(9)** |
| lettre *(f)* | letter **(14)** | matin *(m)* | morning **(4)** |
| se lever | to get up **(8)** | médecin *(m)* | doctor **(17)** |
| lèvre *(f)* | lip (SV) | médicament *(m)* | medicine **(17)** |
| librairie *(f)* | bookshop (SV) | se méfier | to beware **(15)** |
| libre | free **(1)** | meilleur | better **(7)** |
| limonade *(f)* | lemonade **(9)** | mélanger | to mix **(18)** |
| liquide *(f)* | liquid **(2)** | même | same **(4)** |
| lit *(m)* | bed **(2)** | ménagère *(f)* | housewife (SV) |
| litre *(m)* | litre **(9)** | mener | to lead **(11)** |
| livre *(f)* | pound **(2)** | menu *(m)* | menu **(11)** |
| | | mer *(f)* | sea **(6)** |
| | | merci | thank you **(1)** |

| | |
|---|---|
| mère *(f)* | mother **(20)** |
| mériter | to deserve **(14)** |
| en mesure de | in a position to **(16)** |
| météo *(f)* | weather forecast **(14)** |
| mètre *(m)* | metre **(3)** |
| mettre | to put **(17)** |
| mettre à la poste | to post **(14)** |
| midi *(m)* | midday **(2)** |
| mime *(m)* | mime **(10)** |
| minuscule | tiny **(6)** |
| minute *(f)* | minute **(2)** |
| mode *(f)* | fashion **(7)** |
| moderne | modern **(16)** |
| modiste *(f)* | milliner (SV) |
| moins | less **(3)** |
| mois *(m)* | month **(16)** |
| moment *(m)* | moment **(1)** |
| monde *(m)* | { world **(4)** / people **(6)** |
| monnaie *(f)* | small change **(3)** |
| mont *(m)* | mount **(18)** |
| montagne *(f)* | mountain, hill **(18)** |
| montée *(f)* | climb **(10)** |
| monter | to climb **(10)** |
| montre *(f)* | wrist-watch (SV) |
| monument *(m)* | public building **(3)** |
| mot *(m)* | word **(19)** |
| moteur *(m)* | engine of car (SV) |
| moto *(f)* | motorcycle (SV) |
| mouchoir *(m)* | handkerchief (SV) |
| mouiller | to wet **(18)** |
| municipal | municipal **(4)** |
| municipalité *(f)* | municipality **(8)** |
| musée *(m)* | museum **(4)** |

**N**

| | |
|---|---|
| nager | to swim **(14)** |
| naissance *(f)* | birth **(16)** |
| national | national **(15)** |
| nationalité *(f)* | nationality **(16)** |
| neuf | brand new **(11)** |
| neveu *(m)* | nephew (SV) |
| nez *(m)* | nose (SV) |
| nièce *(f)* | niece (SV) |
| niveau *(m)* | level **(18)** |
| noir | black **(19)** |

| | |
|---|---|
| nom *(m)* | name **(8)** |
| nombreux | numerous **(10)** |
| nord *(m)* | north **(15)** |
| normal | normal **(6)** |
| normand | Norman **(7)** |
| notaire *(m)* | solicitor (SV) |
| note *(f)* | note, mark at school, bill **(18)** |
| nouveau | new **(16)** |
| nuit *(f)* | night **(12)** |
| numéro *(m)* | number **(1)** |

**O**

| | |
|---|---|
| oblitérer | cancel (ticket) **(3)** |
| occuper | to occupy **(20)** |
| oeil *(m)* | eye (SV) |
| les yeux *(pl)* | |
| oeuf *(m)* | egg **(7)** |
| officiel | official **(3)** |
| offrir | to offer **(10)** |
| omelette *(f)* | omelette **(7)** |
| on | one **(6)** |
| oncle *(m)* | uncle (SV) |
| optimiste *(m)* | optimist **(5)** |
| orage *(m)* | storm **(14)** |
| orange *(f)* | orange **(7)** |
| ordinaire | ordinary **(18)** |
| ordonnance *(f)* | prescription **(17)** |
| ordre *(m)* | order **(18)** |
| oreille *(f)* | ear (SV) |
| origine *(f)* | origin **(11)** |
| ou | or **(2)** |
| où | where **(3)** |
| oublier | to forget **(3)** |
| oui | yes **(1)** |
| ouverture | opening **(4)** |
| ouvrier | workman (SV) |

**P**

| | |
|---|---|
| palais *(m)* | palace **(11)** |
| pain *(m)* | bread **(9)** |
| paisible | peaceful **(15)** |
| panier *(m)* | basket **(17)** |
| panne *(f)* | breakdown **(18)** |
| pantalon *(m)* | trousers **(8)** |
| panorama *(m)* | panorama **(10)** |
| papeterie *(f)* | stationer's **(20)** |
| paquet *(m)* | packet **(9)** |
| par | by **(6)** |
| parapluie *(m)* | umbrella (SV) |
| pardessus *(m)* | overcoat (SV) |

| | | | |
|---|---|---|---|
| pareil | similar (15) | phare *(m)* | headlight (SV) |
| paraître | to appear (14) | pharmacie *(f)* | chemist's (17) |
| parce que | because (2) | pied *(m)* | foot (3) |
| pardon | excuse me (1) | pile *(f)* | battery (SV) |
| pare-brise *(m)* | windscreen (SV) | piquenique *(m)* | picnic (12) |
| pare-choc *(m)* | bumper (SV) | piscine *(f)* | swimming-pool (4) |
| parfois | sometimes (10) | | |
| parfum *(m)* | perfume (2) | place *(f)* | square (3) / seat (4) |
| parler | to speak (8) | | |
| partager | to share (19) | plage *(f)* | beach (6) |
| partie *(f)* | part (10) | se plaindre | to complain (6) |
| partir | to leave (10) | plaine *(f)* | plain (14) |
| partout | everywhere (15) | plaisir *(m)* | pleasure (1) |
| passage *(m)* (souterrain) | (underground) passage (SV) | plaire | to please (7) |
| | | plan *(m)* | plan (3) |
| passager *(m)* | passenger (17) | plante *(f)* | plant (3) |
| passeport *(m)* | passport (1) | plaque *(f)* | number-plate (SV) |
| passer | to pass (2) | plat | flat (7) |
| se passer | to happen (15) | plateau *(m)* | tray (7) |
| pâté *(m)* | pâté (7) | plein | full (16) |
| patiemment | patiently (7) | pleut | rains (6) |
| pâtisserie *(f)* | cake-shop (SV) | plombier *(m)* | plumber (SV) |
| patron *(m)* | owner, boss (SV) | plus | more (4) |
| pâturage *(m)* | pasture (14) | plusieurs | several (14) |
| pauvre | poor (17) | pneu *(m)* | tyre (18) |
| payer | to pay (6) | poche *(f)* | pocket (SV) |
| pays *(m)* | country (SV) | poisson *(m)* | fish (18) |
| Pays de Galles | Wales (SV) | poissonnerie *(f)* | fishmonger's (SV) |
| paysage *(m)* | landscape (10) | poitrine *(f)* | chest (SV) |
| pêche *(f)* | peach (SV) | poivre *(m)* | pepper (7) |
| pêcheur *(m)* | fisherman (SV) | poivrer | to add pepper (18) |
| pendant | during (8) | | |
| se perdre | to lose oneself (8) | police *(f)* | police (8) |
| | | pomme de terre *(f)* | potato (9) |
| perdu | lost (8) | | |
| père *(m)* | father (20) | pommier *(m)* | apple-tree (14) |
| période *(f)* | period (15) | pompier *(m)* | fireman (SV) |
| personne *(f)* | person; nobody (9) | pont *(m)* | bridge (10) |
| | | porc *(m)* | pig, pork (SV) |
| personnel *(m)* | staff (2) | port *(m)* | port (2) |
| personnel | personal (16) | port *(m)* | postage (19) |
| personnellement | personally (13) | portefeuille *(m)* | wallet (SV) |
| | | porter | to carry, wear (6) |
| petit | little (2) | porteur *(m)* | porter (SV) |
| petit-déjeuner *(m)* | breakfast (5) | portion *(f)* | portion (7) |
| petit-pain *(m)* | bread-roll (17) | portugais | portuguese (SV) |
| petits-pois *(m,pl)* | green peas (SV) | Portugal | Portugal (SV) |
| peu | (a) little (6) | poser | to put a question (13) |
| peuple *(m)* | people (19) | | to place |
| peut-être | perhaps (6) | possible | possible (6) |

| | | | |
|---|---|---|---|
| possibilité *(f)* | possibility **(14)** | quand | when **(4)** |
| postal | postal **(12)** | quand même | nevertheless **(6)** |
| poste *(f)* | post office **(14)** | quant à | as for **(19)** |
| poulet *(m)* | chicken **(18)** | quart *(m)* | quarter **(4)** |
| pour | for **(1)** | quartier *(m)* | district **(7)** |
| pourquoi | why **(2)** | quel? | what? which? **(2)** |
| poursuivre | to pursue **(15)** | quelque(s) | some **(5)** |
| pouvoir | to be able **(1)** | quelque chose | something **(7)** |
| pré *(m)* | meadow **(14)** | quelquefois | sometimes **(5)** |
| préfecture *(f)* | police HQ **(11)** | qu'est-ce que? | what? **(2)** |
| préférable | preferable **(6)** | question *(f)* | question **(8)** |
| préférence *(f)* | preference **(12)** | quincaillerie *(f)* | hardware store |
| préférer | to prefer **(2)** | quitter | (SV) |
| premier | first **(3)** | | |
| prendre | to take **(2)** | | |
| prénom | first name **(8)** | | **R** |
| près de | near **(3)** | race *(f)* | race **(15)** |
| présenter | to present **(1)** | raison *(f)* | reason **(13)** |
| presque | almost **(12)** | radiateur *(m)* | radiator (SV) |
| pressé | { in a hurry **(8)** | rapide | quick, swift |
| | { pressed **(11)** | rapide *(m)* | express train (SV) |
| pression *(f)* | pressure **(18)** | ravi | delighted **(5)** |
| prêt | ready **(2)** | rayon *(m)* | department **(6)** |
| prévoir | to have in mind | rebâtir | to rebuild **(15)** |
| | **(5)** | recevoir | to receive **(19)** |
| prévu | foreseen **(12)** | recommander | to recommend |
| prier | to request, pray | | **(14)** |
| | **(16)** | recommencer | to begin again |
| primaire | primary **(15)** | | **(16)** |
| printemps *(m)* | spring **(17)** | reconnaissant | grateful **(19)** |
| probablement | probably **(11)** | reconnaître | to recognise **(8)** |
| problème *(m)* | problem **(2)** | reconstruction *(f)* | rebuilding **(15)** |
| prochain | next **(11)** | rédacteur *(m)* | newspaper editor |
| professeur *(m)* | teacher **(8)** | | (SV) |
| profession *(f)* | profession **(8)** | rédiger | to draw up a |
| profiter | to take | | document **(16)** |
| | advantage of | réfléchir | to reflect **(19)** |
| | **(16)** | regarder | to look (at) **(6)** |
| promenade *(f)* | walk, ride **(10)** | région *(f)* | region **(7)** |
| se promener | to go for a walk | régional | regional **(15)** |
| | **(8)** | réglé | settled **(2)** |
| prononcer | to pronounce | regretter | to regret, be |
| | **(19)** | | sorry **(2)** |
| proposer | to suggest **(14)** | régulier | regular **(10)** |
| provision *(f)* | provision **(17)** | rejoindre | to rejoin **(12)** |
| prune *(f)* | plum (SV) | remarquer | to notice **(14)** |
| puis | then **(10)** | rembourser | to reimburse **(19)** |
| pullover *(m)* | pullover **(6)** | remettre | to put back **(19)** |
| | | remonter | to go up **(10)** |
| | **Q** | remplir | to fill **(16)** |
| quai *(m)* | platform, **(11)** | rencontre *(f)* | meeting **(18)** |
| | quay **(5)** | rencontrer | to meet **(19)** |

| | | | |
|---|---|---|---|
| rendre | to make (12) | **S** | |
| rendre visite | to pay a visit (16) | sac *(m)* | bag (9) |
| rentrée *(f)* | return (19) | sac à main *(m)* | handbag (SV) |
| rentrer | to return (home) (8) | sacré | holy (10) |
| | | saignant | bloody, rare (7) |
| renseignements *(m,pl)* | information (3) | sale | dirty (18) |
| | | saler | to make dirty (18) |
| renvoyer | to send back (16) | | |
| réparer | to repair (19) | salle *(f)* | room (9) |
| réparation *(f)* | repair (19) | salon *(m)* | sitting-room (8) |
| repas *(m)* | meal (7) | sandwich *(m)* | sandwich (12) |
| répondre | to answer (8) | sans | without (12) |
| se reposer | to rest (8) | satisfaire | to satisfy (14) |
| reprendre | to take again (12) | satisfait | satisfied (8) |
| | | sauce *(f)* | sauce, gravy (18) |
| représentation *(f)* | production (theatre) (4) | sauf | except for (4) |
| | | sauter | to jump (18) |
| réserver | to reserve (9) | savoir | to know (3) |
| résoudre | to resolve (15) | scolaire | educational (15) |
| ressembler | to resemble (14) | seconde | second (17) |
| rester | to remain (1) | secondaire | secondary (8) |
| retard *(m)* | delay (13) | secrétaire | secretary (1) |
| retour *(m)* | return (10) | section *(f)* | section (16) |
| retourner | to return (10) | séjour *(m)* | stay (1) |
| se retrouver | to meet up (14) | sel *(m)* | salt (18) |
| réussi | successful (18) | semaine *(f)* | week (1) |
| réussite *(f)* | success (19) | sentiment *(m)* | feeling (16) |
| se réveiller | to wake up (8) | se sentir | to feel (19) |
| révéler | to reveal (19) | sérieux | serious (17) |
| revenir | to return (10) | serveuse *(f)* | waitress (2) |
| revoir | to see again (1) | service *(m)* | service (2) |
| rhume *(m)* | head cold (17) | seul | alone, only (7;14) |
| rhythme *(m)* | rhythm (15) | | |
| richesse *(f)* | wealth (18) | seulement | only (3) |
| rien | nothing (6) | short *(m)* | shorts (SV) |
| rivage *(m)* | bank of river (13) | si | if (2) |
| | | si | yes (6) |
| rivière *(f)* | river (4) | siècle *(m)* | century (14) |
| riz *(m)* | rice (SV) | siège *(m)* | seat (17) |
| robe *(f)* | dress (SV) | signaler | to point out (19) |
| roi *(m)* | king (7) | signature *(f)* | signature (16) |
| romain | Roman (15) | signer | to sign (19) |
| rond-point *(m)* | roundabout (10) | silhouette *(f)* | silhouette (10) |
| roue (de rechange) *(f)* | (spare) wheel (SV) | similaire | similar (19) |
| | | simplement | simply (7) |
| rouler | to drive, travel (14) | sirop *(m)* | cough medicine (17) |
| route *(f)* | road (14) | situer | to situate (11) |
| rue *(f)* | street (3) | snack *(m)* | snack (19) |
| ruine *(f)* | ruin (15) | sobriété *(f)* | sobriety, simplicity (14) |
| russe | Russian (SV) | | |

| | |
|---|---|
| soeur *(f)* | sister (sv) |
| soie *(f)* | silk (19) |
| soir *(m)* | evening (1) |
| soleil *(m)* | sun (6) |
| sommet *(m)* | top, peak (10) |
| sondage *(m)* | public opinion poll (8) |
| sorte | sort (9) |
| sortir | to leave, go out (13) |
| soudain | suddenly (16) |
| soufflé *(m)* | soufflé (18) |
| soulager | to comfort (17) |
| soulier *(m)* | shoe (18) |
| soupe *(f)* | soup (18) |
| sous | under (11) |
| souvent | often (8) |
| souvenir *(m)* | memory, souvenir (12) |
| se souvenir de | to remember (18) |
| spectacle *(m)* | show, spectacle (4) |
| steak *(m)* | steak (7) |
| sucre *(m)* | sugar (18) |
| sud *(m)* | south (14) |
| Suisse *(f)* | Switzerland (18) |
| suite *(f)* | continuation (16) |
| suivre | to follow (3) |
| sujet *(m)* | subject (15) |
| super *(m)* | 4 star petrol (18) |
| supermarché *(m)* | supermarket (17) |
| supposer | to suppose (14) |
| sur | on (3) |
| sûr | sure (8) |
| sûrement | surely, certainly (8) |
| surtout | above all (3) |
| symptôme *(m)* | symptom (17) |
| système *(m)* | system (2) |

## T

| | |
|---|---|
| tabac *(m)* | tobacco (shop) (20) |
| taille *(f)* | size, waist (6) |
| tailleur *(m)* | tailor (sv) |
| tante *(f)* | aunt (sv) |
| tard | late (4) |
| tapisserie *(f)* | tapestry (14) |
| tarif *(m)* | scale of charges (16) |
| taxe *(f)* | tax (18) |

| | |
|---|---|
| tellement | so (8) so many, so much |
| temps *(m)* | weather, time (1) |
| tente *(f)* | tent (9) |
| (se) terminer | to finish (18) |
| terrasse *(f)* | pavement café (2) |
| terre *(f)* | earth (8) |
| tête *(f)* | head (17) |
| thé *(m)* | tea (8) |
| thermomètre *(m)* | thermometer (17) |
| timbre *(m)* | stamp (14) |
| tirer | to pull (17) |
| tomate *(f)* | tomato (17) |
| tomber | to fall (18) |
| toucher à | to come to, reach (16) |
| toujours | always (8) |
| tour *(m)* | tour, trip (6) |
| tour *(f)* | tower (10) |
| touriste *(m)* | tourist (11) |
| tout | all, everything (2) |
| tous | everybody (5) |
| toux *(f)* | cough (17) |
| tousser | to cough (17) |
| train *(m)* | train (10) |
| tranche *(f)* | slice (9) |
| transport *(m)* | transport (15) |
| traverser | to cross (3) |
| travailler | to work (15) |
| travail *(m)* | work (16) |
| très | very (1) |
| triomphe *(m)* | triumph (10) |
| tripes *(f,pl)* | tripe (7) |
| trop | too much (6) |
| trouver | to find (6) |
| se trouver | to be located (11) |
| truc *(m)* | whatsit (12) |
| typique | typical (10) |

## U

| | |
|---|---|
| unique | unique, only (14) |
| universellement | universally (10) |
| université *(f)* | university (11) |
| URSS *(m)* | USSR (sv) |
| ustensile *(f)* | utensil (9) |

## V

| | |
|---|---|
| vacances *(f,pl)* | holidays (8) |
| vache *(f)* | cow (14) |

| | | | |
|---|---|---|---|
| valise *(f)* | suitcase (sv) | visage *(m)* | face (sv) |
| vallée *(f)* | valley **(18)** | vite | quick **(6)** |
| valoir | to be worth **(18)** | vitesse *(f)* | speed **(16)** |
| vanille *(f)* | vanilla **(2)** | vivre | to live **(19)** |
| varié | varied **(14)** | voie *(f)* | track **(11)** |
| veau *(m)* | calf, veal (sv) | voilà | here is, here are |
| venir | to come **(4)** | | **(1)** |
| vent *(m)* | wind **(8)** | voir | to see **(2)** |
| vérifier | to check **(18)** | voiture *(f)* | car **(6)** |
| verdure *(f)* | greenery **(14)** | vouloir | to want **(7)** |
| vers | towards, about | voyage *(m)* | journey **(12)** |
| | **(4;5)** | vrai | true **(6)** |
| vert | green **(6)** | vraiment | really, truly **(2)** |
| vêtements *(m,pl)* | clothes **(5)** | vue *(f)* | view **(10)** |
| vétérinaire *(m)* | vet (sv) | | |
| viande *(f)* | meat **(7)** | | **W** |
| vide | empty **(17)** | wagon *(m)* | carriage, cart |
| village *(m)* | village **(14)** | | (sv) |
| ville *(f)* | town **(3)** | wagon-lit *(m)* | sleeping car (sv) |
| vin *(m)* | wine **(7)** | | |
| vinaigre *(m)* | vinegar (sv) | | **Z** |
| violent | violent **(13)** | zone *(f)* | zone **(14)** |